THE AMERICAN STATE UNIVERSITY

THE AMERICAN
STATE UNIVERSITY

Its Relation to Democracy

*

By NORMAN FOERSTER

CHAPEL HILL

THE UNIVERSITY OF NORTH CAROLINA PRESS

1937

MANUFACTURED IN THE UNITED STATES OF AMERICA

ACKNOWLEDGMENT

Cordial thanks are due the following persons who read part or all of the manuscript and offered valuable suggestions, but who are, of course, wholly free of responsibility for the opinions expressed in this book: William T. Couch and Edgar W. Knight, University of North Carolina; Forest C. Ensign, Harrison J. Thornton, Wilbur Lang Schramm, Joseph E. Baker, State University of Iowa; Richard F. Jones, Washington University; and Alan Reynolds Thompson, University of California.

N. F.

CONTENTS

INTRODUCTION

That people will be happiest whose laws are best, and are best administered, and . . . laws will be wisely formed, and honestly administered, in proportion as those who form and administer them are wise and honest; whence it becomes expedient for promoting the publick happiness that those persons, whom nature hath endowed with genius and virtue, should be rendered by liberal education worthy to receive, and able to guard the sacred deposits of the rights and liberties of their fellow citizens, and that they should be called to that charge without regard to wealth, birth, or other accidental condition or circumstance.

THOMAS JEFFERSON.

INTRODUCTION

THE AMERICAN STATE UNIVERSITY HAS PRO-
gressively tended to subvert the higher interests of American democracy. It has devoted itself to ends that are not ends, to truths that are only half-truths, to services that have turned out to be disservices, to practicalities that have become impracticalities and absurdities.

Abundant criticism is now being directed against the university, from without and from within, impressing upon it the need of some sort of reform. But most of the criticism and most of the proposed reforms are shallow, concerned with the mechanism of education rather than its controlling spirit and ends. Experiments in the mechanism of education are not enough. If they are now producing the sense of vitality and hopefulness that comes of new activity, they will later produce the sense of disillusionment that comes of reliance upon mechanism. Only a small and ineffective portion of the criticism of our higher education rests upon the conviction that the problem is far deeper and more serious than is commonly realized, that the needed changes are in the realm of spirit and ends, that a decisive shift is demanded in our whole modern philosophy of education and of life, and that without such a shift our institutions of higher learning will assist, rather than resist, the forces that are disintegrating democratic civilization.

This conviction, I believe, will be increasingly forced upon us by the march of events. Today many persons are still well content with the modern world; many others, not content, believe that progress lies in the directions we have been following; and others believe that these directions are dubious but inevitable because of social pressures or the logic of the modern mind. The first two of these groups, it seems reasonable to predict, will hereafter become smaller and smaller, while the third will increasingly hesitate as it begins to perceive whither our social pressures and our logic are carrying us. Sooner or later, after numerous efforts at evasion of the real issues in our social and educational problems, after if not before the catastrophe for which applied science is offering more and better facilities of destruction, the real issues will have to be faced.

The chapters that follow will be concerned with the discovery of the real issues in modern civilization and education, for I cannot but think that the most practical thing one can attempt, in a time of national and international bewilderment, is to find out what is really important. Once that is in view, the general lines of reconstruction will suggest themselves readily enough. Perhaps I should add that no reconstruction can be expected to give us a perfect society and a perfect education. It seems strange that it should be necessary to say this; but the faith in progress and perfectibility which characterized the eighteenth and nineteenth centuries, and which has been rapidly waning in Europe, still has its masses of fundamentalists in the United States, especially in those states where the state universities are strongest. I have no intention of rivalling those who are engaged in forming dreams of education or of society as a substitute for serious thought. I have no desire to offer the reader a refreshing sedative. I shall be content if the reconstruction glanced at in this study is practical in the sense that, by taking into account the whole of human nature and of human experience, it points the way toward that degree of individual and social order which is practically possible, though it may not be achieved tomorrow.

An assumption which I shall have to make from the start is one so old that it has its classic statement in Aristotle. Writing his treatise on education as part of his book on government, Aristotle affirmed that "A given constitution demands an education in conformity with it." Early in the modern age, a hundred years before the foundation of the first American college, Sir Thomas Elyot similarly took it for granted that his plan of education must harmonize with the English constitution by providing for the training of "noble mennes children, who, from the wombes of their mother, shal be made propise or apte to the gouernaunce of a publike weale." So well did he work out his plan for training the prince, the noble, and the gentleman that the *Boke of the Gouernour* may almost be regarded as the Magna Charta of English education. In the nineteenth century, an altered constitution caused the Elyots of the new democratic era to assert, in the same vein, "We must now educate our masters."

The United States of America were committed from the start to a democratic constitution. Although the founders did not set up a national system of education, provision for an enlightened democracy was undertaken by individual citizens and by the states themselves. When state universities were established one after another—the first to open its doors was the University of North Carolina—they were intended to harmonize directly with the state constitutions, indirectly with the Federal Constitution. In time the function of the state university came to be understood as follows: The state university should serve state and nation by providing a type of higher education in accord with a constitutional democracy; specifically, by (1) offering its facilities to all who are educable, (2) educating youth for the full development of mind and personality, (3) educating youth for wise citizenship and leadership, (4) transmitting the social heritage of knowledge and culture, (5) encouraging the development of knowledge and culture, and (6) tolerating freedom of thought and speech.

This view of the function of an American state university merits, I think, unqualified acceptance. But when one begins to ask what these broad phrases imply, how they should be defined and interpreted, one soon perceives that there is room for wide differences of opinion. What is the true genius of our constitutional democracy, our American polity? Who are the educable? In what does a sound development of mind and personality consist? What are the marks of wise citizenship and leadership? What are the essential parts of our knowledge and culture? In what directions should we try to develop knowledge and culture? Are there any inescapable limits to freedom of thought and speech? These and other questions that suggest themselves can be so answered as wholly to justify the state university of today, or to convict it of serious blunders. The university can be given a clean bill of health, or it can be found suffering from grave maladies.

From the point of view to be developed in the succeeding chapters, it will appear that there was something unsound and ominous, almost from the start, in most of the state universities, and that this organic disturbance has become dangerous as they have grown in size and power. To say this is not to condemn them. Their story will always be a source of inspiration. Advancing along with the lower public schools, they have achieved, in the span of a few decades since pioneer days, nothing less than an epic of cultural conquest and settlement, which has been eulogized, quite properly if *ad nauseam,* by no end of educators and politicians. But the first rough cultural settlement is now over, and the time has come for a candid examination of the evils attending that settlement. These evils, as the reader should constantly bear in mind, have appeared not only in the state universities but also in the privately endowed colleges and universities, some of which seem to have vied with the public institutions in the promotion of demoralizing purposes. Private universities have also contributed certain leaders, such as Charles W. Eliot and John Dewey, whose influence on American education will one day be recognized, I cannot but think, as in the main misleading. The subject of this study, however, is not our higher education as a whole, but the American state university. How has it come about that it is possible to assert, in all sobriety, that the state university of today threatens the health and security of American democracy?

PART I

FOUNDATIONS OF THE STATE UNIVERSITY

Chapter One

THE POLITICAL BASIS

§ 1

FASCIST ITALY UNDERSTANDS THE IMPOR-
tance of education; Nazi Germany understands it; Com-
munist Russia understands it. Never, perhaps, were plainer
illustrations of Aristotle's dictum that a given constitution
demands an education in conformity with it. If this dictum
is not so well illustrated by democratic America, the reason
would seem to be that America is less certain of her constitution. Her constitution is, of course, the Constitution
of 1787; but it is also the Declaration of Independence
and the Gettysburg Address, it is also Washington, Hamilton, Jefferson, and Lincoln. It is a document, and it is a
tradition, and both are open to interpretation.

For the purposes of this study, I wish first to deal,
however briefly and inconclusively, with the political views
of the American president who, in composing his epitaph,
omitted his presidency of the United States but included
his foundation of a state university—Thomas Jefferson.

The presidency of Jefferson was, indeed, disappointing
enough. During his eight years in that office, as previously
during the Revolution, he failed to serve his country in
the way that one might expect of the author of the
Declaration of Independence. Throughout his life his

success lay less in transforming his faith into enduring reality than in kindling that faith in others. His accomplishment, in contrast with that of the more practical founders of the nation, consists precisely in expressing and communicating the hope of his own time, and all later times, for a better human life in the New World than in the Old. With "such a country before us to fill with people and with happiness," what could we not hope from our American experiment? More than anyone else, Jefferson gave America faith, without which her democracy could not endure. This was his immeasurable achievement, confirmed, long after, by Abraham Lincoln.

Today America needs once more a renewal of that faith. In a world from which democracy seems to be passing away, we shall do well to turn afresh to the vision of Jefferson, as a number of writers have recently done.[1] Ardent for the promotion of Jeffersonian doctrines, some of these writers look upon the New Deal of President Roosevelt as admirably Jeffersonian, others as abominably unJeffersonian, just as in the past Jefferson has been quoted on both sides of the questions of the day. In part this ambiguity is the normal result of applying old doctrines to new circumstances; in part, the result of what Jefferson himself called the "slipperiness of reason." There is, however, a more particular explanation: the special slipperiness, or rather vagueness, of Jefferson's own mind. His mind was notable for range and aspiration, rather than weight and strictness. Aside from inconsistencies, his thought had the generous looseness of many of the sentimental rationalists of that eighteenth century in which he

[1] See, for example, Herbert Agar, *Land of the Free* (1935), James Truslow Adams, *The Living Jefferson* (1936), Claude G. Bowers, *Jefferson in Power* (1936), and Charles M. Wiltse, *The Jeffersonian Tradition in American Democracy* (1935).

was born and nurtured. It is the thought of a man who conceived that Bacon, Newton, and Locke were the "three greatest men the world has ever produced," and that "The writings of Sterne, particularly, form the best course of morality that ever was written." The sensible and sentimental, penetrating and superficial, broadly imaginative and narrowly literal, magnanimous and small-minded alternate and blend till it becomes possible to view the man as sage and saint, or as sentimentalist and demagogue. And yet, for all the elusiveness of his mind and character, certain things emerge that are still highly pertinent and fruitful—above all, a passionate devotion to human freedom.

Freedom had been won in the Revolution—could it be preserved? Was a "durable freedom," in Hamilton's phrase, possible? Could it be protected against the perils that threatened it from both sides, the peril of despotism and the peril of anarchy? Seeking freedom as a "just mean" between these extremes, Jefferson believed that the greater danger to be averted was that of despotism, tyranny, oppression. Likewise seeking the mean, Hamilton believed that the greater danger lay in anarchy, disintegration, mob rule. Probably each exaggerated the danger he feared, though in the retrospect it seems that the dissolution of the newly formed nation was the more proximate danger. Even Mr. J. T. Adams, writing as one who abominates Hamilton and idolizes Jefferson, admits that "Had we attempted to follow Jefferson completely, the nation might not only not have continued but not have survived its first decade." Hamilton saw, as Jefferson did not, how imperative it was to establish power and authority, if there was to be any central government at all. "The centrifugal," said Hamilton, "is much stronger than the centripetal force in these States, —the seeds of disunion much more numerous than those of union." The seeds of disunion were alarmingly numerous through the years of the Revolution, the critical years that followed, and indeed as late as 1861.

Yet what Jefferson saw—the possibility of losing the freedom for which the Revolution had been fought—was real enough. As he says in his *Notes on Virginia,* as early as 1776 "our circumstances being much distressed, it was proposed in the house of delegates to create a *dictator . . .* ; and in June, 1781, again under calamity, the same proposition was repeated, and wanted a few votes only of being passed." Other states were muddling through; could it be that in Virginia alone "fear was to be fixed in the hearts of the people, and to become the motive of their exertions, and the principle of their government?" Fervidly he answers, "The very thought alone was treason against the people; was treason against mankind in general; as riveting forever the chains which bow down their necks, by giving to their oppressors a proof, which they would have trumpeted through the universe, of the imbecility of republican government, in times of pressing danger, to shield them from harm." In the same spirit he later faced those who would consolidate power in the central government as opposed to state, county, township, and farm. "Were we directed from Washington," he declared, "when to sow, and when to reap, we should soon want bread." While abroad he watched the French Revolution with keen sympathy, commenting even upon the excesses of 1792: "Was ever such a prize won with so little innocent blood? . . . Were there but an Adam and an Eve left in every country, and left free, it would be better than it now is." Sweet indeed is a land of liberty! While regretting the necessity of political earthquakes, he relished a spirited little rebellion now and then—"a good thing, and as necessary in the political world as storms are in the physical."

But is a free democratic nation possible? Are men ca-

pable of self-government? Can they be trusted with freedom? Faith in freedom needed faith in man, and Jefferson
had it. "I cannot act," he said, "as if all men were unfaith-
ful because some are so. . . . I had rather be the victim of
occasional infidelities, than relinquish my general confidence in the honesty of men." Perhaps his confidence was
just as wise, if not so realistic, as Hamilton's deep distrust:
"Take mankind as they are," said Hamilton, "and what are
they governed by? Their passions." Between the two was
Washington. "He sincerely wished the people," as Jefferson
wrote in a letter, "to have as much self-government as they
were competent to exercise themselves. The only point on
which he and I ever differed in opinion, was, that I had
more confidence than he had in the natural integrity and
discretion of the people, and in the safety and extent to
which they might trust themselves with a control over their
government." But *the people,* it is essential to remember,
did not mean to Jefferson what the phrase means to us in
the industrial civilization of today. It meant the American
people of his own day, ninety per cent agrarian. Jefferson
had faith in the farmers rather than the people. Small land-
owning farmers he conceived to be "the most virtuous and
independent citizens," and democracy he conceived to be
safe so long as they preponderated. Though as a practical
politician he was glad to have city workers in his party, he
did not hesitate to term *canaille* those common people of
European cities who were destined so largely to constitute,
by immigration, the people of the United States.

As there is danger of reading too much aristocracy into
Hamilton, so there is danger of reading too much democracy into Jefferson. Recent advocates of Jeffersonian democracy rightly admit that he was "an aristocrat to his
finger tips," "an aristocrat by birth, by temper, and by cul-

ture," [2]—an aristocrat who could be counted on to give a place to the aristocratic principle *within* the form and spirit of democratic government. He held the people to be, as he said, "unqualified for the management of affairs requiring intelligence above the common level." He was even doubtful of the advisability of letting them choose their representatives by direct vote. Inclined to believe that their representatives in the House, like members of the Senate, should be elected indirectly, he was reconciled only because he thought the people should be very close to the chamber entrusted with the protection of their rights. As a leading scholarly authority on Jefferson remarks, "In 1778, as well as in 1789, Jefferson did not hesitate to proclaim that if the source of all power was in the people, the people could not exercise their power in all circumstances, that they had to delegate their authority to men really qualified, retaining only the right to select them. This may not be the common acceptation of the term 'Jeffersonian democracy,' but I have a strong suspicion that on the whole Jefferson never changed much in this respect." [3] Democracy meant, to use his own term, "representative democracy." Government by the people meant government by representatives of the people. Men really qualified were to frame and execute the laws, and the national Constitution was to be altered, if necessary once in a generation, "by assembling the wise men of the State, instead of assembling armies." Representative government, it may be noted in passing, is obviously different from the government by pressure which has so largely developed during our era of industrial and commercial expansion. Rubber-stamp dele-

[2] Adams, *op. cit.*, p. 359; Wiltse, *op. cit.*, p. 40.
[3] Gilbert Chinard, *Thomas Jefferson, The Apostle of Americanism* (1929), p. 238.

gates, who merely register the forces of local and national groups, have more and more taken the place of true representatives, who were permitted a large measure of discretion.

Jeffersonian democracy is thus government by a *natural* aristocracy based on the consent of the people. In words often quoted by students of government but never by practical politicians, Jefferson stated that "There is a natural aristocracy among men. The grounds of this are virtue and talents. . . . The natural aristocracy I consider as the most precious gift of nature, for the instruction, the trusts, and government of society." Leadership was to be vested in leaders, not in followers; public affairs were to be managed by selected persons qualified for their responsibility, not by the people. But the *aristoi,* as Jefferson termed them, must be selected because of their natural superiority to their fellows in virtue and talents, not because of an artificial superiority in birth and wealth. Jefferson early made war upon the landed aristocracy of Virginia, to which he belonged—"a patrician order, distinguished by the splendor and luxury of their establishments." By annulling the privileges of entail and primogeniture, he hoped to abolish the aristocracy of wealth and "make an opening for the aristocracy of virtue and talent, which nature has wisely provided for the direction of the interests of society, and scattered with equal hand through all its conditions." In a well-ordered republic, provision must accordingly be made for the "separation of the *aristoi* from the *pseudo-aristoi,* of the wheat from the chaff," and for the discovery and training of the really good and wise among the common people. "Worth and genius would thus have been sought out from every condition of life." Such is the social democracy of Thomas Jefferson.

§ 2

This social democracy demands an educational democracy. It demands, as Jefferson insisted early and late, "a system of general instruction, which shall reach every description of our citizens from the richest to the poorest." The objects of general instruction, he conceived, were twofold. One was to combat the danger of despotism and oppression by illuminating, "as far as practicable, the minds of the people at large." "Enable them to see that it is their interest to preserve peace and order, and they will preserve them. And it requires," he adds, "no very high degree of education to convince them of this." If Jefferson here seems unduly optimistic, it should be remembered that he held that "common interest in public affairs . . . is possible only when the field of activities is circumscribed" and that, in his own political philosophy, the functions of government were confined within narrow bounds. What he expected of education was reasonable enough; it never occurred to him to assert that education could enable the generality of men to understand such complex problems as those with which government attempts to deal today.

The second object of instruction of the people was also reasonable—"the great object of qualifying them to select the veritable *aristoi*." Like Lincoln, he believed that the people, whatever their passions and impulses, possessed a fundamental common sense, which would guide them in national crises and enable them to entrust public affairs to sound leaders. To implement this common sense they needed little more than an ability to read the newspapers and journals which, in a free country, provided the materials for the formation of public opinion. Furthermore, the plan of instruction which Jefferson outlined would itself mark out the *aristoi* from whom the people should choose their representatives.

According to the plan which Jefferson proposed to the state of Virginia soon after the Declaration of Independence, all the children of the state were to receive three years of training in reading, writing, and arithmetic. From among the children in each primary school was to be chosen, annually, "the boy of best genius in the school, of those whose parents were too poor to give them further education," and this boy was to be sent forward to one of the grammar schools, "of which twenty are proposed to be erected in different parts of the country, for teaching Greek, Latin, Geography, and the higher branches of numerical arithmetic." After a year or two, all of these boys were to be dismissed, except "the best genius of the whole," who was to remain for the full term of six years. "By this means," said Jefferson with more realism than urbanity, "twenty of the best geniuses will be raked from the rubbish." At the close of the six years, half of these geniuses were to be denied further education at public expense, and the other half, "chosen for the superiority of their parts and disposition," were to be sent on to William and Mary College. By means of this selective plan the state would provide an education "adapted to the years, to the capacity, and the condition of every one, and directed to their freedom and happiness." Above all, he hoped to "avail the State of those talents which nature has sown as liberally among the poor as the rich, but which perish without use, if not sought for and cultivated." The people's money, collected by taxation, was not to be wasted by keeping the dull and indifferent children of the poor in school and college. But the expenditure of public funds upon the talented sons of the poor was another matter, since the public welfare demanded that they be not only found but trained for leadership, "rendered by liberal education worthy to receive, and able to guard the sacred deposits of the rights and liberties of their fellow citizens."

Many years later Jefferson outlined a very similar plan of education which led to the realization of his dream—the University of Virginia. In the schools or "colleges," as he called them, preparatory to the University, the curriculum was to be made up of "the Greek, Latin, French, Spanish, Italian and German languages, English grammar, geography, ancient and modern, the higher branches of numerical arithmetic, the mensuration of land, the use of the globes, and the ordinary elements of navigation." In the University itself, "all the branches of useful science" were to have a place: i.e., "history and geography, ancient and modern; natural philosophy, agriculture, chemistry and the theories of medicine; anatomy, zoölogy, botany, mineralogy and geology; mathematics, pure and mixed; military and naval science; idealogy, ethics, the law of nature and of nations; law, municipal and foreign; the science of civil government and political economy; languages, rhetoric, belles lettres, and the fine arts generally"—a programme so diverse as to be prophetic of the modern state university, though the faculty provided to teach all these subjects was to number not over ten professors. When the University at length became a reality, Jefferson was content to say of the faculty, "A finer selection could not have been made," and of the students, "A finer set of youth I never saw assembled for instruction."

§ 3

The modern state university might have been developed on the basis of Jefferson's political theory and educational plan. In fact, however, it mainly followed a different polit-

ical theory and different educational plan. It was dominated by the spirit and purposes not of Thomas Jefferson
but of Andrew Jackson. Jefferson as vice-president had
known Jackson in the Senate, and testified that "He could
never speak on account of the rashness of his feelings. I
have seen him attempt it repeatedly and as often choke
with rage." Undisciplined in character and mind, "emphasizing in the democratic doctrine everything of which
Jefferson . . . had sought to purge it," [4] he was regarded
with distrust by the elder statesman. Both Jefferson and
Jackson were brought up on the frontier, but whereas
Jefferson later acquired standards, Jackson remained intellectually and ethically raw. The one had tempered equality
with quality; the other was satisfied with equality alone.
The one had wished to retain the aristocratic principle
within democracy; the other wished to destroy that principle and give democracy free rein. The one had reflected
the caution of the founders; the other reflected the recklessness of the frontier. The one had insisted upon the
guidance of the majority by talents—virtue and intelligence; the other insisted, simply, upon rule by the majority
—the force of numerical quantity.

The result was a political and social revolution. Opposed, it has been estimated, by two-thirds of the newspapers, four-fifths of the preachers, seven-eighths of the
banking capital, and virtually all the manufacturers, General Andrew Jackson of Tennessee, honest man of the people, rugged individualist of the West, champion of the majority—"the humbler members of society—the farmers, me-
chanics, and laborers," as he put it—won the election of
1828 and inaugurated the era of equalitarianism and exploitation. A disorderly throng of his followers forced their
way into the White House, upsetting the punch bowls,

[4] Wiltse, *op. cit.,* p. 234.

breaking the glasses, administering bloody noses to a number of ladies, climbing in muddy boots on damask chairs "to catch a glimpse of the people's Napoleon." It was natural enough for Justice Story, of the Supreme Court, to see in this episode the triumph of King Mob; it is natural today for historians to see in it the turning point in American manners and the foreshadowing of the destructive exploitation of the country's wealth. Exploitation was also foreshadowed, in another way, by the audacious slogan "To the victors belong the spoils." Within a few years Jackson's henchmen formed the Democratic party into a mutual-profit society, and despotism once more threatened to subvert the stability of freedom.

The cumulative discontent of the agrarian and labor elements in the developing country had at length brought those elements into political power and introduced a new type of leadership, confident, undisciplined, despising tradition, free of the taint of Old World ideas and institutions. The only effective dogma supporting this leadership was that of natural equality, sanctioned not by the Constitution but by the simple conditions of life on the frontier. There every man had to learn, well enough, all sorts of things, without the dubious advantage of "book learning." Doing the same things for the same reasons, the backwoodsmen attained a remarkable degree of community. Everyone took it for granted that he was as good as anyone else, and had no inclination to be "different"—Main Street was to develop easily in a country where roads were few and streets did not deserve the name. At the same time, through a paradox readily explained by human nature, the uncouth equalitarians of the frontier were fervid hero-worshippers, passionately loyal to real or seeming captains and dictators, ever responsive to superiority in those qualities which they themselves shared. But not to other qualities. They were suspicious of the well-trained statesman. They were hostile to the wealthy and to "men of quality," so hostile that the older type of politicians felt constrained to withdraw from public affairs, or, if they still sought leadership, to declare that they were really plain folk and thoroughly respectable in their democratic faith. Daniel Webster publicly apologized for not having been born in a log cabin. The "aristocratic East" had been overthrown by the "democratic West." Henceforth emphasis was to shift from freedom to equality, from representative government to direct democracy, from quality to quantity, from the self-discipline of individuals to reliance upon mass efforts and mechanisms.

As time went on, power passed from the Tennessee and Kentucky frontier to that of the region between the Ohio and Mississippi, of which Lincoln was the transcendent expression. Lincoln represents the practical, forward-looking pioneers who cleared away the forests and established homes in the great Northwest. These pioneers were ambitious to enlarge their clearings, to compete with each other in developing the rich industrial resources of the region, to win a secure place in its social life, to build towns and commonwealths, to give their children a better chance than they had had themselves. If it is true that, as late as 1832, not more than a quarter of the children in Illinois received any instruction during the year, it is also true, as Theodore Roosevelt wrote in *The Winning of the West*, that "Many a backwoods woman, by thrift and industry, by the sale of her butter and cheese, and the calves from her cows, enabled her husband to give his sons good schooling." As the settlements thickened, the old frontier indifference to book learning slowly yielded to the middle-class belief in its practical value and willingness to make sacrifices to provide it.

The equality and practicality of the frontier were destined to shape, in large measure, the universities that were set up by the territories and states of the West. Unlike the state universities of the South, they were from the beginning integral parts of state programmes of education. As early as 1816, the constitution of Indiana announced this programme: "It shall be the duty of the General Assembly, as soon as circumstances will permit, to provide by law for a general system of education ascending in regular gradation from township schools to state university, wherein tuition shall be gratis, and equally open to all." After the Jacksonian revolution, the demand for equality in education was pressed with passionate zeal by leaders like Jonathan Baldwin Turner, who in 1853 published his *Industrial Universities for the People* in Jacksonville, Illinois. On the opening page of this work Turner affirmed, in his earnest and vigorous language, the kind of democratic faith that attended the birth of many American state universities. "Any system of education," he wrote, "adapted to the exclusive or unequal and inordinate culture of any one class or profession in the State, is defective: it generates clans and castes, and breaks in upon that natural order, equality, and harmony which God has ordained. It will create a concentration of intellectual power in the educated head of the body politic,—cold, crafty, selfish, and treacherous,—which will sooner or later corrupt its heart; will exhaust and overlabor and overtask its weak, uncultured, and undeveloped subordinate powers and organs, and produce a bedlam rather than a kingdom on earth." This is obviously something different from Jefferson's plan of educating a natural aristocracy raked sedulously from the rubbish. And the curricula of Turner's universities for the people, while providing for many subjects and preparing for many occupations, were to give special emphasis to training in useful subjects for those who proposed to be farmers, engineers, or business men. "The industrial classes," he said, "want, and they ought to have, the same facilities for understanding the true philosophy, the science, and the art of *their* several pursuits (their life-business), and of efficiently applying existing knowledge thereto and widening its domain, which the professional classes have long enjoyed in *their* pursuits." With other heralds of higher education for the people, Turner spoke for frontier practicality.

He also spoke, in a traditional way, for the idea of a liberal education. "The end of all education," he recognized, "should be the development of a true manhood, or the natural, proportionate, and healthful culture and growth of all the powers and faculties of the human being,—physical, mental, moral, and social; and any system which attempts the exclusive, or even inordinate, culture of any one class of these faculties, will fail of its end: it will make mushrooms and monks, rather than manhood and men." After all, the West could not afford to dispense with manhood and men. After all, there was a sort of democracy, within each man, of the classes of his powers and faculties, no one of which should be permitted to tyrannize over the rest.

But precisely how the liberal and the special ends were to be equally attained, how all the powers and faculties of the human being were to be developed while particular practical training was in progress, was not very clear to Turner or to his contemporaries and successors. For a time the liberal aim tended to be uppermost. Many of the early administrators and faculty members had come from the East, and naturally sought to transmit the traditions of liberal scholarship by which they had been nourished. Especially strong was the conservative influence of the men from Yale.[5] While the universities of the South maintained lib-

[5] The influence of Yale had dominated over the University of Georgia, the first state university to receive a charter (1785), though not opened till 1801, six years after the University of North Carolina. A frontier

eral scholarship better than those of the West, one of the Western institutions, the University of Michigan, was in this respect superior to the rest of her group.[6] In a number of the new universities the conflict between the liberal and the special caused trouble from the very start. As the catalogue of the University of Wisconsin still reminds us, John H. Lathrop, a graduate of Yale who was chancellor of the University from its opening in 1849 to 1858, "insisted upon maintaining a solid classical course as the nucleus about which all possible future developments were to be gathered but which was never to be sacrificed to any other objects, however plausible they might be and however much he desired to meet them. . . . The college was bitterly criticized. There was a feeling abroad, vague but insistent, that the University did not do for the community what it should. A 'practical' education was wanted, without any clear idea of what a practical education might be, or how expensive the equipment for it must be. Chancellor Lathrop resigned. . . ." It would appear that he had made the politically wrong choice. It was safer to embrace both horns of the dilemma, as was done by men like Turner and also by the momentous Morrill Act passed by Congress in 1862, which gave large grants of Federal land to the states "in order to promote the liberal and practical education of the industrial classes in their several pursuits and professions in life."

---

university, placed far up in the hills on the edge of the Indian country, it had as its first presidents Yale graduates, and its first building, curriculum, and instruction followed Yale models. Its location was optimistically named Athens. Practical education was not seriously urged till the time of Andrew Jackson. A department of agriculture was provided for in 1854.

[6] An astonishing institution, the Catholepistemiad, or University of Michigania, was proclaimed in 1817, but the University was not definitely established until 1837.

The task that faced the founders and early administrators of the state universities was not easy. They looked to the eastern institutions for guidance, as the East, in its own beginning time, had looked to Oxford and Cambridge. They felt the momentum of historical forces, of a cultural heritage accumulated through the centuries. But they also felt the influence of their environment, of great forests and prairies almost without human history, of scattered men and women bent upon subduing nature to their ends—men and women not devoid of memories but looking to the future more than the past. The desire for education was clear, the need for it was clear, but the sort of education that would satisfy the *deepest* desires and needs of the community was not clear.

Perhaps enough has now been said to outline the relation of the early state universities to American democracy. Responding to the equalitarian spirit of Jackson and the frontier, rather than the selective spirit of Jefferson and the framers of the Constitution, they were inclined to offer, so far as they could afford it, all sorts of practical education to all sorts of people. They were primarily organs for the exploitation of a continent by a race of pioneers. As early as 1868, "half a million vigorous, adventurous, gold-seeking argonauts"—in the words of President Sproul—"decided that California needed a state university," and in time state universities were founded in every commonwealth south and west of Pennsylvania. Acquiring something of a history, they gradually developed into a fairly definite type of institution, best exemplified in the Middle West.

Chapter Two

THE HUMANITARIAN IMPULSE

§ 1

TO TRACE IN DETAIL THE HISTORY OF THE
American state university would scarcely be the best approach to an understanding of its essential nature and aims.
More to the purpose will be a deeper exploration of the
forces that energized it, even though this may seem to take
us far afield. For the modern state university is not simply
an outgrowth of the old frontier democracy. It is not simply the lengthened shadow of Andrew Jackson. It should
be viewed, rather, as the blending of two vastly greater shadows, which, elongating again and again, have quite swallowed up our man of the people—the shadows of Bacon and
Rousseau, who may be taken to symbolize, the one in the
outer order, the other in the inner, the humanitarian idealism that developed apace in England in the century of our
national birth. Without a fresh understanding of this humanitarian impulse, an impulse far stronger than that of
the equalitarianism that arose spontaneously on the frontier, we cannot hope to comprehend what has given our
universities such exuberant life and such grave disorders.

Beneath the political basis of the American experiment
lies the spiritual basis. Democracy is only a means toward
an end—the good life. But what is the good life? Democ-

racy, whether Jeffersonian or Jacksonian, has never given this question a firmly spiritual answer, equivalent to the answers given by past ages. To the ancient world the good life meant the humanistic ideal of proportionate living, to the Middle Ages the welfare of the soul, to the Renaissance the free expansion of personality. What has it meant to modern America? Ever since the Declaration of Independence we have heard that it is life, liberty, and the pursuit of happiness. But are these real ends, or merely means to ends? If life is valuable, for what is it valuable? If liberty is essential, what is to be done with it, how is it to be used? For the pursuit of happiness? Then what is our notion of happiness? Are we to start with the formula of Beccaria—a writer well known to Jefferson—"the greatest happiness divided by the greatest number" (*la massima felicità divisa nel maggior numero*), and then in the utilitarian manner define happiness negatively as the avoidance of pain, positively as the sum of pleasures, holding all pleasures to be equal in value and each person to be the best judge of what will give him pleasure? This hedonistic calculus, however, scarcely offers an adequate account of our ideal values, nor would any other ready-made set of abstractions satisfy. Let us turn, rather, to the historical record, and undertake a brief survey of the origins and development of the humanitarian ideals which have animated our way of life, and which distinguish the modern period from all other periods of history. The time has long been ripe for such an inquiry, though our historians, absorbed in every manner of peripheral research, have never systematically undertaken it. In the pages that follow I cannot do more than suggest some of the main forces underlying modern civilization, and interpret as best I may the central urge giving the entire complex of forces a certain unity of direction.

§ 2

"Humanitarianism," says George Macaulay Trevelyan, "was an Eighteenth Century product." [1] In sum, it marks the conflux of two great movements of that century, the sentimental movement and the scientific movement, and, correspondingly, it had—as it still has today—two essential motives: a constantly wider extension of sympathy to humanity, and a constantly wider extension of the instruments of living.

Both of these motives had already been present in Francis Bacon. In effect Bacon turned away from the humanistic and religious traditions of the past and fronted the experimental science of the future. Knowledge, he said, is power; if we know and apply the laws of nature, we can control nature. "Professors of any science," he observes in the modern manner, "ought to propound to themselves to make some additions to their science," not for the sake of mere knowing—for what can that be worth in itself?—but for "the glory of the Creator and the relief of man's estate." Owing partly to the influence of Bacon, the glory of the Creator was more and more forgotten, while the relief of man's estate was assiduously remembered. Despite his disdain for the multitude in the concrete, he made science itself finally subservient to φιλανθρωπία, hoping that the advancement of learning might produce "a line and race of inventions that may in some degree subdue and overcome the necessities and miseries of humanity." After Bacon, the Puritans dedicated themselves not only to the glory of the Creator but also to the relief of man's estate. To John Durie, for instance, attention to godliness was one thing, and "the common relief of mankind from outward miseries" quite another, nowise to be neglected. Another Puri-

[1] *History of England* (1926), p. 526.

tan writer, John Webster, a Cambridge scholar who became a chaplain in the parliamentary army, deprecated a
mere knowledge of "natures power in the causes and effects" and called for the use of knowledge "for the general
good and benefit of mankind, especially for the conservation and restauration of the health of man, and of those
creatures that are useful for him." Indeed a recent historian
of ideas has gone so far as to maintain, with good evidence,
that "our modern scientific utilitarianism is the offspring
of Bacon begot upon Puritanism." [2]

As it developed, the humanitarian movement fed upon
the scientific tradition established by Bacon, rather than
upon the religious tradition of Christianity. In the eighteenth century the movement was part and parcel of a growing secular spirit in reaction against Christianity, which affected laymen and churchmen alike. There were always,
then and later, individual Christians who, while responding to the spirit of the time, infused genuine religious sentiment into that spirit; but the central drive of the movement, both within and without organized religion, was directly opposed, none the less, to an otherworldly faith and
the cultivation of the inner life. So it happened that "in
the detestation of cruelty, Benthamite free-thinkers, Whig
philanthropists, such as Fox, Tory humanitarians, such as
Pitt, and Evangelicals who followed Wilberforce, were substantially at one." [3] On the whole, the detestation of cruelty
grew as the Christian faith declined. Faith in the supernatural having substantially disappeared, the most that humanitarianism could properly assert was that it represented
the terminal moraine of Christianity: the old religion of
England, except in limited circles, was gone, and all that
remained was a vague sentiment of brotherhood among

[2] Richard F. Jones, *Ancients and Moderns* (1936), p. 92.
[3] C. Phillipson, *Three Criminal Law Reformers* (1923), p. 156.

men who had no Father. In place of a supernatural relation of souls, humanitarianism offered a natural relation of natural men. Christian love was metamorphosed into natural sympathy, and the old faith in personal immortality yielded to the new faith in social progress. While in England the humanitarian movement flourished along with, but not because of, Evangelical religion, in France it flourished, very definitely, as a revolt against the Church and the horrors committed in the name of Christianity: in France it was skeptical, and finally atheistic. In the worldly society of England and France in which it grew apace, humanitarianism found no meaning in the primary law, *Love the Lord thy God,* and therefore perverted the meaning of the secondary law, *Love thy neighbor as thyself.* It did not value the clear distinctions upon which a seventeenth-century Christian like Sir Thomas Browne had insisted when he said, "I give no alms only to satisfy the hunger of my brother, but to fulfil and accomplish the Will and Command of my God; I draw not my purse for his sake that demands it, but His that enjoined it; I believe no man upon the Rhetorick of his miseries, nor to content mine own commiserating disposition." In the new faith, a commiserating disposition was enough; God dropped out, or at most retained a faint and diminishing *Nachschein.* In the old faith, the essential virtue had been the humility of the spiritual man before God; in the new faith, it was the sympathy of the natural man for other men.

The development of a naturalistic view of man, as opposed to a religious or humanistic view,[4] may be traced in the speculations of a series of moralists beginning with

---

[4] The humanistic view, also declining since the seventeenth century, will be dealt with in Chapter Seven. Here it will suffice to remark that humanistic altruism, like Christian altruism, rests on a dualistic conception of human nature.

Hobbes. According to Hobbes, the central motive in man is his egotism—"a perpetual and restless desire of power after power, that ceaseth only in death." The natural condition of mankind is therefore warfare, and the remedy for this condition is to be found not in the delusive sympathy of men for each other but in the authority of organized society. In conflict with his naturalistic thought but in harmony with the religious spirit of the seventeenth century, Hobbes crowned his picture of a civil commonwealth with an established Church deriving its sanction from supernatural revelation. His successor, Locke, provided little more than a decorative place for the law of God, building up an ingenious scheme in terms of sensations and ideas that rested squarely upon nature and had no need of a power above nature. Mandeville recognized natural pity among the various passions that govern man, but regarded it as a natural frailty, "as much a frailty of our nature as anger, pride, or fear." "The weakest minds," he adds, "have generally the greatest share of it, for which reason none are more compassionate than women and children." In Hume, whose thought dissolves the world and human nature itself into a pure flux, self-love is offset with sympathy, an original, inherent capacity of man to share in the happiness or misery of his fellows, the basis, no less, of a large proportion of human virtues. In Shaftesbury, meanwhile, man is conceived as possessing something called a moral sense: "An inward eye distinguishes, and sees the fair and shapely, the amiable and admirable, apart from the deformed, the foul, the odious, or the despicable." In this aesthetic morality, "conscience" becomes an actuating rather than a restraining power. The genial rhapsodies of Shaftesbury, together with Adam Smith's *Theory of Moral Sentiments,* mark the passage from rationalism into sentimentalism.

While in Britain a succession of ethical thinkers was thus

debating the feasibility of a natural basis for morality, as a substitute for the supernatural basis provided by a disintegrating religion, it was the rôle of a French *littérateur* to draw into himself the new thought and feeling of the age, and to infuse into the humanitarian gospel of the eighteenth century the passion of genius. Though often following the rationalistic method of the Enlightenment, Rousseau was a man of feeling and the spokesman of a view of life resting on feeling. In an age of cold and shallow reason and decadent artificiality, he announced, with the warmth of prophetic inspiration, the supreme authority of natural emotion. Unforgettable are the ringing words with which he began his book on government, "Man is born free; and everywhere he is in chains," and his book on education, "God makes all things good; man meddles with them and they become evil." God—Nature—makes the very heart of man good. It is not accident that the simple heroine of Rousseau's novel "never had any other guide but her heart and could have no surer guide"—this is an answer, in the guise of fiction, to the egotism of Hobbes, which Rousseau had already answered directly in his discourse on the origin of inequality. If the natural man was to be a sufficient basis for a working philosophy in an age that was dispensing with the humanistic and Christian traditions, the natural man would somehow have to be given social respectability. This could be done by boldly making civilization the scapegoat, and by refuting the offensive dogma of Hobbes that "All men in the State of nature have a desire and will to hurt." Rousseau essays this task by simply proclaiming a new dogma: man has by nature an instinct of sympathy capable of holding his egotism in check. There is a principle, he says, "which has escaped Hobbes; which, having been bestowed on mankind, to moderate on certain occasions the impetuosity of egotism, or, before its birth, the desire of self-preservation, tempers the ardor with which he pursues his own welfare, by an innate repugnance at seeing a fellow-creature suffer." Is not pity a feeling "so natural that the very brutes themselves sometimes give evident proofs of it?" And was it not a stronger feeling in primitive than in civilized man, serving in the stead of laws, manners, and virtue before the dubious gift of reason, which so easily subverts the rightness of feeling by specious arguments in favor of self-interest? Reflection separates and isolates; feeling harmonizes and unites. It is important to note that in Rousseau, as among humanitarians generally, virtue is not viewed as involving a restraint upon passion. It is itself a passion—a passion *with* others, or compassion, a feeling *with* others, or sympathy.

The assumption that natural feeling is competent to moderate the self-love of individuals and to produce all the social virtues permeates the *Social Contract*. In this work Rousseau designed a popular absolutism as thoroughgoing as the Leviathan set up by Hobbes, resting on the complete surrender, under the terms of a mythical social contract, of each individual to the social group, "the total alienation of each associate, together with all his rights, to the whole community." Here we have unqualified political equality and unanimous fraternity. Rousseau held it to be possible because, "as each man gives himself absolutely, the conditions are equal for all; and, this being so, no one has any interest in making them burdensome to others." He was himself not entirely unaware of the strangeness of this belief, and hence proposed a distinction, nebulous enough, between the *volonté de tous* and the *volonté générale*. His general will, however, was not the same as the Aristotelian and mediaeval conception of the "common good": it had no need to be just—enough, it was the will of the "sovereign people." Although it is only fair to Rousseau to remind oneself that he was not proffering a scheme for any actual revolution, and might have been horrified had he lived to see the sovereign people cast off their old chains in favor of the new imposed by Robespierre and Napoleon, his treatise became in fact the Bible of the humanitarians who engineered the French Revolution. Here was a "Gospel of Brotherhood," as Carlyle summed it up, "not according to any of the four old Evangelists and calling on all men to repent, and amend *each his own* wicked existence, that they might be saved; but a Gospel rather, as we often hint, according to a new fifth Evangelist Jean-Jacques, calling on men to amend *each the whole world's* wicked existence and be saved by making the Constitution."

Reviewing, late in life, his own epoch-making writings, Rousseau said, "I saw everywhere the development of his main principle, that nature has made man happy and good, but that society depraves him and renders him miserable." "And particularly," he adds, *"Émile* . . . is nothing but a treatise on the original goodness of man." He was right: the work which has exercised the profoundest influence on modern education is a treatise on the original goodness of man. It presents a plan of education "according to nature." The instincts with which nature has endowed the child are right and sound, and must be given free play. But man, the miseducator, interferes: "He will have nothing as nature made it, not even man himself, who must learn his paces like a saddle-horse, and be shaped to his master's taste like the trees in his garden." Away with these prejudices, away with the perpetuation of the customs, conventions, and artificialities of our misguided civilization. "Lay it down as an incontrovertible rule," Rousseau declares, "that the first impulses of nature are always right; there is no original sin in the human heart, the how and why of the entrance of every vice can be traced." Hence the chief function of the educator is to keep vice from entering the heart of the child, by providing conditions which will enable nature to do her positive work unhindered. The child should follow his natural interests as they arise, for "present interest, that is the motive power, the only motive power, that takes us far and safely." "The only habit the child should be allowed to contract is that of having no habits," i.e., no inculcated habits; let him develop habits naturally. As for the duties to elders and to society which seem so important in the adult-centered school, "if you talk to children of their duties, and not of their rights, you are beginning at the wrong end, and telling them what they cannot understand and cannot be of any interest to them." Despite all the bold exaggerations of the *Émile,* one may freely acknowledge, with Paul Elmer More, that "in part the book is admirably wise; in its provision for training the body, in many other details, even, one gladly admits, in its opposition to an unreasoning system of compression, it was not only a wholesome reaction from the practice of the day, but is full of suggestions of permanent value." [5] All this is true; and yet the fact remains that the prestige of Rousseau's educational theory has been out of all proportion to its real value,[6] and that the effects of his one-sided thought upon the practice of education from kindergarten through graduate school, in America at least, have been nothing short of disastrous.

[5] *Shelburne Essays* (Sixth Series, 1909), pp. 229-30.

[6] One example: "A college reported a course in French literature as satisfying the requirement for a history of education. When a question was raised with reference to the propriety of this procedure, the institution made reply to the effect that Rousseau was discussed in the course to an extent justifying the claim that it gave students an insight into the history of education." Charles H. Judd in *Higher Education in America* (ed. R. A. Kent, 1930), p. 173.

§ 3

The central doctrine of Rousseau's writings, the natural goodness of man, was the central doctrine of eighteenth-century sentimentalism. If sentimentalism in general may be defined as indulgence in emotion for its own sake, eighteenth-century sentimentalism may be defined as that indulgence when joined with the assumption that man is naturally virtuous. Diderot admirably conveys the temper of the movement when he writes: "I repeat it—the virtuous, the virtuous. It touches us in a manner more intimate and more sweet than whatever excites our contempt and our laughter. Poet, are you a man of sensibility and of tender feelings? Then strike that note, and you will hear it resound or tremble in every heart. 'Do you mean to say that human nature is good?' Yes, my friend; it is very good. Water, air, earth, fire—everything in nature is good. . . . It is wretched conventionalities that pervert man. Human nature should not be accused." This note was struck by countless poets, dramatists, and novelists of the age, who sought to entertain and edify their contemporaries by awakening tender feelings of compassion for undeserved suffering. Pity and tears became new conventionalities; the man of feeling provided a pattern for imitative living worthier than that of the man of reason. Of Rousseau himself, Hume said that "he has only felt, during the whole course of his life. He is like a man who was stript not only of his clothes, but of his skin." As a man of feeling, Rousseau was sure of his innate rightness of impulse, and in theory credited his fellows with a similar rightness, while in practice, like many another sentimentalist, he could often be suspicious, uncharitable, or even cruel. Individuals were so much harder to love than mankind at large. The typical sentimentalist is wont to declare, like Mr. Pickwick in his oration, "that if ever the fire of self-importance broke out in his bosom, the desire to benefit the human race in preference, effectually quenched it."

The humanitarian movement of the eighteenth century was based not in reason but in feeling; not in religious feeling but in natural feeling, one might almost say physical feeling. It was content to postpone the higher values of living till the lower could be made secure for all. Whereas the religion of the Middle Ages had concentrated upon the claims of the soul, and the humanism of the Renaissance had concentrated upon the claims of personality, the humanitarianism of the eighteenth century concentrated upon the claims of the body. It displayed an unbounded aversion to physical pain and deprivation. It demanded that an end be put to misery and suffering, not because they were increasing but because they existed. What was increasing was simply the awareness of them and the feeling—induced by a materialistic world-view—that they were intolerable.[7] Prison abuses, slavery, mistreatment of the insane, cruel sports, abominable punishments, especially capital punishment for trivial offences, along with other conditions to which men had before given scant attention, were now, one after another, made the occasion of propaganda and reform. There had been plenty of Christian charity back in the Middle Ages, when benevolence might be enjoined as a moral duty resting on supernatural sanctions, but none of the instinctive repugnance to bodily suffering that is so marked in the eighteenth century. On the contrary, the mortification of the body had been regarded as praiseworthy, torture had been allowed by universal consent, and burning at the stake had been viewed

[7] "Mammon hates cruelty; bodily pain is his devil—the worst evil of which he, in his effeminacy, can conceive." Charles Kingsley, "Cheap Clothes and Nasty," *Alton Locke* (ed. 1893), p. lxiii.

with positive satisfaction. It is clear that when humane and enlightened men could endure and approve such repellent sights, the valuation of pain in the great age of Christianity was something quite different from our own. If modern man has been displaying a growing softness of the heart, the real reason may be that he has experienced a growing softness of the body and nerves. Certainly people used to make little of bodily sufferings which today they could not stand, such as floggings of hundreds of lashes and operations without anaesthetics; and men somehow managed to render a noble account of themselves in the days when everybody lived in "slums," that is, in unwholesome physical conditions. The point is not that any of these things is desirable, but that a civilization based on the avoidance of suffering and discomfort is negative and hollow. Irving Babbitt remarks that the obvious answer to the question why medical men are tending to exert the influence formerly belonging to the clergy, is that "Men once lived in the fear of God, whereas now they live in the fear of microbes." The change is signalized in the word *comfort,* which, once a synonym for spiritual consolation, now conveys primarily the notion of physical ease—as the word *comforter,* once applied to the Holy Spirit, is now used in America as the name of a bed cover.

While the Roman church continued its charities on the basis of a firmly spiritual creed, the Protestant denominations, endeavoring to survive and to progress by allying themselves with the enlightenment of the modern world rather than the Light of the world, more and more identified themselves with the humanitarian movement. So it came about that one of the meanings of the word *humanitarian,* which entered our language only with the nineteenth century, is "a person who denies the divinity of Christ." In the nineteenth and twentieth centuries, Protestant churchmen, especially those regarded as progressive intellectuals, were to deny, one after another, the divinity of Christ, the personality of God, the supernatural, the soul, immortality, sin, and free will. In 1834 John Henry Newman, vicar of St. Mary's in Oxford, contemplating the spiritual life of the day, found only "a general coloring from Christianity." "Religion," he observed, "is pleasant and easy; benevolence is the chief virtue; intolerance, bigotry, excess of zeal, are the first of sins. Austerity is an absurdity;—even firmness is looked on with an unfriendly suspicious eye." [8] By the twentieth century, before the first World War, the majority of the Protestant churches of America had become institutions of social service working for the amelioration of the mundane welfare of humanity. Five years before the war their essential creed was well expressed in an address by Charles W. Eliot. Always optimistic, Dr. Eliot saw with satisfaction the support which the churches were giving to many humanitarian movements. "The humanitarian efforts are nowadays directed," he remarked, "against intemperance and the other destructive vices, and against disease, unhealthy modes of living, ignorance, and superstition. . . . It is very fitting that the Christian church should now try to carry on an effective campaign against this world's evil and the resulting miseries in human society; for the Christian church has for centuries been content to hold out the compensatory hope of a happy equality and an equal happiness in another world, while making no effort to combat the wrongs and evils which produce such unnecessary inequalities in this world, and even preaching resignation to them." Therefore he called upon the church now to "abolish root and branch the causes of evil," by means of medicine and other applied sciences

[8] *Parochial Sermons* (1834), p. 359.

rather than through some shaky gospel of regeneration.[9] Expressing similar millennial hopes on another occasion, Eliot noted with slight misgivings that "the universal thirst for the enjoyments of life grows hotter and hotter," and offered the strange suggestion that this thirst might be cooled by the study of economics, a subject which, in the churches of today, seems to be creating more heat rather than less.

One reason, it would seem, why the humanitarian movement has not made a paradise of our feverish planet is that the reformers themselves, both within and without the churches, have so often displayed intemperance, intolerance, and injustice. Their own morality has frequently amounted to nothing more than a naturalistic parody of Christian morality. This was clear enough to Burke by the year 1791, when he declared that "Benevolence to the whole species, and want of feeling for every individual with whom the professors come in contact, form the character of the new philosophy." It was not necessary to wait for Robespierre to illustrate the new philosophy by experiencing—to use his own words, in the midst of the Reign of Terror—a "celestial voluptuousness in the calm of a pure conscience and the ravishing spectacle of public happiness." In Rousseau, in Robespierre, in how many humanitarian reformers down to this day, reform has meant, never the reform of oneself, but always the relentless reform of others, by impassioned haranguing, by brazen advertising, by insidious pressure, by extortion and blackmail, by lobbying and legislation, by sheer force, by war conceived as an instrument of civilization—by any and every means

---

[9] In other words, let the churches abandon Christianity and frankly go in for humanitarianism.—The contrast between the two terms is clearly exemplified by the novelist Huxley in *Point Counter Point* (1928), p. 344, where a Mrs. Quarles is described as "a Christian and not a humanitarian."

available to the imperialistic egotist masked as a benevolent brother. In short, whether we look to the reformers or to the victims of reform, to the ameliorators or to a society that breeds new evils faster than amelioration can work, we see abundant evidence that man, in the humanitarian centuries, has been becoming hotter and hotter in his zest for power after power and enjoyment after enjoyment. In the face of the facts that have accumulated since the seventeenth century, it has become absurd to conceive that the naturalized man introduced by primitivistic reactionaries has a capacity of sympathy capable of holding his aggressiveness in check.[10]

§ 4

If the emotional humanitarianism growing out of the sentimental movement rested on a fatally insecure foundation, it was quite otherwise with the utilitarian humanitarianism growing out of the scientific movement. The failure of modern man to achieve social harmony by the cultivation of natural sympathy has been rendered trebly serious, indeed, by his success in creating more and more instruments of living—and dying—through the advancement of science. The programme toward which the world has been groping for three hundred years is the coördinate progress of "service" and of power, an ever expanding control of man and of nature. But what has actually happened, as Carlyle for example saw in the last century, is that progress

[10] Implicitly, this is now granted by an age that still calls for brotherhood but relies upon economic and social arrangements. What counts with us increasingly is improvement of the environment, not the sentiment of sympathy, still less the inner life as conceived by Christianity and humanism. Outer reform is superseding inner reform. I have discussed this more fully in an article entitled "The College, the Individual, and Society," in the *American Review*, December, 1934.

in power has been a substantial reality while progress in service has been a chimera. In case the twentieth century cannot find something better than this chimera, progress in power may easily destroy the civilization we have been building since the Renaissance and usher in a barbarism in which both power and service will be notably absent. Without some measure of social stability, the future of science itself will not be safe.

The story of utilitarian humanitarianism begins with Francis Bacon. In his view, as we have noted, the value of knowledge lies in power, and the value of power lies in its use for the relief of man's necessities and miseries. In Bacon we find also an idea the implications of which he did not work out, an idea which came, in time, to enthrall the imagination of the Occident: the idea of mundane progress. It contrasts sharply with the humanistic idea of individual progress, which also appears in Bacon, though it is clearer in a man like Sir Thomas Elyot, who had made of it a scheme of education. Individual progress had been offered also by Christianity, and had been vividly portrayed in the *Divine Comedy* and the *Pilgrim's Progress*. Beginning late in the seventeenth century, however, we hear increasingly of progress by coöperative effort. With Fontenelle, writing on the Ancients and Moderns, progress means the progress of knowledge, which Bacon and others had established for past and present and which he now projected into an unlimited future. Fontenelle affirmed as a certainty the contributions of successive generations to an ever growing sum of knowledge.

His friend the Abbé de Saint-Pierre was not content to confine progress to the realm of knowledge. Human beings themselves, he generously conceived, were also capable of indefinite improvement, and he confidently looked forward to social as well as scientific progress. He had an un-

bounded faith in the competence of government and law
to bring about reforms that should lead to general happiness. A nineteenth-century humanitarian and pacifist in an
eighteenth-century environment, as J. B. Bury termed
him, he teemed with benevolence and with concrete
projets of all sorts: "schemes for reform in government,
economics, finance, education, all worked out in detail,
and all aiming at the increase of pleasure and the diminu-
tion of pain." A Benthamite before Bentham, he assumed
the validity of the principle of utility. As he put it himself,
"The value of a book, of a regulation, of an institution, or
of any public work is proportioned to the number and
grandeur of the actual pleasures which it procures and of
the future pleasures which it is calculated to procure for
the greatest number of men." His fundamental principle
was thus quantitative, not qualitative. It could be applied
to anything, poor relief, road improvement, the abolition
of duelling, spelling reform, or world peace. His *Projet de
paix perpetuelle,* later rewritten by Rousseau, tells of "a
war which was to have been the end of war," and proposes
a league of nations as a mechanism to effect progress toward eternal peace. In looking to this end, he was sufficiently realistic to grant that we must deal, not with "men
as they ought to be—good, generous, disinterested, and lov-
ing public good from motives of human sympathy—but
such as they are, unjust, greedy, and preferring their own
interests to everything else." They must also be called
crazy (*insensés*) if utility will not induce them to frame
such a league.

Among the French writers of the Enlightenment, nearly
all of whom (except Rousseau) were permeated with the
new faith in progress, one of the most redoubtable theo-
rists was the author of the *Esquisse d'un tableau historique
des progrès de l'esprit humain.* Ironically enough, Con-

dorcet wrote this work while in refuge from the Revolution in which he had been a leader, and died in prison as an alleged enemy of the cause of man. His fundamental conception is that of a human perfectibility characterized by continuous progress in the past and indefinite progress in the future. Beginning in barbarism, man advanced through nine great epochs; the last of these was inaugurated by Descartes, forwarded by Newton, Locke, and Rousseau among others, and brought to culmination in the revolution of 1789. A tenth epoch lies in the future, which will be marked by the destruction of inequality between nations and between classes and by the endless progress of human nature itself. Man will improve intellectually, morally, and physically. The great instrument of this progress will be education.

In England and America, likewise, typical voices of the new age were proclaiming the certainty of general progress. There was Priestley, for example, who announced that "the end will be glorious and paradisaical beyond what our imagination can now conceive," and William Godwin, whose *Political Justice* appeared in the very year of the Terror and the declaration of war between England and France. In the social order of the new epoch, according to Godwin, "There will be no war; no crimes; no administration of justice, as it is called, and no government . . . neither disease, anguish, melancholy, nor resentment. Every man will seek with ineffable ardor the good of all." If it is objected that this vision disregards men as they are, Godwin will quietly observe that "Nothing can be more unreasonable than to argue from men as we now find them to men as they may hereafter be made." In this transformation Godwin conceives, like Condorcet, that education must be the great instrument. The same year witnessed the publication, in America, of Nathaniel Chipman's *Prin-*

ciples of Government, based on the idea of progress. According to Chipman, man, throwing off the tyranny of traditions, could advance to an ever greater felicity, since man is nothing less than "a being capable of improvement, in a progression of which he knows not the limits."

By the close of the eighteenth century, the central feature of the modern creed, faith in future progress, was well established. Despite the disillusionments of the Revolutionary and Napoleonic eras, it appeared to be supported by history, by reason, by feeling. Nothing now stood in the way except the artificial traditions of Christianity, humanism, and the feudal order; as soon as they could be definitively thrust aside, natural man would enter as master of himself and his earthly estate and proceed to the consummation of his dreams. There would come a day when it could be said, in those glowing words of the poet Shelley which are the full expression of eighteenth-century optimism:

> The loathsome mask has fallen, the man remains
> Sceptreless, free, uncircumscribed,—but man
> Equal, unclassed, tribeless, and nationless,
> Exempt from awe, worship, degree, the king
> Over himself.

In the nineteenth century, the glittering generalities of the eighteenth-century mind were presently felt to be inadequate. Though emotional speculation continued, and found expression in the American anti-slavery agitation and many other humanitarian impulses, the intellectuals of the Victorian era sought to lift the idea of progress from the status of faith to the status of science. Progress must become—no less—a law capable of scientific verification.

Despite temporary set-backs and flaggings of will, mankind would then be enabled to proceed securely toward a

> kindly earth . . ., lapt in universal law.

The paradise man had lost upon his surrender of revelation could be regained in this world by his acceptance of science.

Could science be trusted to bring this about? To the Victorians the answer seemed plain enough; science could be trusted because, unlike religion and philosophy, it is itself forever progressing. The growth of knowledge between the time of Bacon and the Victorian era had been impressive, and the further growth, as the nineteenth century wore on, was nothing short of startling. There was much to justify the quiet optimism of Sir Michael Foster when, in 1899, he surveyed a century of scientific progress: "The story of natural knowledge, of science, in the nineteenth century, as, indeed, in preceding centuries, is . . . a story of continued progress. There is in it not so much as a hint of falling back, not even of standing still. What is gained by scientific inquiry is gained forever; it may be added to, it may seem to be covered up, but it can never be taken away. Confident that this progress will go on, we cannot help peering into the years to come, and straining our eyes to foresee what science will become and what it will do as they roll on." Here was a cause worthy of dedication, or, as it increasingly appeared, sacrifice. For the spiral progress of science to ever greater heights is possible only at the price of an intellectual division of labor equivalent to the physical division of labor demanded by the advancing industrial revolution. Instead of taking all knowledge as his province, as Bacon proposed to do, the modern scientist must limit himself to a plot of ground, becoming himself an instrument of discovery, a tool more complex than any other created in the industrial age. Working in a narrow field, he has the happy realization, however, of comradeship with his predecessors and successors. In the words of Sir Michael, "As each of us feels that any step forward which he may make is not ordered by himself and is not the result of his own sole efforts in the present, but is, and that in large measure, the outcome of the labors of others in the past, so each of us has the sure and certain hope that, as the past has helped him, so his efforts, be they great or be they small, will be a help to those to come." Such is the onward-looking method of science: a process without end, a preparation for preparations *ad infinitum*, an unceasing progress of knowledge after knowledge, power after power.

Trusting science, the nineteenth century set out to establish a scientific law of progress, a law of social man equivalent in validity to the natural law of gravitation. To find such a law was the chief problem of a new science called social physics, rechristened by Comte, in 1838, as *sociologie*, a science so vaguely ambitious that it did not even succeed in defining its subject-matter. More important by far was the advancement of learning in the natural sciences of geology and biology, from which had come, by the sixth decade of the century, such an array of facts that the scientific world was ready for complete acceptance of a theory of pivotal significance in relation to the idea of progress— the theory of evolution. For a time the human implications of this theory affronted the imagination of many people not wholly divorced from the old humanistic and religious traditions. Even an age long accustomed to the idea of change found it difficult to acknowledge that the progress of man began among a simian tribe or even in primordial slime. The dignity of man, assumed by the old traditions and warmly reasserted in a new way by the eighteenth century, was rudely shocked. Then gradually, since enthusiasm for progress represented a stronger current in the age than its Christian and humanistic heritage, it became easy to think in terms of the ascent of man and to conceive that, if man had already ascended so high, he might ascend in the future to heights unimaginable. At this point the public was ready for the philosophy of Herbert Spencer, whom Darwin himself regarded as the "greatest living philosopher in England," a scheme of thought designed to restate in scientific terms the dogma of man's perfectibility. He founded it upon the law of development from simpler to more complex organisms. Applied to man as a social being, this law could lead Spencer to the broadest assertions, such as this: "Progress is not an accident but a necessity. What we call evil and immorality must disappear. It is certain that man must become perfect"; or this: "The ultimate development of the ideal man is certain—as certain as any conclusion in which we place the most implicit faith; for instance, that all men will die." Progress is necessary and inevitable. It is automatic and has an inner momentum. It is a natural law.

Darwin made no such claim, and Huxley conceded that, "so far from gradual progress forming any necessary part of the Darwinian creed, it appears to us that it is perfectly consistent with indefinite persistence in one state, or with a gradual retrogression." But some of the idealists of the Victorian era would not have it so. Engaging in what might nowadays be called wishful thinking, they gave evolution the benefit of the doubt, and among the three possibilities —progress, persistence, and retrogression—they elected to believe in the one they liked best. They elected to believe, without verification, that evolution means progress, that progress means a guaranteed improvement, and that the future improvement of the human species, if not infinite, will end in perfection. They were engaged in doing something closely similar to what they usually conceived was being done by the religious fundamentalists, who, in *their* wishfulness, chose to believe in a spiritual reality which science could not validate. The law of progress, touched with emotion, became the religion of progress.

This new religion, sanctioned by the authority of science, was imported into the United States, where it spread apace. With the splendid recklessness of a pioneering nation born in the optimistic eighteenth century, the Land of Promise more and more faced the future in confidence that it belonged to her. It was no accident that the college chapels which in the late nineteenth century resounded, at Commencement, with prophecies of American greatness simultaneously echoed the praises of science and progress —the progress of science and the science of progress. To assert that progress is a law of nature to be obeyed with gladness for the glory of man, of America, and of one's self, was to send out the new generation fired with energy and hope and the desire for noble experiments. Percolating from the educated classes to the mass of the population, this religion of progress became the unacknowledged religion of the United States, the inspirational basis for American living, which, in ideals as in material things, was assumed to have a higher standard than decadent Europe. While largely a lay religion, it was gradually brought within the Protestant churches to fill out a faith that had become hollow and dessicated. The church buildings themselves were correspondingly modernized by additions intended for social entertainment and social service—additions that not uncommonly dwarfed the house of worship. The humanitarian movement, under the supposed ministry of science, had become a religious movement.

§ 5

The kind of progress which has most impressed modern man is material progress. The public has never been vitally interested in the method of science or in the knowledge attained in the realm of pure science: these it has accepted on authority (as it must, finally, accept everything) without understanding them. But it has received with sufficient understanding and the keenest interest the concrete results offered by applied science, the gifts of machines for work and pleasure, without which the prestige of science would be slight indeed. When the common man is reminded that this is the great age of science, he is reminded, primarily, that this is the age of the machine—of an endless flow of new and astonishing instruments of living. The power of which he is aware is the power of innumerable utilities. To the true scientist himself, this thirst for immediacy is always irritating. Huxley, for example, fulminated at the "blind leaders of the blind" who "see nothing in the bountiful mother of humanity but a sort of comfort-grinding machine," or "a sort of fairy godmother, ready to furnish her pets with shoes of swiftness, swords of sharpness, and omnipotent Aladdin's lamps, so that they may have telegraphs to Saturn, and see the other side of the moon, and thank God they are better than their benighted ancestors." To the true scientist, the first object is knowledge itself, knowledge of the great house of nature in which man lives, not an idle zest for marvels or for appliances to cushion the lazy.

What does a "scientific age" mean? To the man in the street—and in the factory, movie palace, and dwelling—it means the sort of age which announced itself, during the industrial revolution, through the steam engine, spinning machine, water frame, power loom, cotton gin, threshing machine, mowing machine, sewing machine, steamboat, and locomotive, and then gave us the telegraph, telephone, electric lamp, wireless telegraph, turbines, photography, dynamite, stock-tickers, phonographs, motion-picture cameras, talking pictures, automobiles, airplanes, dirigibles, vacuum cleaners, washing machines, electric refrigerators, conditioned air, television, submarines, tanks, and poison gases. A fairly typical instance of the Aladdin lamp of science was selected by one of the authors of a popular survey of *Science Remaking the Modern World,* in his chapter on "The Influence of Coal Tar on Civilization." Once a waste product and a nuisance, this sticky substance became a valued source of dyes, of perfumes, of drugs, and of explosives—German coal-tar products, it is said, nearly caused the Allies to lose the war. Science, the fairy godmother, has made man master of space and time, of earth, water, and air, during a spurt lasting a century or two out of the million years of his sojourn on the planet. "What next?" represents the mood of modern man. Perhaps the control of nature for human use has only begun. Not only have the desires of men grown hotter and hotter, but constantly new means of satisfying these desires have been provided by science. An economic report solicited and signed by Herbert Hoover declared that the experts had "proved conclusively what has long been held theoretically to be true, that wants are almost insatiable; that one want satisfied makes way for another. The conclusion is that economically we have a boundless field before us; that there are new wants which will make way endlessly for newer wants, as fast as they are satisfied." Man has in him a desire for an ever higher "standard of living," and science can engineer the prosperity and produce the things that will satisfy this desire.

A scientific age thus means, or rather is made to mean,

an endless variety of instruments of living. It also means, or rather is made to mean, an ever increasing quantity of these instruments. They are not only produced, but produced in abundance, produced in the mass, so that they become cheap and accessible to an ever larger proportion of the population. In this way, in the nineteenth century, they created conditions making for a large increase in the population, and the increase in population invited a further increase in abundance, cheapness, and accessibility, with the result that, in this single century, the industrial civilization of the western hemisphere suddenly achieved an increase in population of more than 400 per cent, a supreme instance of mass production. In vain did apostles of Sweetness and Light ask, "What is population but machinery?" and ridicule the worship of numbers regarded as an end rather than a means to higher ends. Countries, towns, and even universities came to be esteemed by the mass mind for their progress in population, along with their progress in physical and pecuniary wealth. In England, still more in America, the two countries that led industrial expansion, it became natural to reduce the idea of progress to sheer statistics, to be impatient of qualitative differences and to insist on judging everything by measurement. Greatness meant tables of numbers and jagged graphs; if the numbers and lines soared upwards, this was sufficient proof of man's undying idealism. Perhaps "higher things" would one day rise above these elevations in material greatness, as the notion of progress (which could imply anything and everything) seemed to suggest, but after all it did not matter much. Progress in a material sense, progress in quantity, seemed not only the surest and most tangible sort, but, in all candor, the most satisfying sort.

Enmeshed in an ever larger and more tangled net of desires and things, men soon came to realize that the satisfaction of desires by material things involved a competition for quantity. In the old Christianity, the more abundant life could be won by self-renunciation and charity; in the new materialism, by self-assertion and the Devil take the hindmost. The rawness of the new ethos could be disguised by sympathy with the hindmost and ingratiating "donations" of superfluities; but it was still there, as one might as well admit. Was not life, in its very essence, a sharp struggle for existence? Darwin, a student of Malthus, had shown this to be true in a biological sense, and it was supposedly true in an economic sense also. Let individual men compete, as nature intended, and a world of economic order will inevitably follow. Disturb this balance of nature, intervene in this mechanical process, and there is no telling what will happen. *Laissez faire!* Thus you will not only assure economic order, but release the full powers of men, who will be induced to use every ounce of energy and intelligence they possess in order to survive in the struggle of life. What is wanted is a rugged individualism. The naked, abstract "natural man" of the eighteenth century is now clothed in the garments of the industrial age: he becomes the "economic man" in his first dress, he becomes the rugged individualist. His is life, his is liberty, his is the pursuit of happiness.

The rugged individualism of America's frontier democracy and of *laissez faire* economics at length had to be redefined, in 1929, as ragged indigence. The programme of naturalistic liberty and equality, developed in a materialistic society using science for progress in the utilities of life, led straight to an imposing plutocracy presided over by the Carnegies, Rockefellers, Fords, Mellons, Insulls, and Mitchells and politically engineered by Herbert Hoover and his advisers, and then collapsed. Rugged individualism had pictured the pursuit of happiness, which Jefferson and Jackson had left vague, as the pursuit of wealth and power —as a race which all could enter and anyone hope to win. There were, said Mr. Hoover, no class distinctions in America; nothing counted much except natural intelligence and unremitting energy in the race for materialistic success. The hindmost were legion, an army of men rushing blindly or falling at the roadside, many of whom received the boon of social service, just as in the other kind of war shattered multitudes are repaired in some sort by the Red Cross. If materialism was for all, evidently abundance was for the few. For a brief period a hope was inculcated, by progressive experts in the science of economics, that technological advances joined with mass production were going to mean a new era—an era of endless progress in prosperity and abundance of goods for all. This was just before the crash.

§ 6

The forces that energized the state universities of the early twentieth century are now before us. It is time to examine the universities themselves.

PART II

THE UNIVERSITY BEFORE 1930

Chapter Three

MASS EDUCATION

§ 1

THE UNIVERSITIES FOR THE PEOPLE, ADVO-
cated by Turner and his contemporaries and developed
with splendid energy in the epoch between the Civil War
and the economic collapse of 1929, naturally reflected,
more clearly than most of the private colleges and universities, the public temper which I have tried to charac-
terize in the preceding chapters. They were the expression,
in terms of higher education, of Jacksonian democracy and
the humanitarian movement. They reflected, not so much
the purposes of the founders of the nation or the spirit of
the Constitution, or the diminishing capital of the humanistic and Christian traditions, as the newer impulses making for direct democracy, social leveling, applied science,
and material success. More and more turning away from
the past, with its aristocracies, its Christians and gentlemen, its imposition of human culture upon the natural
man, they concentrated upon the pressing claims of the
present and dreamed of a golden future in which the natural man, free, equal, and fraternal, might at last fully express himself. For the time being, if not forever, the
natural man must be the economic man, the conqueror
of physical nature and the creator of an industrial order.

59

To train the natural man to fulfill his appointed task seemed to be the proper function of American collegiate education, especially in the universities maintained by the public. Assuming this to be their function, the state universities met a warm response from the public. By the twentieth century they came to occupy a prominent place among the modern instruments of education: schools reducing illiteracy, secondary schools with swollen enrollments and curricula, the rapid diffusion of news and knowledge through printed matter, the new ease of travel and communication, the motion picture, the radio, and other agencies through which the economic man, without ceasing to be economic, has become the mass man. In the decade before the depression, the state universities imaged with startling vividness the materialistic society which they served.

§ 2

This society included the students who came to the universities, bringing with them the motives and the point of view prevailing in their environment. In the race for economic success, they were determined not to be the hindmost. They subscribed to what Ruskin had termed the modern religion, the religion of Getting-On, which they rationalized, in their sentimental moments, into the humanitarian religion of getting the world on. Perhaps the best way to further the work of the world was to be, within limits, the type of natural man that came to be known as the "go-getter." Determined to make the most of themselves, they liked to think that they were preparing, not to shoulder their way ahead by exploiting their fellows, but to act as the agents of progress in serving their fellows. Was not the nature of things so happily constituted that Power spelt Service?

They had other motives as well, for after all they were human beings, young human beings, capable of many idealisms. There were times when the idea of making the most of oneself seemed to have little relation with the idea of preparing for a specific "job." At such times they were inclined to harsh criticism of the curriculum, the teaching methods, and their instructors, all three of which had been nicely provided to satisfy the students' prevailing motive. The prevailing motive being what it was, they had little to complain of. They were getting the sort of education demanded by them and the society which they represented. If occasionally they felt intellectually and emotionally starved, they could console themselves with the thought that a narrowly vocational education would prevent their starving physically. It was all very well to talk about preparing to live—how could you live if you could not make a living? They looked upon their education as a kind of insurance against worldly insecurity, a young age rather than old age insurance. In a society valuing sheer prosperity more highly than anything else, in a land supposed to be blessed with a higher standard of living than existed anywhere else and a standard that was constantly rising, a land in which social applause went to those who could keep up with or get ahead of the Joneses, it was perhaps not to be expected that the young generation should display the heroic qualities which had distinguished their pioneering grandparents, above all the willingness to take risks. Like the parents of most of them, especially after the great war, they were inwardly soft.

They came to the universities, in the first place, for a college diploma. This they regarded as a means to economic advantage, which many of them, as someone has suggested, would gladly have purchased for ten dollars without wasting time on a college campus. In the words of a report published in 1933 by the American Association of University Professors, "Though it is now commonly accepted that increased education does not of itself guarantee greater earning power, this does not seem to discourage parents or students. As one elderly cab-driver whose son was attending college stated it, 'Parents have no right to bring children into the world unless they expect to see them through college. You can't get anywhere nowadays without a college diploma.' " How many students in the decade preceding 1930 heard and repeated this brisk reminder, "You can't get anywhere nowadays without a college diploma," it would be difficult to say; certainly the conduct of a large proportion of them would suggest that it was their educational motto. The diploma is what counts. It must be got, if not earned. Everyone should get it, everyone who has suffered the accident of birth. Perhaps the process of getting-on should be facilitated by inscribing the college degree on the birth certificate.

In the second place, the students came to the universities for the so-called student activities. The term suggests the possibility of student passivities, with which I shall deal later. While most of the activities were, in themselves, wholesome and admirable, the attitude toward them was not. To the wealthier students, who already had insurance against worldly insecurity, and who abounded in the private universities, activities were synonymous with "college life," an experience of carefree enjoyment to be cherished in memory through the years of annoyance and ennui which were sure to follow. To the less privileged students, who abounded in the state universities, such activities were a serious means of education, that is to say, a means of getting on in the world. If one could succeed in the little world of the college campus, one could hope to succeed in the big world outside. Activities, it was perceived, developed the kind of character one was going to need in later years. By the sheer fact of "going out" for recognized activities one showed one's willingness to coöperate, to do one's part, to be loyal and unselfish. The American zest for organization was well exemplified by the development of every manner of activity within the college. A student who could not play football or debate could at least secure advertising copy from hard-pressed local merchants or subscriptions from a reluctant town and gown. A student who could not play the saxophone could perhaps aid in the reformation of his fellows through a religious organization. Much admired was the rare student able to engage in no end of activities while getting by comfortably in his studies. Most admired was the still rarer student who could do these things and substantially "earn his way" by typing, dish-washing, and what not. Earning one's way seriously interfered with study, less seriously with activities. In the state universities the majority of students, even in prosperous times, earned part of their expenses and at the same time largely occupied themselves with coöperative play. It was understood that character implies a willingness to work hard—in play. Play, indeed, became work: time-consuming work to gain positions for oneself and for others, routine in the service of organizations and publications, endless rehearsals for plays, concerts, and diverse contests, hard labor for months on the athletic fields for the good of Alma Mater, with or without a subsidy. Occasionally one heard of a freshman who, having enjoyed football in high school, went out for it in college but gave up when he found it to be not a sport but a highly exacting business. Often sport became not only a business but a war; especially in the smaller places, if a crucial battle ended in defeat, the whole community went into prolonged mourning. Character, again, was understood to imply sociability, a certain gregarious ease and warmth not to be derived from the dry fodder of book learning. Least admired was the student devoted to study, caricatured as the grind or bookworm, boring his way through tome after tome; much admired was the student who had many friends and acquaintances; most admired, he who knew everybody. Incidentally, it was borne in mind that the forming of "connections" might prove very useful in making one's way in later years.

The point is not, of course, that student activities (along with fraternities and sororities) are to be deplored. A student should be more than a student: he should be a person and a member of a group. His preparation for mature living should be of the generous sort described by Emerson in his address on the American scholar. He has much to learn by engaging in debate, or playing in an orchestra, or acting in amateur dramatics. The mere fact of association is valuable, for a society of young persons, as Cardinal Newman maintained, will teach each other. In the state universities of the early twentieth century there was a special justification for activities, owing to the narrowly vocational education of the great majority of students. Their programme of studies was not satisfying. They sensed, clearly or obscurely, the danger of becoming badly warped and mutilated, and turned to student activities as a means of protecting and developing their humanity.

The objection is not to activities as such, but to their quantity and quality. In the well-known metaphor of Woodrow Wilson, the side-shows swallowed up the main tent, though the comparison with a circus is a little hard on the faculty performers. A disproportionate pursuit of activities is especially to be deplored in American universities, in which schooling occupies so large a part of the year and in which it is not traditional to use vacations largely for study. Vacations have usually meant play for the wealthy and gainful work for the rest. It is literally true that students had little time for study. When attendance upon lectures, participation in activities, and earning of expenses had been provided for, scant room was left for the central task of study itself, or even for sleep. As for the quality of the activities, they were too often not worth the sacrifice. Many were essentially empty, frivolous, or ridiculous. If one estimated the quality of student life by the quality of student conversation—probably the soundest single criterion—one was appalled by its triviality and ignorance. The fact noted by foreign observers that Americans cannot converse but only talk, could be illustrated by the student "body" of any institution of higher learning, especially any state university. Students had no interest in general ideas, nor any usable fund of knowledge and information. Their close association in organizations and in fraternities and sororities was necessarily all but abortive. Despite all their zeal for organizing, they established few clubs for reading papers or for discussion. Occasionally they indulged in a long, rambling "bull session," in which the three favorite subjects were sex, God, and athletics, in the order named; but the discussion was crude and puerile, chiefly because those who took part had never been taught to reason and reflect and had pitifully little knowledge of what others, their ancestors and contemporaries in the story of mankind, had learned or thought. They did not read the books of the day, the month, or the year; as a rule they did not even read the newspapers. When tested by their instructors, once in a while, for their general information about the world past and present, they were found to know almost nothing. They could not well discuss even their activities, since these, like their studies, were of special rather than general interest, and besides most of their activities were, as the word implies, a matter of doing rather than thinking. They repeated in miniature the passion for mere activity and speed which has all but banished reflection from our society. Campus life, instead of serving as a leaven for the elevation of American life, accepted American life as it was. Often it was impossible, for example, to see any difference between campus politics and ward politics. Activities trained men and women for leadership, perhaps, but scarcely for sound leadership. The proof of this was evident in the graduates of the universities, who, entering upon their careers, quickly merged into the mass of American life, undistinguished by superiority either ethical or cultural.

§ 3

In the expansive materialistic society of the early twentieth century, students came to the state universities in ever increasing numbers for a third reason—to prepare for jobs. The diploma they wanted for social applause, though the applause naturally lessened as the number of graduates increased. The college activities they wanted as a means of character development, though the type of character they had in view was largely unsound. In addition they wanted, upon coming to the universities or within the next year or two, a mode of training that should be very definitely useful and fruitful.

Responding to the temper of the acquisitive society from which they came, they wished to learn to "do something" that would yield revenue. In their choice of a course of study, their guiding principle was that proposed by Herbert Spencer: direct utility. When Spencer wrote his essays on education, in industrial England of the middle nineteenth century, the prevailing motive of education was, as he conceived, social applause, which demanded an "ornamental" discipline, "the education of a gentleman," while the idea of "direct utility" was "scarcely more regarded than by the barbarian when filing his teeth and staining his nails." By the time that students were thronging to the universities of industrial America of the early twentieth century, a civilization had arisen that cared little for gentlemen or their ornamentation and frankly extolled the economic man. Direct utility and social applause were no longer in conflict. The applause now went to utility itself. In a business civilization built upon applied science, it became conventional for students to attend universities in order to learn something which they could sell. Mr. Selfridge was not alone in insisting that "All men are merchants": "the lawyer sells," "the doctor sells," "the artist sells," "the teacher sells." Even a more ornamental person like Stuart P. Sherman agreed that "A good teacher is a good salesman." Did not all men earn their livelihood by selling their skill, their knowledge, their ideals, their affections? Did they not—to come right down to brass tacks— did they not "sell themselves"? Wasn't there good authority for the commandment: "Sell all that thou hast"?

This form of the vocational motive is hardly to be commended; but the motive itself, always prominent in the history of education, need not be frowned upon. In one of its senses, the word *vocation* signifies a call given by God to the Christian life. The vocation of being a gentleman, even a merely ornamental gentleman, may be more valuable to society than many another occupation. In any case, we may agree with Shakespeare when he represents Falstaff as affirming that it is no sin for a man to labor in his vocation. But this is not to say that all vocations, and all vocational trainings, are equally estimable. It may be true that "All service ranks the same with God," but it cannot be true with man. A hierarchy, not an equality, ranks the vocations, as everyone grants when he is not being pseudo-democratic.

Too many vocations low in the scale were provided for by the universities; too many students with low vocational aims came to the universities and fixed more firmly the commercial character of these institutions. As might have been foreseen, the lower the vocation the more likely it was to attract to the campus students who had no intention of interesting themselves in what Jonathan Turner called the "true philosophy" underlying their proposed life-business, who in the classroom became dim-eyed and listless the moment the professor spoke of general principles, because all that they wanted was a convenient set of rules and tricks to help them gain a position and hold it. Utility must be exceedingly direct. Each item of information should have its cash-value plainly stamped upon its face.

"The ruling passion just now," said Nicholas Murray Butler in 1921, "is not to know and to understand, but to get ahead, to overturn something, to apply in ways that bring material advantage some bit of information or some acquired skill. Both school and college have in large part taken their minds off the true business of education, which is to prepare youth to live, and have fixed them upon something which is very subordinate, namely, how to prepare youth to make a living." "This is all part and parcel," he added, "of the prevailing tendency to measure everything in terms of self-interest. . . . An educational system based upon self-interest is not worthy the support and the sacrifice of a civilized people." Yet this is the system that the tax-payers and the parents were supporting, even more in 1929 than in 1921, especially in a national university like Columbia and in the many state universities. A state university president found it necessary to declare, with similar indignation, that "A university which is not producing capable graduates filled with a consuming desire to be of service to their fellow-men, may well be considered a menace rather than a benefit to the community. It may indeed prove a curse to the commonwealth if its graduates are merely mediocre, or if they use their trained skill merely to help themselves in exploiting their fellow citizens." [1] The mediocrity of the mass of graduates was obvious; so was the exploitation of fellow citizens, accompanied, often, with expressions of consuming desire to be of service, even in the subscriptions to business letters. They came to the university for increase in power, earning power; and they went forth and earned.

This was true not only of those preparing for the humbler vocations but also of those looking forward to the professions. Deans of medical schools, for example, noticed that they had to deal with an ever larger proportion of students who proposed to be physicians and surgeons for commercial reasons. The doctor sells—and makes a good profit. This attitude could be found even among the abler students, whose consuming desire, if they had one, was often not for knowledge or service but power. The same motive may be still better illustrated by the profession of teaching, in which the pecuniary rewards, it would seem, are modest enough to discourage the mercenary. Yet undergraduates planning to teach, as one writer complained,

[1] Said by "one of the greatest presidents of a state university" (President James, of the University of Illinois), according to Ernest Bernbaum in a paper on "The Idea of a State University" first published in *Literary Studies for Rhetoric Classes* (ed. B. L. Jefferson and others, revised, 1932).

A selfish vocationalism also made great headway in England. As H. G. G. Herklots observed in his study of *The New Universities* (1928), a university course there came to be regarded as "a money-making asset rather than a sacrifice of money-making for spiritual and intellectual ends." One may question whether these higher ends really involve a sacrifice of worldly advantage.

"looked forward to certification and not to a broad and liberal education,"[2] and by the time they graduated possessed the teachers' certificate and little else. As for the graduate school, where one might expect the passion for knowledge and self-fulfillment to burn brightly, the temper of the rank and file of students was expressed, without much exaggeration, by a professor at the University of Wisconsin long before the commercial drive had reached its full extent: "Young men and women were straining after the doctor's degree," he noted, "not because they considered that they were bound to develop themselves to the full stature of which they were by natural endowment capable (for the graduate school was no place to go for that), but because without degrees they could get no position." One could see, farther on, "these same doctors of philosophy, now become instructors, laboriously investigating and publishing, and attending the meetings of learned societies—for the most part because, without manifesting such activities, they feared they would receive no promotion," and still farther on one could see these instructors, now become professors, continuing the same strenuous activities for the sake of 'calls,' and inspiring the same ideals in students who were to carry the gospel of education to the lower schools. All, from Alpha to Omega, had been reared from babyhood in the atmosphere of the struggle for SUCCESS."[3]

For the women students, in the coeducational system of the state universities, the normal vocation was marriage. Even in the epoch that witnessed the adoption of woman suffrage and other forms of "equal rights" including the

[2] J. A. Kinneman, *Society and Education* (1932), p. 51. While deploring this situation, the author presents a view of education which would render a liberal education impossible.
[3] Grant Showerman, *With the Professor* (1910).

right to a business or professional career, there were few women undergraduates who did not prefer the old career of being a wife and mother. College offered an unexampled opportunity for the pleasing task of preparing for this career. The method of preparation consisted largely in what was known as "dating." In the giddy decade of the nineteen-twenties signalized by post-war disillusionment, prohibition illusionment, and good automobiles and roads, this association of the sexes was often carried on recklessly. A few of the girls, otherwise indistinguishable from the majority, partly "earned their way" in a dubious manner said to be sanctioned by the new psychology and the new morality. The majority, vaguely if not definitely, thought of the college as a sort of matrimonial preparatory school, leading toward some degree of happiness, comfort, and social standing. The vocational motives that animated the men students were naturally relegated to a subordinate place. But they existed, none the less, since marriage was not a certainty. Besides, the college degree and the marriage certificate might not be secured simultaneously. The young woman must prepare to do something, if only for a few years. She must have insurance against insecurity. Even if her parents could support her, she might prefer, later on, to do something. She must have insurance, in this case, against vacuity. There were many possibilities: business, journalism, medicine, nursing, social service ("social administration"), and what not. But the most eligible seemed to be teaching. For many, teaching was inherently attractive; for others, the least unattractive of callings; for all, a possible resource. The majority of women students accordingly decided to meet the requirements of the state teachers' certificate, usually amounting to more than a third of the work of the upper college. They must also have a "major" subject, occupying the bulk of a year's

work, which in practice had to be selected from the list of
high school subjects; there was no use, for instance, in
selecting a subject like philosophy. In addition, they must
or should have a second and third, preferably a fourth,
subject for teaching. And all this despite the fact that something like half of the students who received the certificate
were never to engage in teaching.[4] Of those who were
actually to teach, the majority would drop out within five
years of service. Vocational training thus came to mean,
not training for a life-work, but for a few years of work or
no work at all.

It would be safe to say that the majority of undergraduates, both men and women, chose their special subject
without having a special aptitude or zest for it, or even any
special knowledge as to what the subject was. They chose
largely at random, like the child who decides that when he
is grown up he will be a grocer or a policeman. Their
problem was well illustrated by the fraternity student who
ran about distraught, in September of his junior year, ex-
claiming, "My God! In two hours I'll have to know what
I'm going to do the rest of my life." As a rule, only the
narrow, illiberal students knew what they wanted to do
the rest of their lives; all the others needed a proper college education to enable them to find out. The most liberal
students, with minds open on many sides, were precisely
those who needed ample time to understand themselves

[4] This ineptness and waste appeared not only in the universities but
also in the teachers' colleges, institutions expressly designed to furnish
teachers for the schools. For instance, President Bizzell, of the University
of Oklahoma, in his address before the Southwestern Conference on
Higher Education in November, 1935, states that fewer than half of the
graduates (both men and women) of 199 teacher-training institutions of
the Southwest between 1923 and 1927 entered the teaching profession.
In the opinion of Dr. Bizzell, this indicates that the teachers' colleges
"have been performing their task reasonably well."

and the world before attempting a choice of vocation. But choose prematurely they must, or believed they must. The direct utility of some plan of "vocational guidance" was a very superficial expedient to slip students into the right grooves. With the best of intentions they made costly blunders—false starts, sometimes a series of false starts, learning a few isolated skills and tricks without relevance to the vocation which in fact became their life-work. Whatever the type of their vocational training, a large proportion of the men, along with most of the women, either never entered the occupation for which they had prepared themselves, or abandoned it within a comparatively few years after graduation.[5]

Naturally, under all these circumstances, study was anything but eager. Students whose interest was centered upon the diploma or the activities cared little for learning. Students who made a half-hearted choice of some kind of vocational or professional training were not likely to be dedicated spirits. While the college activities were beyond question activities, the college studies were in large measure passivities. The tendency was marked to regard knowledge as something to be absorbed in the classroom. Why else did one spend fifteen or more hours in the classroom every week for thirty-three or more weeks? In that time one could learn a great deal, if one gave good attention. And attention was undeniably good. While the self-assured

[5] Those of low scholarly attainments were least likely to follow an occupation implied by their vocational training, though one might suppose them to be just the ones for whom such training was most appropriate.—The whole matter of the relation between choice of majors, standings in major studies, and occupations engaged in after graduation has been considered statistically by V. T. Smith in his doctoral dissertation, *The Correspondence between Occupations and Major Specializations of Graduates of the University of Illinois of the Class of 1923*. University of Illinois, 1933.

students in the private universities, especially in the East, frequently adopted a hostile attitude, as if to say, "Teach me if you can," the more docile students in the state universities, especially in the West, were disposed to meet the instructor half way, as if to say, "Teach me all you can." This was gratifying; but the fact remains that an education cannot be secured by meek listening for one hundred sixty-five hours a year. It does not produce independence of mind; it produces little more than knowledge of a number of items of information. Study was also necessary, but students did not study. According to a pleasant fiction that had become traditional, the college expected a minimum of two hours of preparation for each class hour, but in practice the college was forced to base its standards on the fact that the average student gave less than one hour and that many gave only a half hour. Students who fell into the clutches of professors that required more than that were not likely to recommend the professors' courses. Never having been trained to study actively, they read their daily "lessons" passively. Sometimes they skimmed, sometimes they laboriously conned with their eyes. They confronted the pages as they confronted the instructors, hoping that the pages would do something. They had no inclination to brace the mind, to concentrate all its activities upon the matter in hand. Among the few who really wanted to do as well as they could, the tendency was to measure effort (as the two-hour tradition encouraged them to do) by a purely quantitative standard. If they dawdled over their lessons, they believed themselves entitled to good grades, provided that enough clock hours had been invested. Students low in intelligence and in habits of concentration often suspected that their instructors did not grade fairly or "had it in for them" personally. The best students complained that study was all but impossible in the dormitories and Greek letter houses because of the noise resulting from a proper degree of good fellowship. In the libraries provided by the university, study was difficult because of whispering and ogling.

Since the faculty, while acquiescing in low standards, kept them high enough to make trouble for students who were incompetent or lazy or both, dishonesty abounded. Students submitted papers revised or written by others. Fraternities and sororities kept barrels of papers accumulated though the years, which could be drawn upon at need. Papers written for one class of a large course were submitted by other students in other classes of the course. Passages were plagiarized from books, often without realization that this was a form of cheating. Full lecture notes were gathered, sometimes coöperatively, before examinations, and surreptitiously used in the interest of smooth performance. At quizzes, tests, and final examinations an astonishing amount of dishonesty occurred, a large proportion of the class copying from others or from notes, even when the policing was conscientiously alert. Many students learned to be amazingly clever in deception, but the more stupid usually found that crude methods sufficed. It was difficult for the instructor to prove guilt, and his incentive was not great in view of the lenient attitude and mild punishments adopted by the faculty and the administration. A few state universities tried the "honor system" calling for a gentleman's pledge at each examination and the exposure of dishonest gentlemen by their fellows, an old-fashioned piece of idealism quite out of tune with the go-getting realities of the epoch, commonly reputed to be successful among the gentlemen of the University of Virginia though no proof of its success could be had. How the whole situation compares with that of other epochs or other types of institutions one can hardly estimate; certainly it could not easily have been worse than it was. And this despite the fact that a definite vocational motive, according to the theory of many educators and educationists, produces a desire for self-improvement and a willingness to work hard. The fact would seem to be that a vocational training is just as likely to be vitiated with dishonesty as is a liberal education.

Students animated by the several motives with which I have been dealing could not be expected to display a liberal interest in the few supposedly liberal courses they were required to take, or a friendly concern for the vague thing known as "culture." The thing and the word itself became objects of ridicule. It was an epoch when it was fashionable for young men and women to be "red-blooded" or "hard-boiled," when men wished to be "he-men" and women to possess "It," an epoch, in more philosophical parlance, of primitivistic materialism. It was an epoch notable, not for what Matthew Arnold had called "sweetness and light," but for what he had called "Philistinism." The sons and daughters of this time of materialistic scramble were generally Philistines, sometimes flaming Philistines, materialists in work and pleasure. They were quite right, it is true, in disdaining the sort of culture represented early in the century by Elbert Hubbard, editor of *The Philistine,* a little magazine which would today be called "arty," or the sort of culture represented by the maladjusted heroine of *Main Street,* founder of the Thanatopsis Club. The sentimentalism of those who urged the claims of culture could not well cope with the frank materialism of the decade following the war. Of what use were painting and poetry (mere frills), of what use were foreign languages (dead or alive), of what use was philosophy (mere speculation), or religion (mere wishing), or even history (the dead past)? The subject known as "English" fared better: good writing is useful, even in business correspondence; creative writing gives a certain "kick"; contemporary books mirror our dynamic civilization. Yet a curious thing happened to this subject. In the women's colleges it was widely elected by women, in the men's colleges widely elected by men, but in the coeducational institutions widely elected by women and avoided by men. Subjects like English, foreign languages and literatures, music and the other fine arts were generally looked upon as suitable not for human beings but for women. The cultural destinies of the states and the nation were left to women—not out of deference to women but out of indifference to culture.

Moreover, the men, less often the women, made it clear that there was no room, in the little universe of the undergraduate college, for any person who could be dubbed a "high brow"—a term used to designate anyone who possessed standards of excellence markedly higher than those which satisfied his fellows. It was best to be a regular fellow, but it was certainly better to be a low brow than a high brow. The good "mixer," Jacksonian successor to the outmoded gentleman, was a cheerful and hearty person who could not be suspected of being genteel, because he was, or appeared to be, "like everybody." He was content to belong to the undistinguished average, average in mind and manners, in achievement and ideals. There was no place for superiority. And yet, human nature being what it is, a pseudo-superiority came into being—the superiority of mediocrity. Those who happened to be "well-born" or exceptionally educated were plainly expected, and usually inclined, to conceal that undemocratic misfortune by putting on a "mucker" pose and thus at least outwardly conforming to the ways of the divine average. The average, being divine, regarded its inferiority with complacent indulgence and developed a curious snobbishness—curious because inwardly insecure—toward all who were different from the average. One mark of this pseudo-superiority was the use of slipshod language in speaking, the language of the man in the street, not the racy language of the farm and the factory, but the dull and blurred language of Main Street, a mode of expression made up largely of slang and *clichés* applied to any and every situation, which did not really express because it lacked edges. Perhaps a majority of the university faculty itself, in lectures and consultations, either naturally or artificially avoided language that might be considered too shapely or discriminating, a fact somewhat alarming in view of the rhetorical commonplace that slovenly expression is the mark of slovenly thought-processes. In opposition to the prevailing exaltation of the ordinary there was, to be sure, during the realistic nineteen-twenties, a minority of lusty disciples of H. L. Mencken, brilliant journalistic critic of the American circus, himself a disciple of Nietzsche and exponent of an irresponsible aristocracy. But rawness and cleverness, like sweetness and light, proved impotent to elevate the manners and the intellectual tone of the campus. The psychology of the campus was indeed more than ever the psychology of the mass man: equalitarian and complacent.

Yet one must not paint the picture too darkly. Whatever the motives of the students and the sort of society which they established, they were, as I have intimated, human beings and as such not without yearnings for the culture which they affected to despise. Searchingly interrogated, many of them would have shown an inner sense of the possible meaning of education. Many of them, without being interrogated, deliberately elected certain courses that had no direct bearing on their vocational and technical training, or chose certain professors not because they "knew their stuff" but because they possessed stimulating personal qualities. If they did not select their work more fully in this manner, the reason was often that courses of this kind were hard to get in, that is, scant room was left for electives in the vocational, pre-professional, and professional programmes which they were following. In the psychological jargon of the day, their impulse or drive for self-expression was frustrated by their desire for adjustment to living in their social and economic environments. It was up to them to adjust themselves, and not to hanker after strange gods. Great is adjustment, narrow the way that leads to success!

There was one class of students, however, who could not or would not adjust themselves to any sort of higher education. They were students who came to the universities for no clear motive whatever, and who never subsequently discovered any good reason for being there. Their friends were going to college; there was nothing to do at home. It was easy to go to college—one slid in, by the sheer fact of having attended high school long enough. No examinations; few or no "entrance conditions" to worry about. One might as well attend the university for a year or two anyway. They were well received by the faculty: they would learn a little something, a few might even "find themselves"—that is, wake up to the need of preparing to make a living. In this sense, almost never in any other sense, a few of them did find themselves and at length emerged with a diploma. The great bulk of them, on the contrary, were intellectually or morally incompetent, too dull or too lazy (or both) ever to meet the low standards for "getting by." In certain respects they corresponded to the unemployable who are always so large a part of the unemployed in society. They were the despair of the most patient of teachers. They offered a hopeless problem even when placed in "low" sections, along with badly-prepared but earnest students. They were frequently given more of the teachers' time, and consequently of the tax-payers' money, than the average or superior students. Notwithstanding every effort to "save" them, they were in fact incurable. And in proportion as they augmented what was grimly called "student mortality," they reduced the standards of the university by making other students seem comparatively passable. While the university did all it could to be of service to them, they did not render any service in return, because they could not. Unless in athletics, for it was hard to discountenance a class of students who contributed at least as many able athletes as any other class, in view of the sentiment of the student body, the alumni, and the faculty as well. And so these slow-witted Spartans were tolerated. The state universities, founded for persons who could not afford to study in the private universities, became asylums for persons who would not or could not study anywhere. The state universities, founded for all classes of the social structure, generously opened their doors to all classes of students and non-students.

§ 4

Opening their doors wider and wider, the state universities grew with a rapidity that they viewed not with alarm but with pride. They reflected the expansive mood of industrial America, its indiscriminate faith in magnitude and development, its tremendous energy and its belief in progress. Their chief standard, like that of the public, was quantitative. In America the first question asked about an educational institution was, "How large is it?" "How many students has it?" The question did not annoy professors and administrators, unless they had to report a surprisingly

low figure. Certain small colleges, it is true, did not want
to grow, though they sometimes found reasons to enlarge
the sphere of their usefulness, while the state universities
took it for granted that their usefulness was unlimited and
sought every means to advertise and extend their offerings.
Like the public, like the students, they believed in getting-on, even in go-getting. They themselves became a
form of big business, they themselves attempted mass production. They were ever looking for new markets in which
they might sell their wares. They engaged in advertising
and propaganda to convince the public of its "right" to
higher education and of the need of such education for
success. They engaged in imperialistic competition, lowering their standards to get ahead of or keep up with rival
universities. They deliberately encouraged, instead of resisting, the unsound expansionism of the decade of prosperity following the World War. They "whooped it up"
till Mr. Hoover was able to felicitate the country upon
having, in its "institutions of higher learning" ten times as
many students as any other country.[6]

A large part of the growth of the state universities, especially before 1900, was the proper concomitant of the development of the country. How the country developed between 1833 and 1933 was clearly illustrated by the celebration in the latter year in Chicago. In 1850, when the state
universities were infantile or unborn, the population of
the United States amounted to only 18 million souls, few
of whom were in the new West. A quarter of a century
later, the total enrollment in the state universities was only
2,340 students. As late as 1903, when the number of such

[6] Once in, the students had to be got out again. In at least one state
university, the registrar sent a form letter to the instructor, at the close
of the year, stating that a certain senior could not graduate unless he received a certain grade, such as B, in that instructor's course.

universities had increased to thirty-six, the student enrollment amounted to only 41,369 and the faculties to 3,471.
Up to this time they grew with population; after this time
they grew, rather, with business. By 1928, the state universities enrolled 183,805 students and their instructing staffs
reached 13,505. The University of Michigan alone had
9,807 students on the campus in the regular session, and
the University of California (Berkeley Campus) 11,061.

We may take the University of Illinois as sufficiently typical. As described by Ernest Bernbaum, "When it first
opened its doors, it was housed in one building, located
halfway between two small villages, and 'set down in the
black mud of the prairie, with not a tree or shrub, a spear
of grass, nor a fence,—as desolate a place as possible.' It
numbered fifty students; and, including the President,
three teachers. The curriculum was meager; the standards
were elementary; and the supply of books, instruments,
and laboratory materials, was absurdly small." Only sixty-
five years later, "instead of one building rising up like a
stump from the bleak earth, we now behold more than 100
buildings embowered among trees and lawns and gardens.
Instead of fifty students, there are more than 12,000; instead of three teachers, more than 1200. The curriculum
has been expanded until it covers nearly every conceivable
subject (except theology); and such is the variety of the
courses that to comprehend merely what the titles of all of
them mean would require an almost omniscient mind.
There are more than ten museums—of art, of natural history, and of engineering. The library contains nearly
1,000,000 volumes. The extent and value of the laboratory
facilities is beyond description. If one wished to obtain
even a superficial knowledge of the buildings and the other

material facilities of the university, one would have to spend at least a month in inspection of them."[7]

This engages the imagination, and there is much in the story thus sketched that bears witness to a fine passion for knowledge and an admirable energy. But the story has other aspects. If citizens of the state would have to spend a month inspecting the plant, they would also have to spend a considerable share of their earnings in support of the institution. Tax-payers must be convinced that the public funds required for construction, maintenance, and continuous expansion were wisely invested. Construction and maintenance being a sort of *fait accompli,* emphasis was boldly placed upon the desirability of a policy of continuous expansion. To the economic man, the most convincing argument was economic. It seemed that the university, like the student, had a vocation, the vocation of getting on and on, because in getting on it took the state with it, endowing the commonwealth with continuously growing material advantages. In the end, research meant goods that really counted, health, comfort, and revenue; at least certain kinds of research meant this. As Professor Bernbaum states the argument, the University's "professors of agriculture, by their discoveries in agronomy, crop rotation, fertilization, animal husbandry, farm and dairy management, and horticulture, have been of substantial help to the farmer. Its professors of engineering have increased the wealth of the public, and promoted its ease and security, by finding better ways of building domestic and public edifices, of ventilating dwellings and tunnels, of improving sanitation, of constructing modern roads, of firing locomotives, and of safeguarding railway traffic by scientific testing of rails and wheels. Its professors of chemistry, biology, or medicine,

[7] *Op. cit.*

have found new substances of wide usefulness, and new uses for substances that were supposed to be valueless; they have reduced the cost of many essentials of life; they have discovered a serum against ptomaine poisoning, and a specific against leprosy. Its professors of commerce have done much to improve the understanding of the principles of banking, of accountancy, of advertising, of international trade, and of the relations of capital and labor. On the basis of the work accomplished in such colleges alone, it is conservatively estimated that the practical services rendered by the university to the state and the nation are worth $100,000,-000 annually—i.e., approximately forty dollars for every dollar which it costs the state to support it."

Nothing more need be said; the tax-payer was answered in terms he was supposed to understand. He would have to remember that the university was a paying business, that for each dollar he was asked to give he would receive forty dollars in return. His children would give still more dollars, and receive still more forties. Education for utility meant education for profit. The humanities, in this argument, were quietly ignored; as ornamental subjects they might legitimately be abolished. It would be hard to prove that professors of archaeology, Sanskrit, and phonetics added one cent to the citizen's income, or even professors of Latin and French, or philosophy and history. Such professors and such subjects were at least harmless and might be tolerated, especially in view of the fact that provision for them was far less expensive than equivalent provision for the useful professors and subjects.[8]

[8] At Wisconsin, similarly, the University was commonly justified in terms of the profit motive. At the time it was the most widely heralded state university of the country, one heard chiefly of the Babcock Milk Tester, invented by S. M. Babcock of the College of Agriculture. State universities that did not include on the campus a college of agriculture had to find other ways of justifying their existence.

There was, besides, the stirring thought that the university, like the universe, was a place for everything; that, like the department store, it had every imaginable department. A few doubting Thomases from the hinterland might be expected to protest, like the Minnesota legislator who opposed the university's appropriation on the ground that, when he had been a student twenty years previous, the university had offered more courses than he could take. The unuseful subjects having been entrenched in the early days, the subjects constantly being added were mainly of the demonstrably useful variety. Each met a definite need, or at least want; each satisfied the vocational motives of some segment of the public. The dream of the humanitarians was fulfilled: higher education was made to include *"toutes les connaissances"* and much more besides. Early in the modern age Bacon had announced that he had taken all knowledge for his province; early in the American republic, Noah Webster had declared that "The greatest genius on earth, not *even* a Bacon, can be a perfect master of every branch"; early in the twentieth century the American state university itself took all knowledge and all utilities for its province, and offered to each professor and each student one branch to be mastered. Instead of a single curriculum composed of the classical languages, mathematics, and natural and moral science, which had sufficed for education in a simpler age, it organized gradually a host of equally rigid curricula that led to no common center but to all points in the periphery. It was argued that, in the complex modern world, knowledge was of all sorts (first premise), that students were likewise of all sorts (second premise), and that each student should therefore concentrate upon one limited field determined by the sort of person he was (conclusion). The university must offer medicine for those who wanted medicine, German for those who wanted German, journalism for those who wanted journalism, professional education for those who wanted professional education, and so on. To make sure that it offered enough, it must offer everything imaginable.

Turning the pages of the catalogue of the University of Nebraska, for example, one is amazed at the number and variety of the courses, pertinent and impertinent, developed by such an institution in less than a lifetime. This university was not opened till 1871, and thirty years later it had only passed the 2,000 mark in enrollment; but in another thirty years it had 11,000 students enrolled in its ten colleges and three schools, and was operating on a budget amounting to more than $3,700,000. In the register of courses of instruction one's eye is caught by such titles as financing of public education, early Irish, creative thinking (College of Agriculture), celestial mechanics, American English, hygiene and plays of childhood, editorial writing, advertising problems, the League of Nations and international organization, first aid, art orientation, applied shorthand theory, scientific German, advanced clothing, micropaleontology, the bibliography of American history, platform art, psychology of the high school subjects, ice cream and ices, history of botany, upholstery and weaving, third year Czech, philosophy of business, ethical masterpieces, thermodynamics, world literature, business English, specialized reporting, problems in teaching clothing and foods, urban sociology, petroleum technology, agricultural extension news writing, social case work, intermediate typewriting, school buildings and equipment, ornithology and nature study, applied technique of folk dancing, roads and pavements, peoples and culture of Oceania and Malaysia, football, sewerage, a man's problems in the modern home.

Truly, the world is full of a number of things, as Robert Louis Stevenson said in his rhyme on the secret of happiness. Some of the subjects named above have an indisputable place, but the great majority along with no end of others that might have been named are not so certainly within the province of a state university. Once embarked on the policy of giving training in any subject and responding to every want that society feels or can be made to feel, a university cannot well find any ground for discriminating against any subject proposed by anyone either within or without the university. If it gives "credit" for a course on clothing, why should it not do the same for a course on beauty culture? If it gives credit for a course on football or tennis, why should it not do the same for a course on tap-dancing or ping-pong? If it gives credit for a course on first aid, why should it not do the same for a course on urban pedestrianism or the technique of hitch-hiking? If it gives credit for a course on broadcasting, why should it not do the same for a course on hog-calling? Perhaps the state universities have already gone so far that retreat is impossible. A sense of humor might save them, but alas, they do not possess it. What standard has been erected that has not already been violated? The standard of dignity? Scarcely; for the state universities, according to Lotus Delta Coffman, president of the University of Minnesota, "hold that there is no intellectual service too undignified for them to perform."[9]

§ 5

Giving people what they want, and finding nothing too undignified, was a programme which sometimes shocked the teaching faculties. But they could offer no serious resistance because, for one thing, they believed in the equivalence of

[9] "Civilization through Service," in a symposium entitled *The Obligation of Universities to the Social Order* (1933), p. 28.

subjects. Knowledge, they saw, had expanded enormously, adding subject to subject. No one could control all or even most of it. No teaching faculty dare say or could agree to say what knowledge was of most worth. Even Spencer had spoken of the "relative worth" of subjects; but that was long ago, and meantime Eliot of Harvard had introduced democracy in higher education with his "elective system." Then modern psychology demonstrated that a man is *not* a man for a' that, intellectually speaking, but a unique individual, and so the idea of "individual differences" or "individual aptitudes" provided a working basis for the elective system. Besides, higher education meant essentially, not attainment of some body of knowledge about nature and man, but acquirement of a certain way of using the mind—the scientific way. The student could acquire this by means of any subject, provided it were rightly taught. "It has been dinned into our ears," said Dr. Butler in his report for 1920, "that all subjects are of equal educational value, and that it matters not what one studies, but only how one studies it." The president of Columbia, where the dinning was vigorous, asserted that theories like this had destroyed the excellence of the colleges of a generation before without putting anything in its place. The doctrine of the equivalence of subjects, he declared roundly, "has destroyed the standard of value in education, and in practical application is making us a widely instructed but an uncultivated and undisciplined people."

But that too was old-fashioned, and instructors went on instructing in the conviction that studies should be free and equal, and that culture and discipline were entirely relative to the individual. Let me give an example from one of the textbooks that indoctrinated this conviction in the student. A teacher in Dr. Butler's university, fairly representative of the mental set and cultural tone of the newer professors, asked the reader, "Who is the cultured man? The Greek professor who cannot keep his Ford running because he knows nothing about a carburetor or the man who knows no word of Greek but can run his car until it almost falls apart?" Answer: "According to the common definition, the former; but according to the scientific one, the latter, for in the American scene today more people actually use and manipulate carburetors than conjugate Greek verbs or read Greek classics in the original." This is a revealing mixture: the disarming antithesis of common and scientific, the quantitative ("scientific"?) standard of "more people," the telling example of direct utility, the quaint professor of Greek ("Greek professor") who has nothing better than an old Ford and cannot "service" it himself, and the ingenious modernist who knows his car from—shall we say?—Alpha to Omega. "The fact is," continues this teacher in Teachers College, "all forms of education are cultural. Here again we are involved in the principle of relativity. Since culture is a set of human tools for human adjustment its value is relative to the person, place, or period. Educational practice must differentiate the worths of types of culture for types of people in types of places at one or another specified time.. . . . One man may be trained in handling gas-engines; another, Greek verbs." Like everything else if one is scientific enough, the matter can be reduced to a formula: "The actual use per unit of population times experience-moments would give an index of worth far greater for the community in the case of gas-engines than in the case of Greek verbs."[10]

This does not grossly exaggerate the cultural tendencies of the new men of the twentieth century in education, sociology, educational sociology, and many other subjects. Some of the new professors were not so smartly crass; many

[10] D. H. Kulp II, *Educational Sociology* (1932).

of the older professors, more richly disciplined, rarely or never displayed this thin literalness. But the inclination was general to accept the relativity of culture and the equivalence of subjects. There was a disposition to remove all uniformly required subjects, even in the freshman year, with the sole exception of English. "Is there any single acquisition or faculty which is essential to culture, except, indeed, a reasonably accurate and refined use of the mother-tongue?" they inquired with Charles W. Eliot,[11] forgetting that once the essentiality of a single subject is admitted, the theory of equivalence is violated and the way is open for other essentials. They forgot, incidentally, that English is inevitably taught, or untaught, in every subject in the university, and that successful training in a reasonably accurate and refined use of the mother-tongue can be attained only when it is furthered by every department in the institution, as in European schools and universities. In some American institutions, however, fitness for this responsibility was so far lacking that it was necessary to establish faculty classes in English grammar. The low quality of English and of cultural attainments in general, among teachers both in the schools and in the universities, was the result, not only of the indifference toward standards prevailing in our society, but also of the special difficulty of finding suitable teachers for the masses of students admitted in the epoch of rapid expansion. The supply of qualified teachers was suddenly out of relation with the demand. Raw teachers faced the task of refining raw students. Even in the state universities of the South, where it had been traditional to invite to the faculties the type known as "the gentleman and the scholar," and where (when the two were not available in the same man) the gentleman had been preferred to the scholar, a growing proportion of the facul-

[11] *The Cultivated Man* (Riverside Uplift Series, 1915).

ties was composed of men crude in mind, manners, and speech.

Another reason for the complaisance of faculties as they witnessed the dubious educational tendencies of the state universities was their attachment to what may be called departmentalism. The university functioned in terms of departments, each of which was commonly regarded as a self-sufficient unit. The university was, so to speak, international, the departments were national; and, as in the modern world, nationalism grew rampant. The welfare of the university was largely a matter of indifference, while the welfare of the department was jealously guarded and enhanced. That this was possible was owing in part to the feudal organization of the institution: at the top a president—a financier and politician—then the several deans, and finally the heads of departments, to whom the deans delegated large powers. As the departments became more and more isolated through the increasing disparateness of the fields of learning, of the educational programmes, and of the intellectual life of the faculty, they were permitted to control their affairs and forward their mysteries much as they saw fit. In them functioned the real life of the corporation. Each professor, associate professor, and assistant professor in a department was inclined to believe that what counted, in addition perhaps to English, was his own subject—if not for educational, then for political reasons. He must be loyal, above all, to the interests of his department. It must secure or maintain its place in the sun; it must annex as many students as possible, extending its services widely and upholding its honor. The majority of professors wanted large classes, of fit or unfit students, while they urged the pedagogical superiority of small classes. They, like their departments, had in themselves the zest for quantity, or, if not, they felt the pressure of colleagues and superiors urging them to make a brave showing. It was generally stated that the university had too many students, particularly too many incompetent students, but it was rarely stated by any professor that he had too many students. If a professor did not believe in his subject, who else would? And further, if he discouraged students from entering his classes, were they not likely to take some inferior subject, subjects being, after all, not quite so equivalent as one sometimes supposed? And in the forefront of each clamant department was its head—spokesman, organizer, disciplinarian, and "boss"—whose authority touched the professors far more intimately than that of the deans and the president. If the head appeared to be benevolent, wise, and aggressive, the members of his staff were generally well content with his dictatorship; if not, they despised his tyranny, or his foolishness, or his weakness, and urged the claims of democratic rule. If he was aggressive alone, he usually satisfied the administration, since aggressiveness implied activity and development.

Within the little realm ruled by its head, the typical department gave serious thought only to its own affairs. It thought in terms of scientific scholarship, efficiency, power, service, progress, as they concerned the departmental subject. It erected tariff walls against the neighboring departments, more than a score in number and all presumed to be imperialistic. It believed that the major thing in a university is the "major"—a word applied to a subject, a student, a teacher, or a department—and it set about developing an endless array of "courses," amounting in some instances to a hundred segments of one subject. The more courses, the more instructors; and the more instructors, the more din of activity in publication and campus services, pleasing to the ear of administrators. Despite the theory of an elective system based on individual aptitudes, the major student was permitted scant freedom of choice, merely electing one or another set of requirements. Some little room was made for what were known as "free electives," though as likely as not the major department, advising the student, limited or dictated his choice. Each department, while at liberty to count toward the major any suitable courses offered by other departments, found that it needed the full legal number of hours for its own subject. If it formulated some kind of "special course" covering the work of three or four years, it left slight room for free electives, though it criticized the paucity of such provision in the special courses devised by other departments. In general, it thought that other departments were too narrow, or technical, or simply hoggish, but it was loath to mend its own ways. In their intellectual life, as displayed in random discussion and in faculty meetings, the departments possessed only one lively common interest: an interest in the educational machinery.

Chapter Four

TRAINING FOR POWER AND SERVICE

§ 1

THE MACHINERY OF UNIVERSITY STUDY WAS IN keeping with the educational ideal of an industrial and commercial civilization. This ideal President Eliot summed up in the first decade of the century when he called for education for Power and Service—"one of the most baneful phrases," in the opinion of Mr. J. T. Adams, "ever let loose by an educator upon an uneducated people." As a humanitarian optimist, Eliot discerned in the young America of his time "a gregarious enthusiasm for social service" and was led to believe that increase of individual power could readily be made to serve social ends. Each boy or girl would discover, through free election of studies, what he wished to do in the world; then he would train himself for efficiency in his chosen career, go forth to take his place in the workshop of the world, and thus serve society. National education would be directed toward the "efficient nation," and would be effective in proportion as it secured "in the masses the development of this power and its application in infinitely varied forms to the national industries and the national service." In the address containing this doctrine of Education for Efficiency, as in the writings of Eliot generally, there is what Ralph Barton Perry has described as

94

"a touch of the banal, of shallowness, of externality," the more dangerous because of the man's personal character and administrative ability. While it would be as absurd to hold Eliot accountable for all the defects of our higher education as to credit him with all its excellencies, there can be no question that he played a leading rôle in the disintegration of the American college in the early twentieth century.

As education for efficiency progressed, it soon became apparent, above all in the state universities, that an enthusiasm for serving society was not developing among the students on the campus or among the alumni who took their places with the go-getters that set the tone of American life. There was a sentimental unreality about the service, in marked contrast to the solid substance of the power. And the power itself was of a low order, the power of machines rather than intelligences. As will be made clearer farther on, the old education had aimed at the liberation of powers of mind and personality, whereas the new education aimed primarily and directly at efficiency in doing some particular thing, whether that thing was skill in handling gas-engines or in adding to the sum of our knowledge of Greek verbs. The genius of the old education had been the development of free human beings; the genius of the new was the shaping of cogs that should fit into the social mechanism. The old education was liberal; the new, servile. As I have pointed out, the mass of students coming to the universities were looking for direct utility. Receiving them on these terms, the universities devised a mode of training that should satisfy their wants. Even in the college of liberal arts, the central concern of the universities was to teach young men and women to do something useful, something immediately lucrative, in a manner often suggesting the "business college." It seemed futile to attempt anything more, though there were professors and departments that bravely tried it. The ever increasing numbers of students who came to college with a marked disability for the life intellectual, indifferent to the austerities of the scientific attitude and of philosophic poise, could at most be taught a handful of trade tricks that might give them a better start in life, if not a better ending. Their "education" would cost their parents several thousand dollars and a share of the state taxes besides—a burden cheerfully borne, however, because of the American faith in education of any sort.

If education was to be servile rather than liberal, if collegiate study was to be instrumental rather than formative, the old traditional curriculum, definite and limited, must be superseded by a vast new structure or conglomeration that could provide room for everything imaginable and should be extensible in view of unimaginable things to be provided later. Was the result to be an educational chaos? Qualitative distinctions between subjects having been abandoned, could other ways of attaining order be devised?

Putting aside for the moment limitations upon free election, we may say that the university conferred the bachelor's degree upon its annual horde of students on the basis of carefully ordered quantitative requirements. In the diploma mill a degree was four years in the making, and weighed exactly 120 semester hours. According to a mechanical course-credit system, each such hour represented one class hour per week per semester, and the number of semester hours of credit earned in each course commonly ranged from two to four, though fractional credits, such as three-tenths of a credit, also appeared in the records. The number of credits that could be earned in a single semester was fixed. Often a student had to refrain from taking a course that he particularly wanted or needed, because it would have made his total credits for the semester too many or too few. In making up a programme he was often obliged to run through the maze of courses offered in search of a suitable three-hour or two-hour course or even to find a way to earn a single credit. In explaining his progress the student naturally told his friends and teachers that he had "got off" say forty-nine hours, or had eighteen more hours to get off. Occasionally a student who failed in a course in his last semester lacked 1/120 of the information needed for a diploma. There was a case in which a candidate for the doctor's degree—for the course-credit system was actually employed in the graduate school also—asked his adviser how he could work off a desideratum of 0.4 s.h., the last fragment of the 90 hours required for that degree. Students transferring from one institution to another carried their credits with them in elaborate official transcripts, and, in case the modes of computation differed, much mathematical skill might be necessary to achieve a transvaluation. Along with the record of credits for each course was a record of the grades earned, which might be A, B, C, D, E, F, Inc., Abs., Exc., Lt., Dr., etc. "Grade points" were also commonly computed, at the rate of one for each D hour, two for each C, three for each B, and four for each A, an average of two such points for each semester-hour being required for a degree. On the basis of all these figurings it was possible to get a definite "picture" of the scholarship of a student or a group. Thus, Mr. X might be a 3.2 man, fraternity Q might stand .119 higher than sorority M, or the men students might rank .01876 lower than the women.

Once a credit was earned, it was as safe as anything in the world. It would be deposited and indelibly recorded in the registrar's savings-bank, while the substance of the course could be, if one wished, happily forgotten. Each course culminated in a final examination; if one knew one's stuff then, one need never know it again. In a subject like required English, a student deficient in ability might, with effort, get a passing grade and then, without effort, lapse into semi-illiteracy; yet the record would show, to the day of doom, that he could read and write passably. The entire progress toward graduation was piecemeal. How could a comprehensive examination be held at the close of the last year when each student had accomplished an education wholly original and unprecedented? Purchasing a diploma on the installment plan was, besides, much easier. Instead of one crucial examination, there were about thirty examinations. Ordinarily each covered the work of a single semester, so that the student who passed in the first semester of a course and failed in the second received half of the course credits. And this is not all. There were "quizzes," monthly, fortnightly, or even weekly, covering easily managed fragments of subject matter, so that the student earned fractions of the credit at short intervals and, having earned them, could not very plausibly be deprived of them if he "fell down" on the final examination. In some institutions the instructor was required to report delinquent students in the middle of the semester, on the understanding that if he did not report them then he could scarcely be allowed to fail them at the end; in other institutions such reports were called for at intervals as short as two weeks, and a student who was never reported by his instructor was expected to pass even if the final examination showed that he could not grasp the subject as a whole. In final examinations, still more in quizzes, the questions to be answered called for information rather than critical judgment and insight, and the student who returned the information which the instructor had given him passed the test with a comfortable margin. The acquisition of the information was rendered easier by means of very definite lesson assignments from day to day in the manner of secondary school instruction, and also by means of required attendance at the class meetings where information was dispensed. One of the leading state universities secured attendance in the first two years by ruling that any student with "unexcused absences (in no case less than two) equal to the number of credits in the course, will be dropped from the class with a record of failure in the course"—a penalty as severe as that imposed by many institutions for cheating on examination. Assuredly the university administration and faculty, in the era of exuberant expansion, did their level best to discover a mechanism that could turn out an educated product efficiently.

Something like order was introduced into the easygoing elective system by means of what were sometimes called "prescribed requirements." These were based on the apparently reasonable theory that education in the lower college should be mainly general and liberal, and education in the upper college mainly specific and useful. In a few state universities this theory was really carried out. One institution prescribed, in the lower college, two years of English, two years of each of two foreign languages, one year of history (American, changed to modern European), one year of natural science (unspecified), and one year of mathematics (calculus and trigonometry), leaving room for only one or two elective subjects to be chosen from a restricted list. A far more typical state university definitely required of all A. B. candidates in the first two years only rhetoric, hygiene, and physical education, to which were added some "group requirements" of comparative insignificance. Another typical institution definitely required a single subject, rhetoric, together with one course among fifteen courses including chemistry, ancient history, and the theory of investment. Less usual requirements ranged from swimming to the United States Constitution, the latter of which could be satisfied by taking University Extension Division course X7A-7B.[1]

Thus liberally educated, the student was considered ready for a more specialized and practical training. He was now "required to elect" a specific subject upon which to concentrate his efforts during the next two years. Having reached the upper division of the college of liberal arts, he was to become a specialist in one among twenty or thirty subjects as various as home economics and entomology—a choice, for many students, among twenty or thirty evils. In many institutions he might become a specialist by taking just three courses, and thus have two-thirds of his time free for anything that attracted him at the moment. If he had a definite vocation in view, as was usually the case, he gave perhaps half his time, or, if the rules permitted, two-thirds, to his major subject. If he desired certification for teaching (a large proportion of women students did), the whole of his time in the last two years, and part of his time in the earlier years, were preëmpted by courses in education and in the teaching subject or subjects. In some states he must (to use an odd euphemism) "specialize" in three teaching subjects, collecting "10 semester hours in one, 12 hours in a second, and 16 hours in a third," in addition to 15 hours in "Education, including Educational Psychology and Technic of Teaching." [2] If training for a vocation left time

[1] This was at the University of California, where other ways of satisfying the requirement were also provided. I do not wish to imply that the requirement is absurd: see Chapter Six, p. 186, note.

[2] The requirement in "professional education," in the various states, now ranges from 6 to 24 hours, only eight states requiring fewer than 15. Why state certification is made to depend upon hours spent in courses is a mystery of the first order, in view of the uneven quality of such courses in the institutions of the state and the high validity said to have been reached by objective examinations ("scientific measurement"). Why do not educationists urge the establishment of a uniform

for electives, the student had a wide range of choice. Though he had to look out for the system of "prerequisites" which debarred him from many courses, the university generously invited him in almost any and every direction at once. At the University of Illinois, for example, he might elect for A.B. credit Government in Illinois or International Law, Heredity or General Ornithology, Farm Home Equipment or City Planning, Reporting or Newspaper Advertising.

In addition to the major there was another way of proceeding to specialized and practical training: various and sundry "special courses," "combined courses," and "semi-professional courses." These constituted the only curricula outlined in the catalogue by the college of liberal arts. Often they reached back into the sophomore year, and sometimes they even prescribed freshman courses in addition to those prescribed by the college, though the catalogue, as likely as not, advised against specialization by freshmen. Many of the curricula also pointed forward, beyond a curtailed college course, to specialized study outside the liberal college. At the University of Iowa, for instance, the curricula offered by the college of liberal arts were listed under the captions: Chemistry, Home Economics, General Science, Graphic and Plastic Arts, Journalism, Social Work, Music, Liberal Arts and Law, Liberal Arts and Medicine, Liberal Arts and Nursing, Pre-Dentistry, Liberal

---

Staatsexamen? "In the early history of the United States," it has been noted, "certification by examination was the accepted procedure. . . . Methods of teacher certification, other than those involving a definite and specific preparation for teaching by attendance at a teacher-training institution, have fallen into disrepute" (Mark E. Stine, "In-Service Education for Teachers," *School and Society,* April 27, 1935, p. 583). Why? An intelligent student could independently prepare for an examination in "professional education" in a summer—a highly intelligent student in much less than a summer.

Arts and Engineering, Liberal Arts and Physical Education. At the University of Minnesota, the curricula brought to the attention of the student in the college of science, literature, and the arts were as follows: State and Federal Administration (5 years), Diplomatic and Consular Service (5 years), Hospital Library Service (5 years), Medical Technicians (4 years), Preventive Medicine and Public Health (4 years), Social and Civic Work (5 years), Military Science and Tactics, Arts and Music (5 years), Arts and Medicine (7 years), Arts and Law (6 years), Arts and Dentistry (7 years), Arts and Architecture (6 years), Arts and Interior Architecture (4 years). From such arrangements it is evident that, while the college began its task when the freshmen arrived on the campus, it had no definite time or unified programme for accomplishing its task. It was all things to all men.

Furthermore, if the prospective freshman surveyed the offerings of the university as described in the catalogue, he was likely to observe that the college of liberal arts occupied a comparatively humble position. For example, in the 1930–31 catalogue of the University of Illinois, 9 pages were devoted to the college of liberal arts—nearly half of them concerning curricula in Home Economics, Preparatory to Journalism, Preparatory to Law, Preparatory to Medicine and Dentistry, Chemistry and Chemical Engineering, and Optic Arts—while a total of 117 pages were devoted to other colleges and schools, viz., the College of Commerce and Business Administration, (13 pages), the College of Engineering (23 pages), the College of Agriculture (13 pages), the College of Education (10 pages), the College of Law (4 pages), the School of Music (4 pages), the School of Railway Engineering and Administration (1 page), the School of Journalism (2 pages), the Library School (2 pages), the Graduate School (9 pages), Military

Science and Tactics (2 pages), Physical Welfare (2 pages), Summer Session (2 pages), College of Medicine (19 pages), College of Dentistry (9 pages), School of Pharmacy (3 pages).[3]

In this way it was made plain to the entering student that if, amid the bewildering riches of subjects of study, he was to pursue a curriculum rather than a hodgepodge, he would be well advised to consider "electing" one of the definite programmes outlined in the catalogue and other publications. He might enter, or prepare to enter after a year or two, one of the vocational or professional courses offered by the various colleges and schools. If he followed the largest group of students into the college of liberal arts, he would certainly find there something practical, something that promised a return as quickly as possible. Each of the curricula proposed by this college was purposeful and clearly organized, as the curriculum of the old American college had been. More or less rigid in its prescriptions, each of them was at least free of the aimlessness of the elective system. The elective system had exploded into fragments the old definite curriculum, but the human instinct for order had soon reasserted itself in a new form. A few programmes had been introduced, then more and more of them, precisely as the departments had multiplied previ-

3 The number of students in the various colleges and schools of the University of Illinois, as given in the same catalogue, was as follows: Liberal Arts and Sciences, 4232; Commerce, 2225; Engineering, 1905; Graduate School, 1115; Education, 1072; Agriculture, 740; Pharmacy, 703; Medicine, 585; Law, 273; Music, 165; Dentistry, 151; Library, 145; Journalism, 116.

Of a total of nearly 15,000 students, 10,455 were listed as undergraduates, but actually about four-fifths of the total might be classified as students who had not passed beyond four years of study.

Analysis would show that the University of Illinois, like most state universities, was really a vocational and professional school in which premature specialization was the rule.

ously. With scarcely any exceptions, however, the organizing principle in such programmes was frankly vocational,
not cultural. At the University of Wisconsin, it is true, the
faculty devised a Course in the Humanities, which enrolled
eight or ten juniors at a time, out of a total of more than a
thousand in the college; and at the University of North
Carolina a similar course was laboriously agreed upon and
annually printed in the catalogue, though it was never
elected by a single student. A unified cultural programme
was not an object of enthusiasm on the part of either students or faculty. It could not be "sold," at least not without
the high-pressure advertising that its proponents did not
believe in, for the students wanted direct utility and the
faculty wanted specialism.

Thus it came about that the college of liberal arts, having no curriculum but only a vast assortment of courses,
was transformed into what was called a "service college"
and might as well have been called a "servile college." It
was a quarry from which those concerned with building up
vocational and professional curricula could take out such
materials as they found usable for their purposes. It was a
department store, with departments of physics, psychology,
languages, and so forth, which provided the elements of
knowledge, the tool skills, the basic sciences needed for special as opposed to liberal education. There were a few university presidents, like Woodrow Wilson at Princeton, who
sincerely deplored this disintegration of the college and the
growing tendency to confine liberal studies to the first two
years, and there were leaders in legal, medical, and engineering education who proclaimed the bad results of early
specialization and the need of more room for liberal preparation, though they commonly saw no way of finding more
room. In the state universities the process of forming new
departments, multiplying courses, devising vocational cur-

ricula went merrily forward. And meanwhile the old liberal subjects of the lower college were, in many cases, robbed of most of their liberality to suit the practical and technical temper of the epoch. In freshman English, the only serious aim was, often, literacy. In the foreign languages (German, French, Spanish) mere comprehension of the printed word had to suffice, a rough command of a tool useful in case one ever had to read foreign research journals or go to South America. In zoölogy it was possible to take the first-year course, presumably one's only course, without hearing about the evolution of man, and this outside of Tennessee. And so on. Liberal collegiate education was thus pressed down by the weight of vocational and professional training above, while at the same time it was pushed up by the pressure of elementary work left unaccomplished by the high school. Ground between the upper and the nether millstone, the college of liberal arts was all but annihilated.

§ 2

It would be aside from the purpose of this study to embark upon a survey of the work of the professional schools, even if I were competent for the task. Suffice it to say that they carried out with much success the function which they regarded as proper or necessary, that of training business men and women, engineers, lawyers, pharmacists, and the like, who had not the means—or, in a vast number of cases, the capacity—for adequate general study. The most serious complaint that may be lodged against these schools is that they did not sufficiently throw their influence on the side of liberal preparation for a professional career, though it would be hard to say how much they might have accomplished even if they had steadfastly sought, by personal advice and the pressure of requirements, to combat the quick-success formula which their students naturally shared with the American public.

Something must be said, however, of the graduate school, the sole unit within the university admitting only graduates of colleges. In 1930 Dr. Abraham Flexner expressed the opinion that the graduate school was "by far the most meritorious part of the American university." He was right, I think, especially if one has in mind the state university, in which liberal education, as we have seen, had all but disappeared.[4]

The same president of Harvard who, more than anyone else, destroyed the liberal college, also, more than anyone else, built up the graduate school. Eliot perceived that the modern world had dedicated itself to the search for knowledge, which is power, by the method of science, and that America would lag behind in the race unless her institutions of higher learning devoted themselves whole-heart-

[4] Dr. Flexner, in his book, *Universities, American, English, German* (1930), made a vigorous onslaught against the *ad hoc* training which supplanted liberal culture. Of the several functions which he conceived proper for a university, however, the one which he believed in most ardently was not liberal culture but research, a term that he used with the fine austerity which science at its best inspires. Here he spoke with authority. But whenever he turned to "cultural values," "human values," "humanism," and the "pure, appreciative humanistic spirit," or to the university's responsibility for these things, he betrayed, by his tone, his vagueness, and his casualness that he viewed them essentially from the outside. "With the quick march of science," he observed, "philosophy and humanism have gone under a cloud,"—and there they remain when the reader reaches the last page.

And yet he recognized their place at the very heart of his idea of a modern university. "In the modern university," he acknowledged, "the more vigorously science is prosecuted, the more acute the need that society be held accountable for the purposes to which larger knowledge and experience are turned. Philosophers and critics, therefore, gain in importance as science makes life more complex." To this I think we must agree, as I shall try to make plain in Chapter Seven.

edly to specialized research. In the brief span between 1869, when he became president, and 1909, when he retired, Harvard, Johns Hopkins, Yale, Columbia, Princeton, Chicago, and other universities had created graduate schools that could look without shame across the water to their German prototypes.

Similarly, the state universities, following the pattern of Eastern institutions, developed field after field so thoroughly that their scholars and scientists were not infrequently called East until at length, though called, they perhaps declined to move, being satisfied with their libraries, apparatus, and other conditions of work. Sometimes, as at Iowa, a great school was built up within the administration of a single dean. By 1930 many of the state universities had upon their faculties scholars and scientists of national and international repute, and even the rank and file of their faculties were men—and a few women—capable of useful research and effective graduate teaching. In this respect the contrast between the situation in the liberal college and in the graduate school was sharp. In the liberal college there were few liberal teachers; but in the graduate school of specialized study a majority of the teachers were skilled in the training of specialists. For reasons of economy as well as theory, teachers of graduates were generally also teachers of undergraduates—occasionally, by default, the best teachers of undergraduates. Despite the tendency of the more ambitious and promising students to feel the attractions of the older and more famous institutions of the East and of a stimulatingly new environment in a large city, not a few of them attended a graduate school in their own or a neighboring state because of the lower expense or the adequacy of the department in which they were to work. These students, when they received the stamp of specialization, had a fair chance to rise to prominent teaching positions in the

state universities. For whereas liberal teaching in the liberal college was rarely rewarded by promotion in rank and
salary, specialized teaching, whether in the college or the
graduate school, was fully recognized by colleagues and
administrators. Department heads, deans, and presidents
made it plain that the way to advancement in the teaching
profession was the publication of articles and books offering contributions to the sum of knowledge. To encourage
such work the universities provided, not only promotion of
professors, but also the essential facilities: laboratory equipment, large libraries, scientific and philological journals of
research, and university presses able to publish books not
suitable for commercial publication. In every one of the
many and constantly subdividing fields of learning, the
state universities sought to push forward the frontiers of
knowledge; in some of the fields, they led the endowed universities. A feeling of high enterprise was in the air—of exacting standards, of scholarly integrity, of scientific disin-
terestedness, of labor and zeal in the cause of inquiry, of
freedom and loyalty and fellowship in a great human undertaking.

In this fine manner the graduate school institutionalized,
so to speak, what was certainly noblest in the modern humanitarian programme, its passion for the pursuit of truth
through science. But at the same time the graduate school
reflected, in its procedure and temper, the subversive elements of the modern programme. If there was a feeling of
high enterprise, there was also a feeling of low enterprise.
How could scholarship with vision be expected of young
students who had been graduated, raw or misshapen, from
colleges dominated by mechanical vocationalism? How
could the structure of graduate study be expected to flourish when the substructure of undergraduate study was unsound? A few professors and deans saw clearly the impossi-

bility of far-sighted achievement without a broad basis of general education; the majority, themselves deficient in culture, either repeated in lip-service what the few said, or ascribed the difficulties which they felt to other causes.

The other causes were usually real. Chief among them, perhaps, was the drag of incompetent graduate students in whom it was impossible to inculcate a sense of high enterprise, the mass of students who were anything but intelligent minds dedicated to inquiry. Many of them came to the graduate school much as they had come to college: it was being done, it was the obvious next step, especially if no other step presented itself. Far more of them, however, saw very clearly what they wanted: degrees as a means to success in life. Generally they were teachers; perhaps they wished to become good teachers, and hoped that a higher degree would automatically produce this result; but mainly they just wanted pleasanter and better-paid positions than they held. Some of the incompetent had plenty of industry; a few were pathetically eager to do all that was expected of them, and were quite unable to understand why they did not therefore please their instructors. And by dint of long plodding even the poorest students might hope eventually to "get through." For the benefit of incompetent students it was necessary to employ in the high enterprise of the graduate school virtually the whole paraphernalia of credits, regulations, red tape and many-colored cards, clerks, offices, and factory bustle—the whole paraphernalia of mass production. There was even added machinery, much for the complicated doctorate, less for the simpler master's degree. The work for the master's degree ordinarily included a final examination, written and oral, in the major and minor subjects, with appropriate arrangements respecting the same, and a thesis due at a certain date, typed in a certain way, fully decorated with footnotes, charts, graphs, and bibliographies. In the unrealistic language of graduate school catalogues, the thesis must present a contribution to the sum of human knowledge, as evidence of the candidate's capacity for independent and original investigation, a requirement which was maintained in the interest of "standards" despite the fact that standards cannot be upheld by any requirement that is not enforced. In general, the faculty was highly ingenious in devising requirements and safeguards, and highly delinquent in making use of them. When the results were bad, they devised more requirements and safeguards, which in turn were not used. That is, in courses, theses, and final examinations they pronounced shoddy work passable.

For the scientific passion of the faculty, which implied high standards attainable by the few, was undermined by its humanitarian passion, which implied low standards accessible to the many. This humanitarian passion took two forms, one general and one particular. Thinking of students generally, professors, along with administrators, "tacitly conspired," as Dr. Zook puts it, "to encourage mere numbers." They were genially inclined toward the theory that the graduate school, like the college, should welcome the bulk of students who came or could be induced to come. A few might be weeded out, the rest must be allowed to set the standard for passing. The graduate school in a state university had the social function of raising the level of the intellectual life of the state by serving as many individuals as it decently (or indecently) could. The inferior students would emerge, after a year or so, with a better knowledge of their subject and some glimmering notion of the meaning of research, improved in their capacity to serve as teachers or otherwise. Thinking of particular students rather than students in general, professors displayed a sympathy which, at times admirable in itself, unquestionably had the effect of depressing stand-ards. Mr. A is a likable, hardworking person who has greatly improved; he may have the benefit of the doubt, even if there is no doubt. Miss B, though a weak student, is financially pressed and wears unsightly shoes; she has done her best, will never do better, and might as well be passed. Mr. C, gaunt and worried, has unluckily a wife and child, but little else; if he does not get through, he and his will be stranded. Miss D, also gaunt and worried, sore beset with want of funds and brain power, is actually in danger of losing her mind; a pass may save her. And so it goes. In each case a service is rendered to human beings with whom the instructor has been rather closely associated for a year or two. This was not graduate education, but personal charity overriding professional duty. So far as it signified an interest in individual students, it was admira-ble; so far as it resulted in giving students that to which they had no right, it was subversively sentimental. And, as happens with sentimentalism, generous impulses were sometimes mixed with ignoble motives: by passing enough students the instructor made his teaching attractive rather than forbidding, and, if his teaching seemed attractive to students, it would look well to an expansive administra-tion.

While the feeling of low enterprise was especially occa-sioned by the sort of work tolerated in the programme of the master's degree, it extended all the way to the end of the programme for the doctor's degree, the highest degree in course, "the indispensable prehensile tail for academic climbing," as someone has called it. Through a series of decades the significance of this degree steadily declined. At one time awarded to exceptional students whose prepara-tory work had been liberal and whose advanced work had been professional, it came to be awarded to large numbers of degree-seekers whose education, properly speaking, had been neither liberal nor professional. Although the faculties, in theory, jealously guarded the highest degree in their keeping, they countenanced, in practice, standards which they knew to be inadequate. Merely average students were accepted as candidates and eventually pronounced scholars, despite the device of a series of hurdles to be leaped. Generally there was a preliminary examination, but as likely as not it was either perfunctory, limited to revealing "gaps" in knowledge to be filled in later, or else so searching that it had to be postponed till it was no longer preliminary—till the student had lived in the departmental family so long that he could scarcely be disowned. Furthermore, if the student performed badly, it might be that he was unduly nervous, or that the questioning had not been altogether happy, or that his course record, implying piecemeal competence, should be taken into consideration; and, in any case, there were more hurdles ahead. But a duty postponed becomes a duty hard to execute. As the years went on—the minimum period was three, but the plodding student could continue indefinitely—as the student's sacrifice of money and time grew larger and larger, as his industry and determination and worry became more and more intense, the prospect of "failing him" gradually faded away. The department found itself wishing it had not passed him at the preliminary examination, but to fail him now might mean a tragedy, a life career blasted. And the department took refuge in a theory of justice which was only a theory of precedent: Miss C was as good as Miss B or Mr. A who were passed last year or the year before, *ergo* Miss C should be passed. Or the department went in for something akin to log-rolling: a vote against the candidate might be interpreted as a vote against the professor supervising his work, who might later vote against one's own candidate. Besides, there was always the consoling reflection that the new doctor, deficient in ability, would probably secure a position as teacher in an institution so humble that he could hardly attract notice. Nor, being infecund as a scholar, would he shame his former instructors by rash publication. On the surface things looked well: the department had many students and turned out a goodly number of doctors each year.

Success for the plodder was rendered the easier by a certain hesitation on the part of the graduate school as to the central objective of graduate instruction. Was it a thorough grounding in scientific principles, or an erudite command of a subject, or attainment of skill in a technique? And how should the graduate school guard against the narrowing effects of premature and excessive specialization? As for unwise specialization, this might be prevented well enough by the requirement of a minor subject, and a minor was usually required; but the value of this expedient was vitiated in practice by the tendency to advise the choice of a closely neighboring subject or even the choice of a subdivision of the major subject. In the latter case registration could be kept comfortably within the major department, and the department would thrive. Furthermore, the horror of over-specialization was not very real. The serious problem was, rather, whether instruction should aim at basic principles, or at erudition, or at technique. Ideally, it was supposed to aim at all three. In fact, however, despite the high enterprise of the graduate school, only a small proportion of the students and by no means all of the faculty were competent to undertake the serious pursuit of truth. The basic principles of science, the exploration of the unknown were made incidental or trivial. In many departments the main object was merely erudition, the accumulation of the largest possible mass of knowledge and information: a rich absorption in every field of the subject and a saturation in one special field. Probably the main object in most departments, however, was training in technique, or more properly techniques—ways of doing this, that, and the other. The methods and attitudes of the trade-school, which dominated undergraduate education in a practical epoch, occupied a large place in the graduate school as well. The skills and tricks of the profession of scholarship, rather than its essential nature and procedure, were placed in the foreground. The emphasis on methods in the department of education was often derided by members of other departments equally engrossed in methods. A short-sighted mechanical dexterity, not a far-sighted searching for lands beyond the frontier, gave the intellectual tone of both teaching and learning. It also gave the incompetent something to do.

In such an atmosphere true research—creative scholarship—inevitably breathed with difficulty, and was sometimes smothered. Exceptional young men and women, broadly developed and gifted with powers of insight, were loath to enter the graduate school. In various departments of learning, they did not enter; the best "material," as the athletes say, kept out. Able students who did enter were often rebellious, for sound as well as unsound reasons, and felt hampered at every turn—by their incompetent associates in the dormitories, by the weight of numbers in courses where discussion was desirable, by lesson assignments, tests, and the like, by lectures addressed to slow minds, by the professors' lack of time for superior students, and so forth. Occasionally a fine relationship sprang up between a gifted student and some of his instructors, but on the whole the graduate school quite failed to make adequate provision for those who could best use its facilities. In fact it was a

busy place where small-minded technical experts and in-
experts could be turned out expeditiously, not an intellectual home for leisurely growth and quiet creative achievement.

§ 3

In the anarchy of specialisms that characterized the entire
university—liberal college, professional schools, and graduate school alike—a certain semblance of unity of purpose
was achieved by means of indoctrination. Not that indoctrination was deliberate, for the great majority of the
faculty held any attempt to influence the opinions of students to be a violation of their code of intellectual morals.
It was conventional for professors to declare that their
teaching was strictly neutral, and to wax indignant at colleagues who might be suspected of propaganda. Apparently
the supposedly neutral professors were unaware that the
history of education—a subject which did not concern
them, though it dealt with their own calling—shows that
education has always indoctrinated, and equally unaware
that the philosophy of education—a subject which they
found too flimsy for serious consideration—indicates that
education in its very nature is indoctrination, not merely
because it dispenses selected knowledge but also because
it inculcates, directly or indirectly, doctrines, opinions, and
attitudes. Thus, in its entrance requirements the university
indoctrinated. In its prescribed courses the university indoctrinated. In its bristling array of curricula the university indoctrinated. In its zeal for efficiency, for power
and service, for the entire programme of the humanitarian
movement, the university indoctrinated. Among all its
teachings, however, one stood out as the most significant:
in its unquestionable form, a belief in science; in its ques-
tionable form, a belief in what may be called scientism.

By a belief in science I mean an intelligent appreciation of the fact that science has provided a method of learning and a body of knowledge which are of incalculable value for human purposes. By a belief in scientism I mean a more or less exclusive devotion to the methods, mental attitudes, and doctrines appropriate to science, ordinarily culminating in some form of naturalistic speculation. The distinction between the two, as I wish to show in a later chapter, is of the highest importance, and may affect profoundly the future history of the state university. And yet the distinction is rarely made in our time. A belief in science is all but universal; and so is a belief in scientism.

The two were already hopelessly confused in the thought of Herbert Spencer, whose dogma of progress we have already glanced at, and who concerns us here because of his influential book on *Education,* if we are to credit the assertion of President Eliot, in his edition of the book, that "the wide adoption of Spencer's educational ideals awaited the coming of the state university." Spencer formulated his ideals in an epoch in which education suffered from an excess of tradition and convention, against which he rightly protested in the name of science, though it does not follow that he protested in the right way. Common sense dictated the necessity of recognizing, throughout the educational system, what modern science had done, was doing, and was in a way to doing; but this did not suffice. A belief in science was needed; but Spencer went further, and called for a belief in scientism. The two were deeply blended in all his thinking and feeling. A sufficient instance is the well-known peroration of the essay on the question "What Knowledge is of Most Worth?" "The uniform reply is—Science. This is the verdict on all the counts. For direct self-preservation, or the maintenance of life and health, the all-important knowledge is—Science. For that indirect self-preservation which we call gaining a livelihood, the knowledge of greatest value is—Science. For the due discharge of parental functions, the proper guidance is to be found only in—Science. For that interpretation of national life, past and present, without which the citizen cannot rightly regulate his conduct, the indispensable key is—Science. Alike for the most perfect production and highest enjoyment of art in all its forms, the needful preparation is still—Science. And for purposes of discipline—intellectual, moral, religious—the most efficient study is, once more—Science. . . . All Science concerns all mankind for all time." Neglected and obscure, a mere household drudge ministering to her haughty sisters, Science is fast coming into her own. "Science, proclaimed as highest alike in worth and beauty, will reign supreme."

Ecstatic proclamation of this new absolute monarch was natural enough during the "orgy of scientific triumph," as Professor Whitehead has called it, which occurred in the middle of the nineteenth century. In that century as a whole, according to Eliot, the growth of organized knowledge was "greater than in all the thirty preceding centuries put together." [5] Along with this knowledge came into the world, as Eliot reminds us elsewhere, the temper of mind called scientific—and, he might have added, scientistic—bringing about in many men nothing short of an inner revolution. The scientific search for truth, Eliot declared in terms as reckless as Spencer's, is "the new passion and religion of today. . . . That is a wonderful prophecy in John viii, 32: 'Ye shall know the truth and the truth shall make you free.' " [6] From the eighteen-fifties to the nineteen-thirties, rapturously muddled utterances of this sort abounded, not, to be sure, among the best scientists, but

[5] Op. cit.

[6] Education for Efficiency (Riverside Educational Monograph, 1909).

among lesser scientists and especially journalists and educators. It became conventional to open an article, a university address, even a sermon, with the words: "This is a scientific age," pronounced with a certain complacence. By the end of the third decade of the twentieth century, when the freshly accelerated pace of science suggested no end of new possibilities, the formula sometimes read: "We are at the beginning of a scientific age." [7] Whenever the scientists were balked—and this usually happened at the points of deepest human import—they were accustomed to promise, "We are about to know . . .", or to grant with proud modesty, "We do not yet know . . .", implying the correlative "but soon" or "eventually." Journalists began their scientific and pseudo-scientific news stories with the words, "Science says," as if they had just had an interview with the Highest. Educators like John Dewey observed that, despite all our science, the spirit of Science had not descended upon us, and insisted that "Every course in every subject should have as its chief end the cultivation of the scientific attitude." [8]

Both science and scientism were taught by the universities. A recognition of the importance of science was taught when one after another natural science was introduced into the curriculum and constituted the subject of an academic department. It was taught whenever a more or less extensive study of natural science was required of all students. It was taught whenever administrative leaders and professors of any subject pointed out the value of understanding and controlling nature. It was taught when one after another applied science was given a place in the university.

[7] These are the opening words of a typical textbook on high school teaching—J. A. Kinneman, *op. cit.*

[8] From an address by Dr. Dewey in honor of Dr. J. McKeen Cattell, December 27, 1933.

Above all, a recognition of the value of science was inculcated by the doctrine that the method of science will yield results, not in the natural sciences alone, but in any subject whatever.

Closely connected with this genuinely scientific indoctrination, however, was another kind of indoctrination which must be called scientistic. This took place when required courses and curricula pointed the student toward an education primarily scientific. It took place when the guides of youth insisted, with Eliot, that we must have not only an understanding of but also a "sympathy" with nature. It took place when faculties contrived ways of using science as an educational instrument for attaining quick success in an acquisitive society. Above all, it took place when students were imbued with the notion that the only respectable way of studying any subject was by the method of science and in the light of a naturalistic interpretation.

The subjects that lent themselves most readily to indoctrination of a scientific and scientistic sort were the natural sciences, along with some of the applied sciences. In respect to effective indoctrination of this sort the best taught subjects in the curriculum were physics, astronomy, geology, biology, chemistry, and applied subjects like engineering and agriculture. Rigid observation, controlled experiment, exact quantitative research, laborious verification, creative imagination held to its task by fact and reason—these could be readily taught in the observatory, laboratory, and experimental station. The soundness of such teaching is obvious. But something more was taught. The clear results attainable through scientific method frequently led the teacher to adopt some kind of naturalistic faith—a view of the universe in which matter or natural forces occupied the central position, a tendency to apply the relativistic and evolutionary doctrines of natural science to human in-

terests and affairs, a disposition to believe in general progress and to attach one's hopes, not to any traditions or
folk-ways carried over from a dying past, but to the contributions of science in the vital present and the unborn
future.

I do not wish to imply for a moment that devotion to the
sciences called natural *necessarily* leads to adoption of the
philosophy of naturalism. A professor of physics or biology,
if he is a dualistic Christian, for example, can certainly believe in the supernatural as well as the natural. There is
nothing to prevent a professor of geology or chemistry, if
he happens to prize the wisdom of Plato or Aristotle or Pascal, from conceiving of human nature in a manner nowise
suggested by his professed subject. I mean simply that a certain mental set is encouraged by an exclusive devotion to
the natural sciences, that the professor who seeks *all* his
knowledge and wisdom within the doctrines and implications of science will turn out to be a naturalist in the
philosophic sense.[9] Certainly this is what occurred in the
state universities of the early twentieth century, in which
devout Christians and ardent Platonists were scarcely in the
ascendency. All but a negligible number of our professors
of natural science were naturalists, not humanists or supernaturalists. They taught not only natural science and the
method of science, but, consciously or unconsciously, a naturalistic interpretation of life. Despite their disparagement
of mere "authority," they taught with pronounced authority, because natural science was manifestly a substantial
subject and the method of science as exacting as fruitful.
It was inevitably suggested to the student that any conclu-

[9] "Naturalism . . . *Philos.* The doctrine which expands conceptions
drawn from the natural sciences into a world view, denying that anything
in reality has a supernatural or more than natural significance" (*Webster's New International Dictionary*). It is opposed to both humanism and
religion: see Chapter Seven.

sions of a philosophical kind that seemed logically to grow out of so substantial a subject and so exacting a method possessed a high degree of probability, if not an irrefragable certainty. In time this sort of indoctrination attracted the attention of unscientific portions of the American public and was denounced as atheistic. For a few years a number of states, notoriously Tennessee, displayed an obscurantist attitude that did not stop to make fine distinctions between science and scientism.[10]

If the natural sciences lend themselves readily to both forms of indoctrination, it might be supposed that a subject like religion would prove intractable, that science and religion were two things, reconcilable if one were ingenious enough, but yet distinct approaches to reality. But the age had announced that it was scientific, that every subject of interest to man must be scientized. Could not religion be redeemed from its confusion and passionate intolerance and be quietly and securely based upon science and scientific method? I am not here concerned with the way of attaining this end suggested by the new science of psychology, which seemed to show how religion, once esteemed as a cure for the soul's sickness, should be regarded as a sign of the soul's sickness. I have in mind, rather, the attempt to render religion fit for scientific research by classifying it with the so-called social sciences. Admittedly, the difficulties were formidable. There might be some doubt about the classification, and even if that doubt were removed, the subject would inherit all the handicaps of social science. Obviously social science could never hope to rival natural science in respect to rigid observation, controlled

[10] Since the war, the university subjects that have roused the antagonism of small-town folk and state legislators have been, rather, psychology and sociology. The indoctrination going on in these subjects has been costly to the state universities in dollars and cents.

experiment, exact quantitative research, laborious verification, and creative imagination held in check by fact and
reason; obviously, it could not enjoy the use of such ob-
servatories, laboratories, and experimental stations as natural science enjoyed. Its problems could not be tested by
tubes, or microscopes, or telescopes. They were almost
hopelessly intangible and almost endlessly complex. And
their complexity was due mainly to the fact that the unit
with which they dealt, the human being, is itself endlessly
complex. Besides, the personal equation of the investigator,
himself a human being, would offer enormous difficulties
of a sort against which the natural investigator had considerable protection.

But the attempt was made. For example, let us glance at
the science of religion as presented by the professor of
comparative religion in the University of Chicago, who in
1929 offered his findings in popular form in *The Quest of
the Ages*. Professor Haydon made bold to call for a religion based on authority, but a new authority "consonant
with the age of science." "Scientific method in religion,"
he averred, "is a new thing under the sun, growing out of
a modern understanding of the nature of religion in the
history of the race." The nature of religion was displayed,
it seems, even before the human race began, for "a shared
quest of the good life" animated "lowly organisms at the
dawn of time." At length came man, a child of Mother
Earth (not of God the Father). Man created many religions, including some supernatural faiths compensating
for his mundane defeats, all of which are found by the
scientific historian to have had one aspect in common: all
were instances of social aspiration. Religion is simply social aspiration. "There are no peculiarly religious values.
Politics, industry, science, education, morality, art . . .—
religion includes them all in a synthesis of the ideal of the

good life." In the future, religion will continue because men will always want a good shared life. The programme of religion hereafter should be to undertake, with the aid of scientific method, the task of "guaranteeing economic freedom and security," as the first step toward making all the goods of life on the planet available to everybody. The signs are auspicious, for today "the world peoples draw together."

Such is the scientific view of religion, and such the programme of religion in an age of science. For his programme the author is content to use the name *humanism* favored by Dr. Charles Francis Potter and other churchmen, though he rightly regards *naturalistic idealism* as a more accurate label. As a naturalistic idealist, he proposes to build his hopes for a rationally ordered human life upon the foundations of science, optimistically ignoring the fact that these foundations have been sketched rather than constructed. Scientists themselves, when sober, recognize that theirs is a quest of the ages, also. In words which deserve close reading, Professor P. W. Bridgman remarks: "No one who has not thought about it can realize how pathetically deficient we are at present in even the preliminary data which are necessary before a start can be made in living a rationally ordered life." [11]

The subject of religion, however, occupies a small place, if any place at all, in the courses of instruction offered by the state universities. We shall find a far more representative example of scientific and scientistic indoctrination in the subject once known as pedagogy and now known as education. This subject, furthermore, has come to be of pivotal importance because of the power of those who profess it. "The 'educationist' is firmly intrenched. Persons of

[11] "The Struggle for Intellectual Integrity," *Harper's Magazine*, December, 1933.

the same stripe occupy the professorships in education, the offices of the state departments, and even the superintendencies and principalships of our schools. They are administrative in their outlook, and desirous of building up a strong bureaucratic guild." [12] Increasingly, in the early twentieth century, they determined the work of the schools in which students were shaped for college, and in college shaped them further through majors in education [13] and the studies they prescribed for the teacher's certificate.

Whether this situation involved a beneficent or a vicious circle depended on one's opinion of the point of view and the practices of the department or school of education. Certainly the general faculty opinion in most universities, for reasons not altogether clear, was overwhelmingly unfavorable. There was envy of the power possessed by educationists, together with resentful charges of imperialistic abuse of that power. There was a widespread belief, natural among specialists, that prospective teachers need all available time for the mastery of the subject or subjects they expect to teach. There was a common charge that the subject of education is flimsy or flimsily taught—though many of the critics were themselves teaching subjects that might appear to be flimsy or flimsily taught. There was the opinion, already mentioned, that educationists are too much concerned with method—though many who held this opinion were engrossed in mere technique and the paraphernalia of learning, or even practical shortcuts and trade

[12] R. M. Ogden, professor of education and dean of the College of Arts and Sciences, Cornell University, in the *Journal of Proceedings of the Association of American Universities*, 1935, p. 89. See also H. M. Jones, "Betrayal in American Education," *Scribner's Magazine*, June, 1933.

[13] An exception is the College of Education at the University of Iowa, which has for many years required prospective teachers to major in some academic subject; only graduates preparing for administration or supervision are encouraged to major in education.

tricks. And there was the reproach that teachers of teaching appear to be rather less likely than teachers of subjects to be good teachers, that they do not practice what they preach. Yet the fact is that professors of education had loyally subscribed to the unwritten law of the university that every subject that has worth—and what could be worthier than a field recognized by all professors since all were active in it?—should be studied by specialists in a scientific manner. The science of education was virtually created in the first thirty years of the present century. It had no doubt the earmarks of a young and impatient science; it was faddish, it made vast claims, it rarely surpassed, and often fell short of, common sense. As late as 1929 a well-known educationist found the work of his colleagues "still marked by an embarrassing lack of a positive science of the subject." [14] But could not the same be said of other sciences struggling to be born?

Much of the unfavorable judgment of education was due, I think, to the fact that professors of other subjects believed that long observation and experience had given them an understanding of the nature of good teaching. Here was one field, in addition to their specialty, in which they possessed knowledge and conviction. After all, they were not merely physicists, historians, and so forth, but professors of physics, history, and so forth. They might defer to specialists in other fields, such as astronomy or hydraulics, but in education they claimed a certain competence. Educators themselves, they believed that most of what they saw going on in the science of education was superficial, or trivial, or simply misguided, and that at best education could never hope to become a really important science. (At times they suspected as much of other alleged sciences, but inexpertness made them cautious.) While a few things

[14] Edgar W. Knight, *Education in the United States* (1929, 1934), p. 45.

might be learned in a scientific way, education was first of all an art. Teaching ability, like literary or graphic ability, was chiefly a matter of endowment. It could be greatly enhanced by emulation of one's own best teachers, and by the discipline of long effort and experience, but very slightly by the method of science. Good teaching was a vital, not a mechanical process; the teacher himself, his personality, his quality of mind, was centrally important. The generality of professors were inclined to agree with Spencer's view that "Bad teachers will fail even with the best methods" and that they will fail the more signally in proportion as the methods are good. For this reason professors were not impressed with the educationist argument in its most modest form, that the function of the department of education is to prevent bad teachers from doing harm.

They perceived, furthermore, that the type of men going into the science of education were not likely to accomplish valuable results. The best scientific minds were going into other sciences. There were exceptions, to be sure, but the number of really distinguished scientists and wise administrators who had been trained extensively in professional education was extremely small. And certainly the richly cultivated minds were rarely attracted to the subject, a most deplorable fact if it be true, after all, that education is primarily an art. The rank and file—and they were many, because the educational aspirations of America were many —were men in whom the curious "thinness" of American academic life reached its maximum attenuation: hard, brittle men, matter-of-fact, literal-minded, practical unto impracticality.

A single example of educationist science and scientism must serve to illustrate. It is, I think, an average specimen. It presents the results of an analysis of the normal "life activities" of college graduates, with a view to determining a selection of studies that would prepare all students for adult living. A woman's college was chosen, with the remark that "Undoubtedly the extracurricular activities of men do not differ essentially in title" (whatever that may mean) . "It was found that the activities common to all college graduates irrespective of vocation, and at the same time subject to training, might be divided into seven groups, as follows: communication; the maintenance of physical health; the preservation of mental health; aesthetic appreciation; participation in social, economic, and political activities; the integration of personality; and the art of consumption. This does not include child-training, because it is not an extravocational activity of unmarried women." Careful analysis having revealed the seven activities of adult living, the investigator was ready to set down the corresponding "constants in a curriculum for a woman's college," which are obviously "English composition; physiology, hygiene, and physical education; psychology; a general course in aesthetic appreciation; a general social-science course for the woman citizen; an integrating course in philosophy, religion and ethics to give a life point of view; and a course in consumption to instruct women how on the financial side to buy intelligently and on the spiritual side to get the highest quality of satisfaction from expended effort." [15]

[15] W. W. Charters, director of the Bureau of Educational Research, Ohio State University, in *Higher Education in America* (ed. R. A. Kent, 1930), pp. 40-41. The example given above suggests how scientism builds a college curriculum. For an example of how it builds a curriculum in a single subject, see *An Experience Curriculum in English* (1935), a report of the curriculum commission of the National Council of Teachers of English.—This sort of thing has been running rampant ever since the time, say, when Charles W. Eliot advocated school training of ear and nose to offset the bad sounds and smells of modern civilization (*Education for Efficiency*, p. 7).

It may be that the literal mind, as distinguished from the liberal mind, has its place in some of the natural sciences, where it is quickly checked if it attempts more than it can do, but it works havoc in subjects like sociology and education, where it is free to run wild in disregard of complexities and intangibilities. These it either cannot see or does not wish to see. Like the unscientific mind, the literal mind spends much of its time in thinking what it wishes—a practice apparently approved by one educational sociologist who maintains that "it is a task of science and hence of education" to encourage "thinkful wishing."

Despite its insistence on definiteness, the literal mind is usually a vague mind. The books and articles which it produces, and which form the daily pabulum of students and teachers of education, are not only dull and pedestrian (one cannot expect all scientists to write like Tyndall and Huxley), but astonishingly low in intellectual tone, the work of unbraced minds, crude, loose, illogical, at times illiterate. These facile scientists might have written otherwise if they had had what they seemed to need, ten years of discipline in the precise statement and close reasoning of the much-despised schoolmen of the Middle Ages, who attained a finesse rarely equalled by the human mind since; something like this might have given our educationists and social scientists the clearness and cogency which they do not have, without loss of scientific integrity. If this suggestion is laughed out of court, one might recommend, with Paul Shorey, some of the writers of the scientific nineteenth century, such as John Stuart Mill, from whom students may today learn "lessons of comprehensive and consecutive thinking, judicial weighing of all considerations pro and con, temperance and precision of expression, and scrupulous fairness to opponents, which they will hardly get from the undigested mixtures of biology, nervous anatomy, anthropology and folk-lore, answers to *questionnaires*, statistics, and reports from the pedagogical or psychological seminar, with a seasoning of uncritical historical and illiterate literary illustration, that compose the made-to-order textbooks of pedagogy, sociology, ethics, and psychology on which their minds are fed."[16] Certainly a scientist equipped for his task should be incapable of beginning a chapter in a book named *Educational Sociology* with a definition that reads: "Educational sociology is what sociology can do for education." Nor should a scientist who writes about society and for society declare his rhetorical incompetence by saying that "Rhetoric has been studied from the viewpoint of memorizing definitions of figures of speech, with no effort having been made to teach an ability to use effective language." The remedy for such ineptness is not a course in Educationist English, nor even a general course in English grammar and syntax, for the difficulty concerns far more than the art of putting words together. What, one may well ask, is the "correlation" of such feeble expression and the total intellectual quality of the writer? Is one not justified in questioning whether a mind that behaves in this manner can cope with any large and difficult problem, no matter how full the statistical data "is"?

Since most of the energy of educationists in the period from 1900 to 1930 was expended upon the collection of data concerning teaching methods, and since the basic science in the investigation of methods was psychology, something must here be said of this science as well. As one educationist put it, "Methodology cannot progress faster than psychology which supplies the basis for thinking about teaching methods." Is the basis solid? "Psychology," he an-

[16] Address delivered in 1910, included in *Representative Phi Beta Kappa Orations* (ed. C. S. Northup), 1930.

swers, "is no longer a mere introspective analysis of mind, whatever the term 'mind' may mean. It concerns itself, in the main, with measurable phenomena. It is rapidly becoming an objective and quantitative study of environmental influences of an inherited mechanism." [17] This statement suggests a degree of unity in the subject which was belied by the conflicting doctrines and violent controversies in writing on psychology and educational psychology.[18] More cautiously, the director of the psychology laboratory at Harvard refers to the common criticism, "often spoken and sometimes written, that the new science has not quite succeeded, that it has been, as compared with its ambitions, relatively sterile, that it set out to study mind by the experimental method, and that it has gained a mass of knowledge about sensation (which the physiologists might have gained), a little else, and nothing of great moment about the rational mind, the personality, and human nature." [19]

The reasons for this dearth of positive results Professor Boring believes to be, first, a dearth of great psychologists, and, secondly, the continuing interpenetration of psychology with philosophy. In regard to the second reason he goes on to say: "Often the very men who cry out most loudly against philosophy in psychology are the men who regard psychology as a system and who write of epistemological matters. All the movements in psychology that have led to self-conscious schools—Wundt's physiological psychology, introspectionism in America, functional psychology, *Gestalt* psychology, behaviorism, but not animal psy-

[17] Paul Klapper, introduction to R. D. Cole, *The Modern Foreign Languages and Their Teaching* (1931).

[18] See, for example, *Psychologies of 1930* (ed. Carl Murchison, the International University Series in Psychology).

[19] E. G. Boring, *A History of Experimental Psychology* (1929), pp. 658-59.

chology nor the mental tests—have been philosophical movements, conducted, for the most part, by men who would eschew philosophy and rely solely upon the experimental method." However scrupulous in their data, these men made their data serve extra-scientific interpretations, and then claimed the authority of science for their findings. A sufficiently typical instance is that of the dean of American psychologists, Dr. J. McKeen Cattell, who, as editor of *Science, The Scientific Monthly,* and *School and Society,* had a wide opportunity to shape opinion among scientists and educators. When awarded the medal of the Society of Arts and Sciences in 1930, Dr. Cattell expressed a series of views that were the outcome, not of experiment, but of the hateful practice of "armchair philosophy," among them these: "The selection, training, and directing of men are problems of applied psychology; it is also for psychology to determine what does in fact benefit the human race. . . . Applied science, based in large measure on scientific research whose utility was not at the time obvious, has been the cause of the political and social institutions that we have and of the lives that we lead. The applications of science have done more to control our behavior than efforts made with this object directly in view, such as those of the churches, the schools, the courts, and the state. . . . Psychology can do more by placing individuals in surroundings where they will act in the way that is wanted than by attempting to change individuals." [20] These are indeed arresting and ambitious dogmas, resting upon philosophic assumptions that are not stated and raising a host of philosophic questions that are quietly ignored. As is the case with most dogmas, they could be supported with reasons, and some of the reasons, in turn, could be supported with selected facts. A university professor, be it

[20] "The Usefulness of Psychology," *Science,* September 19, 1930.

said, has a right to indoctrinate in this manner, if he so desires; only, he has no right to claim for his doctrines the authority of science.

Though inexpert in philosophy, the psychologists seemed to sanction the naturalistic and humanitarian philosophy held by the educationists, who were also inexpert in philosophy and sometimes in psychology as well. The educationists then passed on this philosophy to the teachers and administrators, who passed it on to the pupils in the schools. And through this series of indoctrinations, together with the journalistic indoctrination of adults through popular magazines and the raucous Sunday supplement, it came about that the American public was confirmed in its inherited faith in the humanitarian ideology, which seemed to rest upon the authority of science.

PART III

THE UNIVERSITY AFTER 1930

Chapter Five

DOUBTS AND DRIFTS

§ 1

WHEN THE YEARS OF THE DEPRESSION AR-
rived, the universities found themselves in a new intellectual and social milieu. The confidence and energy that
had been carried over from the nineteenth century were
suddenly shattered; their place was taken by bewilderment and paralysis. While the prevailing mood continued
to be quite as materialistic as in the preceding phase of the
humanitarian movement, there was a marked tendency to
question the forces characteristic of the movement. The
natural man's democracy, utilitarian science, and faith in
progress, though they had apparently enabled society to
create some sort of order, had prevented neither the greatest war in history nor the world chaos which followed the
war and finally overtook America. Could they, unchanged,
be relied on for the building of a new and secure social
edifice?

It was hard to remember that, as lately as the year 1917,
Woodrow Wilson had rallied the spiritual forces of the
country for the completion of the conquest of the world
by democracy. In the tidal waves after the war, democracy
foundered in one European country after another, and in

America, when the depression arrived, it threatened to follow the same course. The incompetence of the people's representatives in Congress was now the favorite target of editors, cartoonists, and humorists. A public which had been indifferent to or resentful of such attacks as H. L. Mencken had made in his *Notes on Democracy* in 1926, chuckled over similar attacks which appeared in the daily newspapers of the nation in the nineteen-thirties over the name of Will Rogers. Faith in democracy, as that term had been understood, was shaken as it had not been in previous depressions. The glory had departed. If the humanitarian movement was to go on, it would somehow have to put new meaning into democracy.

In the midst of the celebration of a Century of Progress, the newspapers of the United States announced, one day, that "Merchants signing the NIRA agreements will each receive two indoor cards, two outdoor cards, two hangers, 10 large stickers, 20 small stickers, 20 consumers' tickets, and 20 consumers' statements of coöperation." During the same summer, state after state, by voting for the repeal of the Prohibition amendment, recorded its belief that the people could not be legislated into virtuous efficiency. A noble experiment had failed; a much nobler experiment was now to be tried, a new deal on a grand scale symbolized by multiplying initials, every manner of act and organization to produce virtuous efficiency. Power and service, the twin gods of the humanitarian movement, had turned out to be power and service for the few; they must hereafter be for all. America, the land of liberty, having made liberty unendurable, next proposed to give a serious trial to equality. Would equality likewise be made unendurable? No one could say. All government involves a compromise between individual and social control, the precise nature of which should depend upon each situation viewed in all its aspects. It was widely believed that the emergency situation of America in 1933 called for a marked shift of emphasis in the direction of social control. To many it seemed that something like governmental and industrial socialism, which might have horrified Thomas Jefferson even more than a *laissez faire* plutocracy, must now be attempted, whether temporarily or permanently. In deference to Jefferson, it was often called democracy. Russian communism now had its admirers, though nobody knew just what it actually was; Italian fascism, prior to its application of a deadly technology to Ethiopia, had its admirers; a thousand and one varieties of socialistic utopias had their admirers; Senator Long, Father Coughlin, and Dr. Townsend had their admirers. Even the intellectuals turned against democracy, Old Style, partly because it had not worked, and partly because its dogmas could not endure the facts being amassed against them by political scientists, psychologists, and biologists. While a few diehards clung to democracy as the system that produces the minimum slavery, the up-and-coming apparently wished to transform the old American dream of life, liberty, and the pursuit of happiness to the new American dream of life, regimentation, and the guarantee of security.

Along with democracy, science lost prestige. Since the problems of the day were urgently practical, it was natural to look to the science of economics for guidance. But when Montagu Norman, governor of the Bank of England, admitted his inability to understand the forces behind the depression, despite his access to vast information, he also admitted the impotence of economic science to devise measures of assured applicability. The strange and often contradictory theories evolved by the experts, including the "brain trusters" summoned to Washington, left the public confused and apprehensive. The blessings of tech-

nological science came to be suspect. The chronic fear of
the Machine, symbolized early in the industrial revolution
by a Frankenstein monster turning upon its creator,
symbolized less grimly in the prosperous 1920's by the
robots of Capek's play, became acute during the seven-
days' wonder of Technocracy. Apparently the cool-blooded
scientists, abjuring social responsibility, were unleashing
forces, in war and in peace, that might defy "adjustment"
and bring our civilization to ruins—how could they answer
that charge? "Not since the days when they were under
close surveillance of the Church," said Dr. Harvey Cushing, "have scientists been put in a defensive position of
this kind. But in this instance it is not the theologian but
the man in the street and on the farm who is asking his
neighbor, 'What price science?' " [1]

Nor was the situation more promising if one turned
from the machine of our external life to the machine of
our internal life as conceived by the new science of psychology. The widespread interest in this subject between
the war and the depression had been due mainly to the
hope that through it man might learn to control himself
and his fellows; but if psychology proved anything, it
seemed to prove not only that people differed in intelligence but that in the aggregate they had very little of it—
that, if not a great beast, as Hamilton had opined, the people were certainly a great fool. Before 1929 this conclusion
seemed interesting; after that, discouraging and unprofita-
ble. Although the depression was said to be largely psychological, psychology was powerless to devise a remedy. Becoming weary of the procession of psychologic *isms* and
noting the failure of the *isms* to coalesce into an impres-

[1] Presidential address, 1935, before the History of Science Society.

sive science, the public turned its attention to other matters.[2]

But what of the old sciences of nature? The magnificent structure which physical science had erected in the full flush of nineteenth-century enthusiasm had crumbled. As Robert A. Millikan declared, "The childish mechanical conceptions of the nineteenth century are now grotesquely inadequate." [3] Science was now grown up, and was about to discover God, or ultimate reality, or nothingness—the layman could scarcely tell which. Certain distinguished scientists, addressing the public in a reckless mood, seemed to be in favor of God; but more cautious scientists, like Kirtley F. Mather, were content with saying, "Today we are beginning to suspect that the mind of man is incapable of grappling with ultimate reality in any truly scientific way." [4] The layman was sorely puzzled, again, when told that freedom of will had been proved in one science and disproved in another, nor was he comforted when it was explained that the term had different meanings in physics and in psychology. He could hardly hope to penetrate to the meanings; for that matter, he could not see, save through a glass darkly, the significance of any of the most celebrated discoveries of twentieth-century science. Layers of rocks accompanied by layers of monkeys or men had seemed fairly simple, as well as scandalous, to the Victorian mind, but the ways of relativity, of protons and electrons, are not easy to visualize, or to relate to one's philosophy of life, or to use in business and conversation. Whether a science engaged in these remote speculations will itself

[2] The history of the vogue has been traced by Grace Adams, "The Rise and Fall of Psychology," *Atlantic Monthly*, January, 1934.
[3] *Has Science Discovered God?* (ed. E. H. Cotton, 1931), p. 30.
[4] *Ibid.*, p. 41.

come to seem remote, whether bepuzzlement will beget indifference, remains to be seen.

While science itself is not responsible for the welfare of society, professors of science have often invited indifference, if not hostility, because of their complacent disregard of public concerns. If the parties responsible for an exposition celebrating a Century of Progress in the setting of the Great Depression gave a singular example of ironic humor, one might expect a more objective and critical attitude on the part of the American Association for the Advancement of Science, which gathered at the exposition for its summer meeting. Typically inept, however, is the letter circulated from its Washington office before the meeting, inviting scientists and non-scientists alike to join and pay dues. In the high-flown and reckless language of American advertising, this letter informs the prospective wearer of a membership badge that "The work of the Exposition has been directed particularly to a demonstration of the progress of science upon which our nation-wide advancement has been built up." "The great Hall of Science," it continues, "with its demonstrations of scientific discoveries in all fields during the past century discloses the way in which the marvellous advance in human efficiency, safety, and comfort has been realized during this period." This is not the language of science, but of salesmanship. It is not the language of science, but of materialism. One would suppose that our nation-wide advancement, if it is a fact, has been built on other foundations in addition to science; and one would imagine that the appropriate fact in 1933 would have been, not a celebration of marvellous human efficiency, safety, and comfort, but an inquiry why so many millions of men had none of the three.

The average American, according to Dr. Frederick P.

Keppel, trusts science only because of its power to provide comforts and conveniences and to create dividends. "He trusts science, he doesn't understand it and doesn't pretend to."[5] But a public that largely neglected the great Hall of Science at the exposition and thronged to the picturesquely human, "old-timey" villages and the plays of a writer who lived over three hundred years ago is conceivably on the way to trusting science in the manner in which it today trusts the church.[6] Clearly, the old literary education was far more successful in instilling a warmly literary attitude toward life than the modern scientific education has been in instilling a coolly scientific attitude. The remedy proposed by many scientists and educationists is more training in scientific method. A well-known zoölogist at Johns Hopkins, for example, suggests a fundamental reform of our whole educational system based upon the need of beginning the "research game" (sic) with the pre-kindergarten child in the home, a vastly expensive reform the cost of which, as he conveniently adds, could be met by abolishing war.[7] Yet even this remedy might fail to produce the results intended if it is true, as observation seems to indicate, that many scientists are scientific only within the province of their own particular science. It may well be that the development of the scientific attitude is the most difficult task which education has ever undertaken—indeed, an impossible task.

As the fortunes of democracy and science declined, faith in progress lost its fervor. In Europe, disillusionment set in with the war of 1914 and deepened during the "peace"

[5] "American Philanthropy and the Advancement of Learning," *School and Society*, September 29, 1934.

[6] On "This Unscientific Age" see the article, so entitled, by Robert L. Duffus, in *Harper's Magazine*, December, 1934.

[7] Maynard M. Metcalf in the *Bulletin of the Association of American Colleges* (1930).

that followed. In America, though more and more intellectuals, after 1914, found themselves unable to maintain the enthusiasm for progress characteristic of the intellectuals of the nineteenth century, that enthusiasm continued to rise until it reached its apogee, in a popular sense, during the expansive years before the crash of 1929, when it began to fall rapidly. Today, progress has no vital meaning on the Continent, and little in England or the eastern United States. While its prestige is still to be reckoned with in the Mississippi Valley [8] there are no signs that it will ever recover, anywhere in America, its old dogmatism and imaginative ardor.

By 1934 it was natural for academic addresses, for example—in striking contrast with those of the nineteenth century—to be conducted in some such vein as this: "As most of us read history a generation ago, it was with a deep belief, a rather blind belief, if you please, in the reality of progress. . . . You and I are today citizens of a world in which this whole philosophy has been thrust out of the mind of nation after nation. . . . This is not merely a question of what has happened to the liberalism of a generation ago. It is more significant even than that. We seem rather to be witnessing the ebbing of a tide of human thought that had been flowing more and more strongly since the Renaissance." [9] The next year President Conant, in his baccalaureate sermon, proposed that we "lay aside entirely the

[8] Over the entrance to the House chamber of the new capitol of the State of Missouri, completed in 1918, one reads the typically nineteenth-century saying: PROGRESS IS THE LAW OF LIFE. As recently as 1936 an editor of the *New Republic* characterized the West as "the region where everyone automatically and instinctively assumes that things are getting bigger and better and that change is synonymous with improvement."

[9] President Harry W. Chase, of New York University, in an address quoted in the *Bulletin of the American Association of University Professors*, October, 1934. p. 370.

problem of progress or no progress." Utterances of this sort began to invade the state universities of the Middle West, where the traditional faith in progress still has intellectual adherents. A person who in 1934 quietly spoke of "the next world war" was regarded not as pessimistic but as exceptionally profound—he was no longer so exceptional a year later, when European dictators seemed to make the next war "inevitable" and it was generally scheduled for 1938. Correspondingly, a person who spoke too earnestly of *progress* came to be looked upon as superficial. Indeed, the very word is gradually passing out of ordinary currency, its place taken by the safer and cooler word *change*. Who can deny that changes are going to occur? Yet the new word, like the old, is especially attractive to the superficial, who, in troubled times, always exaggerate the amount of change that has occurred or may be expected to occur. Vast, revolutionary changes, they tell us, lie just ahead, and the thing to do is to "adapt" ourselves, our institutions, and everything else to them. What we want is not a shaping of events according to fixed standards derived from the past, but an ingenious opportunism in getting ready for tomorrow's weather. Let us study the trends, and, allying ourselves with the strongest of them, secure the advantages at one and the same time of drift and mastery. This is the typical gospel of the nineteen-thirties, something very different from the glad old gospel of Progress. One seems forced to conclude with Burke that, on the whole, "Men are as much blinded by the extremes of misery as by the extremes of prosperity."

§ 2

In a spirit of resentment that naturally grew out of the bewilderment of these years, men looked about for the cause of their troubles and found it in the machine, or Wall Street, or the Republican party, or prohibition, or the motion picture, or the educational system. Not infrequently, it was asserted that the primary responsibility lay with the universities, because they had failed to provide the sound leadership without which the inefficiency of democracy is certain to lead to disaster. This charge could not easily be refuted by the state universities, which had frankly given their main energy to everything except the problem of leadership. Yet they had an answer, of a sort. They had faithfully carried out their obvious function of giving the public, not what it needs, but what it wants. A state university, it was said, is in its very nature not a guide but a servant. It must serve the society which supplies its students and its funds. Accepting its duty of responding to social pressure, had not the state university conducted itself, in the years prior to 1930, in a manner quite above reproach? Had not the education which it dispensed satisfied the dominant aspirations of the public, the students, the faculty, and the administration? Indeed, with a fine political instinct it had succeeded in sensing social pressures before they had taken form, or even in creating and promoting them, so zealously did it serve. And yet there was criticism; it was increasing before the depression, and it increased apace during the depression. A writer in the *Journal of Higher Education* said, with truth, that "the public is in a good deal of haze as to the results of higher education, both actual and desired. . . . The conventional phrases about the culture, breadth of vision, social tolerance, and flexibility growing out of the experience of college and university life are greeted with considerable incredulity these days." These conventional phrases had been carried over from the old liberal education and applied to an education aiming at efficiency in a specific calling. A large part of the recent confusion and skepticism is simply due to the disparity between the liberal conception of what higher education can do for men and women and the servile practice of shaping them into useful tools.

But tools are not useful unless there is opportunity for using them, as students promptly realized when the depression came. Of what use, they asked, is power if we have no chance to serve? Does it not appear that a "practical" education, so long in favor, is today an impractical education? Is there not some other kind of education, which a wise faculty might define for us, that will be a sound investment no matter what we may do in the uncertain years that lie ahead? Will the style of education in fashion today clothe us decently for life? And what of leisure, enforced or earned, in the new era we are entering—does not this imply an education for living as well as an education for making a living? What *is* culture, and is there anything in it? We want to learn to do something, but cannot we also be something—is there no training for personality, for ideals, for values? We are serious; we are willing to work; we realize that we aren't in the easy-going college of the coonskin period. Can't we find something really worth while? Such questions were now asked by the students of the new period, in the vaguely searching manner of young people.

Administrators and faculties, on their side, at first welcomed the depression as a blessing in disguise. A great period of expansion had closed; a period of concentration was beginning, and concentration also had its virtues. Energy could now be expended, not upon the introduction of novel or larger facilities, but upon the improvement of the existing facilities. Financial stringency would make for higher quality, not lower. The merits of every enterprise would have to be closely scrutinized. Promotions and new appointments, when they could be made, would be approached with meticulous care. Above all, improvement in teaching could be undertaken; confessedly, research had been stressed at the expense of teaching, but now the balance could be restored. In the end the universities would emerge from the depression stronger, if not larger.

Among the internal reforms that interested the universities as they entered this period of transition, one of the most laudable was the substitution of a simple and humane way of conducting education in place of the complicated mechanism carried over from the great period of expansion. In the words of the new president of the Carnegie Foundation, "There has been widespread clamor for efficiency, with its statistical analysis, teaching load, student clock hours, and Pearson coefficient. Colleges found it all too easy to set up more or less mechanical checks upon the movement of these students through the institutions. Emphasis came to be placed upon course schedules, hours of credit, attendance at class, and laboratory exercise. All too frequently the essential contact between the student and the institution came to be centered in the office of the registrar, and while it might not be quite true to say that the institutions lost sight of the trees in contemplating the forest, it must be admitted that the campus patter reflects all too much emphasis on the part of student and staff on the mechanical and bookkeeping relationships of college life." A long overdue reaction now set in. "Within recent years, Dr. Jessup continues, "there has come uneasiness in many quarters in regard to this situation. This uneasiness has become so widespread that it is hard to find a college so lowly as not to be conducting at least one experimental project with a view to improving the situation." The uneasiness and the experiments are, at least, healthy signs of the growth of a self-critical spirit, and may in time produce a new convention better than the old, though today nearly all the state universities remain enslaved to the old mechanism.

Closely related with this desire to find a more humane procedure in the conduct of education was a new concern for good teaching. In part this was the result of a changed economic situation. The value of research depreciated. Students trained as research workers faced a world in which it was difficult to find work, and professors accustomed to regard research as their one responsibility to be taken seriously could no longer expect to be called to spheres of larger usefulness in other institutions. Turned in upon itself, the university developed a mood favorable to interest in the art of teaching. An interest which a few years before had been regarded with indifference and even suspicion (for how could a seeker after truth divert any of his best energy to mere instruction?) actually came to be viewed as enlightened and praiseworthy. In most institutions it acted as a mild ferment, in some it led to organized discussion and plans for improvement. Perhaps the clearest indication of the temper of the times is the *Report of the Committee on College and University Teaching* published in 1933 by the American Association of University Professors.

This report is the result of a belief that outside criticism of college teaching, which had been frequently voiced, should be followed by "a self-study of the situation made by the teachers themselves"—the twelve thousand members of the association. The inquiry roused great interest, was conducted with energy and skill within the limits set by the committee in charge, and culminated in a document that discussed the existing situation and possible improvements with the poise characteristic of the profession at its best and in a mode of expression free of the jargon that supplants thought in many professional studies of education. In a word, the report is, on the whole, a civilized document. And yet it scarcely can be called more than vaguely "stimulating," because, operating within artificial limits, it does not press to the heart of the problem. At the very beginning it asks the question: "Can anything be accomplished in the way of improving the quality of college and university teaching unless it is preceded by an agreement concerning the purpose for which the teaching is done?" The obvious answer would seem to be: "No, nothing important can thus be accomplished." But this is not the answer given. Instead, we are simply informed that the investigation "could not go afield into such highly controversial questions as the underlying purpose of undergraduate education, or the means of inducing secondary schools to send better prepared students to the colleges, or the proper standards for admission, or the organization of college curricula, or the general relation between college faculties and governing boards." Our procedure in all of these matters may be unsound; yet by some magic we are to raise the quality of teaching.

Disregarding the underlying purpose, we are to deal with the superficial purpose of undergraduate teaching. And what is this? "The purpose of college teaching," we are told, "is to induce self-propelled intellectual activity on the part of the student. Accordingly a frank recognition of this principle of self-education under guidance will suggest a sufficient definition of good teaching." At first blush this looks modest and superficial enough, but on a closer inspection one perceives that the use of the word "guidance"— which describes the teacher's function, as self-education describes the student's—reintroduces the highly controversial question of the underlying purpose of undergraduate education. The special function of the teacher is described in one more sentence, "To teach effectively is to lead, to inspire, and to guide the learner," and there the matter is dropped. To lead the student toward what goal? To inspire him to what kind of intellectual activity? To guide him in what direction? These awkward questions are not to be asked. But unless they are asked, we can have no criterion to distinguish between the effective pedagogue and the effective demagogue. It may well turn out that the professor who succeeds in making his students work hard for themselves is at the same time misleading, misinspiring, misguiding them. If the underlying purpose of education happens to be a bad purpose, the effective teacher will create more mischief than the ineffective teacher. Not only in education but in every field of social activity, the world abounds in people who are unfortunately only too effective.

Because of this side-stepping of the main issues, the report of the professors does not offer any important conclusions, though it may eventually be found to have served a valuable purpose in giving the problem of collegiate education national recognition. And it does at least touch upon one serious problem, lying outside the scope of the report, concerning which much will have to be said and done hereafter. Among its profoundest observations is this: "Inability to learn is a far more prevalent phenomenon in the American college than is inability to teach." American colleges and universities can hardly be expected to accomplish much in the advancement of teaching when they suffer from "the virtual necessity of admitting many students who have not been trained in sound habits of study and whose widely varied interests do not comport with the curricula of the colleges which they enter. This deficiency in intellectual maturity and interest on the part of many undergraduates is the outcome of an urgent demand, on the part of great numbers of people, to be given a share in the social and other opportunities which institutions of higher education afford." Here is the fatal handicap to which the state universities have long been and are increasingly subject. In these institutions, far more than in the better endowed colleges and universities, a dishearteningly large proportion of students permitted to enter upon a higher education are hopelessly incompetent to study in ways which their teachers regard as appropriate to higher education. The quality of teaching—so the report asserts—has been improving through the years. This may or may not be so, according to one's conception of good teaching. But there is little question that, on the whole, the quality of learning by the student has been lowered as the universities have expanded.

Notwithstanding their awareness of this fact, and notwithstanding their awareness of the virtues of concentration, the state universities of the lean years beginning in 1930, like those of the preceding period, have shown themselves eager to serve as widely as possible by maintaining or increasing their enrollments. Naturally they did not want their great plants to lie idle, like the factories. Naturally they did not wish to dismiss like factory hands a large proportion of their teaching staffs. Naturally they believed that their product, advertised to be educated men and women, would be wanted even during a depression, though admittedly they were increasing unemployment, at each commencement, in all the vocations for which they provided training. Both the motive of self-preservation and the motive of service led them, even in the period of concentration, to continue to think in terms of expansion. In the decades following the turn of the century the number of students enrolled in American institutions above the secondary school had increased by 600 per cent. In the years of the depression the rate of increase fell off, but actual decline in the number of students was either prevented or minimized by expedients reducing the cost of education (in-

cluding an ambitious programme of Federal aid) and by a
slackening or abandonment of requirements designed to
exclude or dismiss unfit students. It was conceived, rightly,
that many students deficient in intellectual maturity and
interest would be better off as undergraduates in a university than as unemployed persons idle in their homes or
wandering about the country. There was little disposition
to ask whether the university also would be better off—
whether its spirit, methods, and aims could stand dilution
by this new admixture of the inferior and incompetent. A
further lowering of standards seemed to be dictated by a
social emergency.

But a policy to be pursued during an emergency is one
thing, and a policy to be pursued afterwards is quite another. As the economic situation improves, the state universities find themselves at the parting of the ways. One
way leads toward higher standards and a redefinition of
function; the other, toward lower standards and aimless
miscellaneity. Which will they choose? The former is the
way of strong resistance, calling for departure from tradition and habit. Both the universities and their supporting
publics would have to undergo a progressive transformation of their views of education and their whole conception
of human values. Undertaking leadership, the universities,
and eventually the lower schools, would have the task of
educating the young in terms of some framework of ideals
better than that of the old humanitarianism, as various European countries have tried to do with more passion, alas,
than wisdom. The second way that invites us is the way of
least resistance. The programme of lower standards and
aimless miscellaneity is familiar and easy, calling only for
an intensification of the old education for efficiency in a
materialistic society. Our American society, it must be admitted, still appears to be dominated by materialism, even

though other interests may eventually emerge from its bewilderment. If the state universities are content to give the public not what it needs but what it wants, what it wants at the moment, they will continue to follow the line of least resistance, they will go on dispensing education for efficiency, they will devise lower standards and multiply aimless miscellaneity.

Not only administrators but faculties as well believe that they confront a "virtual necessity" of opening the doors of the universities to students wanting in ability to study and indifferent even to the varied assortment of curricula that has been provided. What is a virtual necessity? Is it a necessity? Not quite; it is something that looks like a necessity but may actually be subject to choice. Whether it is conceived as an absolute necessity is naturally decided by the desires of those who confront it. If their main passion is for quality rather than quantity, they will not take the responsibility of assuming that an undesirable course of action is unavoidable. They will not wish to play a part in bringing about something undesirable which was not necessary. If, on the other hand, their main passion is for quantity, if ever greater expansion and power and service appeal strongly to their imagination, they will wish to be a party to the consummation of the event, and will assume that a virtual necessity is a necessity indeed.

From the latter point of view, the prospects are alluring enough. The growth of the state universities depends largely, of course, on the growth of the secondary schools, especially the public secondary schools. Within the fifty years from 1880 to 1930, the pupils in the public secondary schools advanced from 3 per cent of children between 14 and 17 years old to more than 46 per cent of such children, and the number of pupils increased from about 110,000 to

4,399,000.[10] Just five years later the number had leaped to 6,719,000. Adding 450,000 pupils in private schools, the total number of pupils in the secondary schools in the year 1935 was 7,169,000.[11] As the National Survey of Secondary Education indicates, this growth was achieved at the price of "increased representation in secondary schools of intellectually less competent youth." Meanwhile, institutions of higher learning were also expanding greatly [12]—but not proportionately. In fact, "Ever since 1890, enrollment in institutions of higher learning has been diminishing relative [sic] to high-school enrollment. In 1890 it was two thirds as large as secondary school enrollments; in 1930 it was little more than one fourth as large." [13] But this tendency may well be reversed, and if it is, the colleges and universities will have abundant room for growth. Besides, the growth of the lower schools from which they recruit their students is almost certain to continue till the population of the country becomes stationary, perhaps in 1950. And again, there is the fact that widespread unemployment of youth will for many years encourage attendance at the

[10] "The Secondary School Population," a report of the National Survey of Secondary Education.

[11] Counting the high school ages as 15 to 18, this means that "approximately 70 per cent of the American young people of high school age are actually in high school. In such highly developed countries as Great Britain, France, and Germany, while elementary schools are as universal as in America, secondary education is highly selective, not going above 15 or 18 per cent of the young people of secondary school age." Edwin R. Embree, "Rural Education," *School and Society,* November 2, 1935.

[12] According to *Recent Social Trends in the United States* (1933), the number of students in higher education in 1900 was 284,683 and in 1930 was 1,178,318.

Incidentally, the number of graduate students increased from fewer than 900 in 1885 to 67,000 in 1934; the number of doctors of philosophy, from 164 in 1890 to 2,620 in 1930.

[13] S. H. Slichter, in a paper read at the meeting, in October, 1934, of the Association of American Universities.

higher institutions. Above all, however, is the fact that these institutions may themselves substantially decide how many students they will have. As Professor Slichter reminds us, "It is impossible to estimate the saturation point for colleges and universities, because this must be determined largely by the educational standards which these institutions choose to maintain." Apparently, the opportunity for almost indefinite expansion exists. Should it be embraced?

Those who welcome the prospect of much greater expansion in the state universities are not looking toward an important increase in the number of students capable of profiting by higher education. The new students, it must be assumed, would be mainly of the type that, according to the report of the American Association of University Professors, now tend to subvert any attempt to improve the quality of university achievement; indeed, they would probably be still more conspicuously lacking in ability to study and in interest in the curricula. The difficulty created by the influx of inferior students, it is suggested, could be successfully met by a familiar piece of university mechanism. Already it is customary to "section" students according to ability, placing the good, the average, and the deficient in separate classes within the same course of study. If the new students were deficient they could be put into the classes where they would be able to follow a simplified programme and to work at their naturally slow pace. The remedy, however, is delusive. In the long run, a great increase in the number of deficient students would produce a shift in the standard employed in sectioning. Since the sections designed for average students always tend to be most numerous, the quality of students in these sections would be lowered by invasion from the deficient students. Once the average sections had suffered this dilution, they would in turn lower the quality of the advanced sections. This process of deterioration has often been seen in action, and appears to be automatic and inevitable whenever an influx of the unfit has been allowed.

Despite this tendency, this law one may almost call it, apologists of expansion cherish the hope that the university may somehow learn how to serve good, bad, and indifferent students with equal solicitude. Cannot the university undertake the task it has confessedly slighted, that of caring for the welfare of good students, and at the same time undertake the task of caring for the welfare of the growing multitudes of average and deficient? Can it not encourage high standards of achievement among the talented and at the same time give the untalented as much as they can or will acquire? Cannot the university, standing at the parting of the ways, audaciously decide to take both ways? The answer suggested by experience is not comforting. The experience of educational institutions, as of other institutions of civilization, suggests that failure attends efforts to concentrate everywhere at once. A university emphasizing everything emphasizes nothing. It cannot exert its best efforts all along the line; the very concept of *best,* as of *emphasis,* implies a declared preference. If a preference is not established of set purpose, it will finally establish itself. It will attach itself to the weightiest task, that of caring for the mass of untalented. In the long run the mass will determine the materials of elementary and advanced courses, the methods of instruction, the teaching assignments of instructors, the quality of instructors, the standards of success and failure in study, and above all, in ways often too subtle for analysis, the prevailing intellectual tone of the institution.

But this will not convince the sentimental, who, disdaining such generalities as "standards" and "intellectual tone," like to think in terms of particular students to be served. If many students do not care for the present curricula, why not devise new curricula? It may be difficult to imagine that we now have students, and shall have more, "whose widely varied interests do not comport with the curricula" already offered, except on the assumption that such students would not be interested in anything. But the proponents of increased public service are not willing to make this assumption. They prefer to believe that there is something which anyone could study with enthusiasm, if that something could only be found. Surely there is *something* within the range of even the most inert. Let us devise new courses of instruction—it matters little what they are—that will catch their interest. At this point certain expansionists abounding in vision come forward with the theory that *every* human vocation can be made more or less learned and training for it be made accessible. A number of vocations (for instance, journalism?) for which a low order of training is already offered can be elevated to professions in company with law, medicine, dentistry, and the like, and at the same time more and more vocations for which academic recognition has not yet been won can be introduced into the college and formed into two-year and ultimately perhaps four- or five-year curricula. Has any one ever asked our women students, for example, whose vocational opportunities are still very limited, whether they would be interested in a training for beauty culture which should fit them for useful service of society? The suggestion is not frivolous. Beauty culture is a vital activity in our civilization; it has been said to be the fourth largest "profession" in the world; it calls for efficient, thoroughly trained persons; it has already won recognition through the establishment of innumerable beauty culture colleges and institutes throughout the country. As at least one state university president has suggested, why should not the public's university, in its all-serving spirit, give this subject its due place, select a dignified Greek name for it, and devise a curriculum mainly practical (for example, a course in Hair Waving) but partly cultural (for example, a course in Relations of Cosmetics to Civilization)?

In this manner one after another of the multitudinous vocations of our complicated modern civilization could be brought within the scope of university education. Opportunity for progress of this sort is almost unlimited. A century ago, in the typical self-contained American community, the number of vocations was something like twenty-five. Today, according to the last national census, the number of vocations has reached a total of more than twenty-five thousand.

§ 3

Let us remember that the idea of the American state university was worked out within the span of a single lifetime. It was worked out in accordance with the supposed needs of the citizens of a democracy in a time of eager industrial expansion. It embraced the object of education for efficiency, and provided for an astonishing variety of types of power and service. It was the educational expression of an acquisitive society keen in the arts and sciences of the production of things, willing to leave to the future the problem of the distribution of things and the development of human values. It was the educational expression, also, of a people confident of the progress of its institutions and imbued with the notion that the remedy for the evils of democracy was always more democracy. Whatever the differences between the universities of the various states and of successive decades, one pattern dominated throughout, a pattern sharply enough defined and firmly enough fixed to survive the three crises that came in the twentieth century: the crisis of a great war, the crisis of a great prosperity, and the crisis of a great depression.

Down to the present time this pattern has not been seriously questioned. Discontent is voiced, experiments are discussed or tried, educators are looking forward toward readjustment and change, but, by and large, the result is a continuing extension and complication of the pattern rather than a fundamental alteration of it. Attempting to deal with the problems of the present and future in terms suited to American needs of the late nineteenth century— if, indeed, they ever truly suited American needs—the state universities are in danger of becoming anachronistic. The time has come, it would seem, not for further uncritical attempts to enlarge the pattern, but rather for a stream of fresh thought that might help us wisely to alter the pattern. The time has come when social prudence dictates, not the fixation of our inherited idea of a state university, but a free and creative reconsideration, conducted in view of the permanent nature of man as well as the special concerns of the time, of what should be the rôle of higher education in a constitutional democracy.

Something of the sort is implied, for example, in the inaugural address of Eugene A. Gilmore, president of the University of Iowa, who calls for "less emphasis on vocational and immediately utilitarian considerations and more emphasis on fundamental things; a clearer perception of the unity and solidarity of learning now so much obscured by the great diffusion and elaboration of courses; acceptance of the principle that there are many things that do not need to be taught and confidence in the ability of really educated persons to do some things for themselves; less of standardization and educational ritualism and more of individuality and individual responsibility; more inspiring teachers who can interpret knowledge and instill enthusiasm and love for it; a realization that the chief object of all sound education is to teach a way of living rather than a way of making a living." This passage bristles with phrases that call for far more than the facile assent and lip-service which they will generally elicit. Before any such set of changes can be brought about, we shall need, obviously, an earnest reconsideration of what the "fundamental things" really are, an envisagement of the "unity and solidarity of learning" and a plan for revealing it to youth, a way of determining the nature of the "many things that do not need to be taught," a careful definition of the best meaning of "individuality," a clear conception of what "knowledge" after all is and why it should be loved, and, finally, an unflinching confrontation of the problem of human values to the end that an admirable "way of living" may be found and encouraged.

It is with matters of this kind that I shall be concerned more particularly in the last chapters of this book. But first I wish to deal, in the ensuing chapter, with some of the relations of the universities to the political system with which they ought to harmonize—the democratic polity, outlined in the national and state constitutions, of which they are the creatures and should be the wise servants.

Chapter Six

EDUCATION OF CITIZENS

§ 1

ONE SIGN OF THE WEAKENING OF THE PRES-
tige of democracy in America is the recent agitation for and
against freedom of speech. According to a newspaper story
that appeared in 1934, a radical-looking young man in
Cleveland was arrested, searched, and questioned for hours
for boldly reading aloud, in a public square where there is
an outdoor forum dedicated to free speech, from a book
containing these incendiary words: "Congress shall make
no law respecting an establishment of religion, or prohibit-
ing the free exercise thereof, or abridging the freedom of
speech or of the press, or the right of the people peaceably
to assemble. . . ." This was amusing enough; but presently
the subject took on a serious aspect when in state after state
laws were urged, and sometimes enacted, menacing freedom of speech on the part of teachers in the schools, colleges, and universities. By the requirement of "loyalty
oaths" one group of American citizens was singled out for
attack and oppression. "Consider the utterly ridiculous condition," says the president of Yale, "which compels President Conant of Harvard, under the Massachusetts law as it
now stands, to take such an oath, while at the same time it
allows a recently naturalized foreign priest to escape such

an oath and pour out weekly over the radio, under the blessed name of social justice, the most poisonous and inflammatory economic and social nonsense!" At least temporarily, no attention is being paid to such agencies of public education as the radio, the motion picture, and the press; but their turn may conceivably come.

Academic freedom is menaced today because democracy is seen to be insecure. Fearful for the stability of the American polity, many people are persuaded that they must do something to preserve it, though they may have only the dimmest notion of what it is. At a time when the American public imperatively needs to reillumine and revitalize its conception of democracy, these super-patriots are seeking to preserve what is little more than a parody of democracy. Perceiving that education is a powerful instrument while educators themselves are easy victims, they are prepared to remove the sense of freedom which is essential for democratic education, on the ground that certain teachers are engaged in propaganda in favor of communism or something of the sort. A few such teachers, to be sure, undoubtedly exist—a few persons who want the right of free speech in order to destroy free speech and subvert the American polity. Included among those who are defending or attacking free speech, it must also be recognized, are many that are actuated primarily by self-interest, identifying it, in the one case, with the perpetuation of the American polity and, in the other, with the promotion of some sort of collectivism.

The whole situation is lamentable, and full of peril. Freedom of speech is one of the freedoms most hardly won and easily lost, and the loss of it is likely to breed, sooner or later, the direful series: fear, hatred, revenge, chaos. As far back as the threshold of the modern age Sir Thomas Elyot exclaimed, in his book on education, "O what do-

mage haue ensued to princes and their realmes where lib-
erte of speche hath ben restrayned!" It took four hundred
years to create the structure of civil and political liberty,
including the liberty of speech, which is now being assailed
or abandoned in many countries. In America this structure
of liberty was formulated in the Constitution, which many
of our advanced idealists are inclined to regard as just a
scrap of paper. Force, not liberty, is the baleful genius of
the new collectivistic polities which have been springing up
in Europe, and which our idealists would like to emulate
in some undefined "American" way. Within our universities and teachers' colleges, many planful idealists, particularly in the fields of education and the social studies, are
enthusiastic for a planned society and for the planned
thinking that might bring it about. They are apparently
content that in America, as in Europe, a whole generation
should be taught that freedom of thought and speech is unsocial or unpatriotic,[1] and that in our universities academic
freedom should be regarded, as it is in those of Russia, Germany, Italy, Jugoslavia, Hungary, Rumania, as outmoded if
not positively vicious. An unsound type of individualism
having led us toward chaos, they propose instead, not a
sound type of individualism, but what they choose to call
"coöperation" or "social control," which is with difficulty
distinguished from sheer tyranny. They thus dissent from
the old-fashioned view of Edmund Burke, lover of liberty
as well as order, expressed in these pregnant words: "It is
better to cherish virtue and humanity, by leaving much to
free will, even with some loss to the object, than to attempt
to make men mere machines and instruments of a political

[1] In 1935 the London *Times* saw "half Europe in shackles worse than
it knew before the French Revolution." About the same time an American journalist (Bruce Bliven in the *Social Frontier*, February, 1935)
estimated that two-thirds of the world was under complete censorship and
eight-ninths of it under serious restrictions.

benevolence." This was also the view of the men, contemporary with Burke, who framed the American Constitution, and will be the view, I think, of those who will seek wisely to guide the future of American democracy. In any case we may lay it down that, if freedom of thought and speech be a good thing, democratic government offers it a degree of security superior to that offered by any other government.

The educational indoctrination proper in the light of our Constitution is nothing other than indoctrination in the principles of democratic government—indoctrination, above all, in freedom of thought and speech. "If there is any principle of the Constitution that more imperatively calls for attachment than any other," said Justice Holmes, "it is the principle of free thought—not free thought for those who agree with us but freedom for the thought that we hate." Like other citizens, teachers are expected to accept the national Constitution, while at the same time they are permitted an area of experimental thinking looking toward orderly revision of the Constitution. Under the American polity, happily, the faculty of a state university may continue that tradition of academic freedom in the quest of truth which the universities of the modern world have regarded as indispensable for the attainment of their high ends.

Our modern conception of academic freedom goes back to the foundation in 1810 of the University of Berlin, the first university dedicated expressly to original scientific investigation. As Wilhelm von Humboldt perceived, the pursuit of truth implies the possession of liberty. "The State should not treat the universities," he said, "as if they were higher classical schools or schools of special sciences. On the whole the State should not look to them at all for anything that directly concerns its own interests, but should rather cherish a conviction that, in fulfilling their real destination, they will not only serve its own purposes, but serve them on an infinitely higher plane, commanding a much wider field of operation, and affording room to set in motion much more efficient springs and forces than are at the disposal of the State itself." If this view is sound, the American state university serves the state, in the highest sense, by conserving and increasing intellectual illumination. It serves the state by preserving in a vital way the knowledge and culture of the past, which tend to prevent a hasty embrace of the aberrations of the hour, and by creating new knowledge and culture, which tend to prevent a blind attachment to old forms of thought and will. The state university conceives of freedom of thought as something to be prized not in disregard of the interest of the state but *in* the interest of the state. It conceives of this freedom, not as a natural right to be proclaimed in defiance of the good of the state, but as a wise expedient in harmony with the good of the state. The results, at times, may be awkward. The truth, or what appears to be the truth, is not always comfortable. But even so, it is better for the state generously to provide the auspices of frank criticism than to witness the growth of such criticism, in an uncritical or bitter form, outside the institutions which it expressly controls. Equally from the point of view of scientific inquiry and the point of view of human dignity as respected by a democratic polity, freedom is the breath of life. While evils may result from academic freedom, still greater evils result from suppression of academic freedom.

Furthermore, most of the evils that result from academic freedom are the consequence of the abuse, rather than the use, of that freedom. The state university is, properly, free to exercise the dispassionate pursuit of knowledge; it is not free to apply its knowledge to the practical direction of affairs. Its function is intellectual, not political. The moment it claims the privilege of directing society, it is in danger of losing its privilege of studying society. "This danger becomes real," as President Gilmore observes in his inaugural address, "if the state university yields to the temptation, and sometimes to the pressure, to participate directly in government activities and to assume responsibility for the immediate application of its expert knowledge or the formulation of policies based upon such knowledge." President Gilmore goes on to remark that "The notion has been expressed, and it has been disastrously tried in some jurisdictions, that a state university, operating through the members of its staff, should be an agency for the direct accomplishment of all kinds of government objects, many worthy, but as often partisan," to which he replies: "It may be difficult to draw the line between research and the application of its results in the promotion of state activities, but it is a line which, if not drawn, will eventually lead to the impairment, if not the loss, of the university's freedom." Permitting its uncritical zeal for service to carry it beyond its real function, the state university must finally submit to a political control that will imperil or destroy its real function.

Academic freedom is also menaced by individual professors who abuse it. Prone to proclaim this freedom as an abstract right, they often forget that, whether a right or an expedient, it has its correlative in responsibility. Not without justice did Harold H. Swift, president of the board of trustees of the University of Chicago, complain that the American Association of University Professors "should have incorporated in its platform the idea of responsibility to the university, and prevention of misunderstanding by the public, as forcefully as it has proclaimed the right of free speech." [2] There are always a few professors who do not stay to make a distinction between free speech and foolish speech. They may be absurdly wholesale, or recklessly belligerent, or inclined to exhibitionism. Those who attract public attention are generally given to violent emotive language, which lends itself only too well to the irresponsibility of a sensation-mongering press. They come to be marked as themselves sensational or at least picturesque figures, and their words are watched in expectation of something that may alleviate the drab routine of the campus. Failing to win the confidence of their classes, they are quoted, more often misquoted, by students who thoughtlessly or deliberately disregard the context of their bold remarks. Often they could say substantially the same thing, as many of their colleagues do, in a way that would not attract attention outside the university. Indeed, most of the limitations to which academic freedom is subject are merely matters of good manners and good taste. They call for a decent degree of restraint and modesty, not for an abandonment of the quest of truth. If the behavior of professors were more seemly, there would be less temptation, on the part of administrators and governing boards, to act in contravention of the principle of permanent tenure.

One limitation upon academic freedom, however, appears to be inescapable: the limitation implied by the fact that a university chooses the professors who carry on its work. With a singular lack of humor one of Columbia's publications displays this quotation as a motto: "Teachers College, as an institution, holds no position, advocates no theory of education. It selects its faculty and, as every such institution must, permits each member untrammeled to present whatever his reflections and his researches lead him

[2] "College and University as Seen by the Trustee," in *The Obligation of Universities to the Social Order* (1933), p. 77.

to believe." This pious statement loses much of its force be-
cause of the seemingly artless phrase, *It selects its faculty.*
There was a similar lack of humor in the founder of the
University of Virginia, who, at about the same time he
was proclaiming "the free right to the unbounded exercise
of reason and freedom of opinion," sagely remarked to
Madison that "In the selection of our Law Professor, we
must be rigorously attentive to his political principles."
Determined not to let his university "slide into Toryism,"
Jefferson was going to see to it that "within a dozen years
a majority of our own legislature will be from one school,
and many disciples will have carried its doctrines home
with them to their several States, and will have leavened
thus the whole mass"—with sound Whig principles. The
German universities in their great days, proclaiming *Lehrfreiheit* while they selected professors, faced the same problem, and the result was often *Lehrfreiheit* for professors
who had the right point of view, especially in the fields of
theology, philosophy, and political economy. In the American state universities of recent years, the fields of theology
and philosophy have given little trouble because the former
has no place and the latter has been neglected, but the field
of the expanding and subdividing "social sciences" is one
in which the difficulty of making impartial appointments
has been serious and is likely to become more so.

Impartiality in the selection of a university faculty is in
the last analysis impossible. To select at random, irrespec-
tively of the candidates' points of view, is not to attain impartiality but to accept the partiality of chance. This
scarcely commends itself. But to select purposefully is to
accept the partiality that inheres in any principle of intelligent selection. This seems to be the best we can do. Upon
what principle, then, shall a purposeful selection be based?
Equal representation of all points of view is scarcely the an-

swer, for it can hardly be that all merit equal emphasis. Shall selection be made with the object of assuring a predominance of the best point of view? In this case what is the best point of view? One institution will reply that it is the point of view of the gentleman, and it will look primarily for gentlemen who are scholars. Another will respond that it is the point of view of the Catholic Church, and it will look primarily for Catholics who are scholars, especially in such fields as philosophy, history, and literature. Another will respond that it is the point of view of science, and in all fields it will look primarily for men distinguished in scientific investigation, not caring much whether they are gentlemen and not caring at all whether their interpretation of human life is naturalistic, humanistic, or religious, in which case, as we have seen, the faculty will turn out to be overwhelmingly naturalistic.

Selection implies a principle of selection, and a principle of selection implies a preference of one thing to other things. Accordingly, it becomes the responsibility of those who determine appointments to seek to assure the predominance of what, according to their lights, is the best point of view. At the same time, since they cannot hope to be infallible in fixing upon the best, it is equally their responsibility, in conformity with our American democratic system, to seek to assure the representation of other points of view that appear to be respectable. Predominance is not the same as the uniformity now sought in Russia, Germany, and Italy. Predominance implies both a majority and a number of minorities, and minorities have their place in university faculties as in legislative bodies. The health of the democratic university, and indirectly the health of the democratic state, is served when it is willing to recognize both radicals and conservatives, both individualists and collectivists, both humanists and naturalists, both Christians and Jews. In the long run the soundest policy of the American state university will consist in being firm in its preference of what appears to it best, and at the same time generous in its inclusion of what seems best from other points of view. Only by means of this policy can it conform to the political constitution upon which it rests and secure the academic freedom which has been lost in many of the great universities of Europe.

The corollary of *Lehrfreiheit* is *Lernfreiheit*. Freedom of thought is appropriate not only to the professor but to the student. He should be free, first, to learn what the faculty, predominantly, considers to be of most worth; and he should be free, secondly, to learn a great diversity of interpretations and convictions. The latter opportunity will exist, it is sometimes suggested, if the faculty is one aiming at complete neutrality, each professor making a studious effort to present all sides of a question without arriving at any conclusion. But the objections to this view of *Lernfreiheit* have already been demonstrated by experience. If the neutrality is real, the student is encouraged to develop an "academic mind," expert in the pros and cons but incapable of any decisions. Having come to the university with a handful of prejudices, he leaves it at last with no beliefs at all and goes forth, paralyzed, into a world of action. On the other hand, if the neutrality is unreal, if there is an insidious indoctrination beneath a show of impartiality, the student is the victim of conscious or unconscious deception, and merely exchanges his callow prejudices for more sophisticated prejudices—a very common occurrence in the modern university. If we are aiming at freedom, it would seem that neutrality is as disastrous as uniformity. What is needed for assurance of freedom to learn is a faculty made up of men who are aware of the assumptions on which their thinking is based, who make their assumptions clear to

their students, and who show how these assumptions affect
their whole structure of interpretation and belief. If they
do the same thing for points of view contrasting with their
own, they will readily convince their students that they are
not dogmatic, that they welcome honest differences of opinion, and that no one who disagrees will be penalized.

§ 2

Freedom to learn implies an antecedent freedom—freedom
to attend the state university. In a democracy, all students
capable of higher education should have equality of opportunity for that education. This is the theory; but not the
practice. In actual practice many students capable of higher
education are being denied an opportunity for it, and multitudes of students incapable of higher education are being
admitted to the universities. Obedient to the mixed motives of aggrandizement and humanitarian service, the state
universities are bent upon providing all sorts of education
for all sorts of students, and are thus transforming higher
education into what is now commonly termed, with increasing misgivings, "mass education."

The paradox of a "higher" education for "all" is becoming apparent to a public less and less subject to illusions as
to the perfectibility of average or sub-average humanity.
The view which Helvétius and other humanitarians of the
eighteenth century urged with fervor, and which was
widely accepted in the early days of the American state universities, the view that human intellects are equal, is now
seen to be fallacious. The public is no longer in a mood to
be impressed by a prophet like Victor Hugo, who, an-
nouncing that free compulsory education would achieve
social salvation, asked, "How long will it take?" and
blithely answered, "A quarter of a century." A growing

number of people would be inclined to agree, rather, with a skeptic like Montaigne when he said, "It is not for knowledge to enlighten a soul that is dark of itself, nor to make a blind man see." Many persons are now appalled at the sensational, trivial, and unsound reading material encouraged by the growth of literacy and are reluctantly drawn to the conclusion that the reading material reflects only too accurately the limits of the reader.[3] In an editorial it was recently suggested that the trend against democracy in this country has been reflected by the so-called "comics," which now delight in "making a monkey of the everyday, commonplace man who is the backbone of democracy. His face has been simplified into a stupid forehead with no jaw." At the time when America went into the war, the Army Tests, while leaving some doubt as to the intelligence of the testers, left much graver doubt as to the intelligence of ordinary citizens. This gave a shock to many patriots, and other shocks were soon administered by psychology and pseudo-psychology, which reduced human nature to a bundle of conflicting, obscure emotional drives or reactions, also by a realistic and naturalistic literature that emphasized everything in human nature which is hopelessly disorderly, irrational, and ignoble. Today we hear less and less of the power of education to work the wonders envisaged by the rationalist utopists of the eighteenth century, and more and more of its humbler value in filling harmlessly the vacant time promised to humanity by the machine age. We wish to have fewer people, in our society, like the unemployed working woman whom a relief investigator found sitting on a porch, and who, when asked how

[3] See the book by R. S. and H. M. Lynd, *Middletown, A Study in Contemporary American Culture* (1929), and H. R. Huse, *The Illiteracy of the Literate* (1933).

she spent her time, replied, "I just set. When I get tired set-tin' here, I go inside and set."

In spite of all the popular education developed by mod-ern nations, we can no longer assume that a wide diffusion of knowledge, such as Washington and Jefferson desired, is in itself a guarantee of political wisdom and stability. As Clarence W. Barron remarked in an address before the Eco-nomic Club of New York, "Of the people in Germany 98 per cent could read and write when Germany went to pieces." In America, the general public is as much the vic-tim of herd emotions as before the great extension of popu-lar education, and there is scant reason to believe that it will come to think and act more intelligently through a further development of popular education. If it is true that the remedy for the failures of democracy is not merely more democracy, it is also true that the remedy for the fail-ures of popular education is not merely more popular edu-cation. The attitude of the common man toward public affairs is well indicated in an incident mentioned by Gov-ernor Gardiner of Maine at a conference on the obligation of universities to the social order. "I was campaigning," says Mr. Gardiner, "in some of the islands off the coast of Maine in a spell of particularly foggy weather that had lasted two or three weeks. I had assumed that, being in the campaign myself, every one else was equally interested in this great event. I went into a small store and found one man sitting by the stove. I approached him quietly and asked him if he were interested in politics, and he never moved a muscle. I thought he might be deaf, so I walked around to the other side of the stove and came up quietly and asked, 'Are you interested in politics?' He finally took the pipe out of his mouth. He didn't look up. Then he said, 'I ain't interested in a damn thing until this fog lifts.' " If it is not a fog, it is always something else. When prosperous, common men want to be let alone; when in adversity, they still want to be let alone. Only when adversity is profound and widespread do they develop deep interest in public affairs, and then their interest is expressed mainly in irrational impulses. Electrons, as someone has remarked, cannot be stampeded by an emotional appeal, but men apparently refuse to follow the example of electrons, even when a whole nation has been supposedly impregnated with the spirit and method of science, as the case of Germany indicates. Men being what they are, there is no reason to believe that a programme of popular education aiming at a critical, intelligent citizenry can ever succeed, no matter how elaborately it may be organized from elementary school to university. People, in fact, do not want this sort of education; rarely, alas, do they want any sort of education that makes any serious demands upon them.

Since the generality of children can never be made into rational and independent thinkers, the only type of popular education that can abundantly serve the purposes of citizenship, it has been argued, is one that is frankly authoritative. Those who cannot or will not think must, in this view, be given thoughts. By the most overt sort of indoctrination, based essentially on force, the few will impose their views upon the uncritical many, and inculcate social attitudes in harmony with the dictatorship then prevailing. This type of popular education, in vogue today in fascist and communistic polities, is a powerful weapon at our disposal if we care to use it, and adoption of it is being urged by certain educationists thirsting for power and service, who choose to interpret the purpose and tradition of the American state according to some kind of socialism. They wish to see to it that the common man—the man sitting by the stove, the woman sitting on the porch—shall become an enthusiastic supporter of some variety of regimented society selected by themselves and dispensed directly, if possible, from Washington. This the educationists could no doubt accomplish if given an opportunity; but the opportunity is happily not in sight.

Disappointed by the results of popular education in a country dedicated to liberty and equality, we are today more willing to recognize that in education, however it may be in other social institutions, we must accept the fact of natural inequality, or, to use the term preferred by modern psychology, "individual differences." Now, the fact of individual differences was clearly discerned centuries ago, by Montaigne, for example. As he said, "Such as, according to our common way of teaching, undertake, with one and the same lesson, and the same measure of direction, to instruct several boys of differing and unequal capacities, are infinitely mistaken." If a boy's interests are mean, why then, says Montaigne, "I see no other remedy but that he be bound prentice in some good town to learn to make minced pies, *though he were the son of a duke.*" Enlarging upon a saying of Plutarch's, Montaigne declares that "There is more difference between such and such a man than between such a man and such a beast," and that "There are as many and innumerable degrees of minds as there are cubits between this and heaven." With equal clarity Sir Thomas Elyot saw that "God gyueth nat to euery man like gyftes of grace, or of nature, but to some more, some lesse," and, long before there was such a thing as humanitarian democracy, exclaimed, "Howe farre out of reason shall we iudge them to be that wolde exterminate all superioritie, extincte all gouernaunce and lawes, and under the coloure of holy scripture, whiche they do violently wraste to their purpose, do endeuour them selfes to bryng the life of man in to a confusion ineuitable." Yet it was still necessary in the year of our Lord 1931 for an American college president to complain that "We believe so thoroughly that all men are created equal that we attempt to keep them so throughout their lives." [4] Our public opinion, as interpreted and formed by those responsible for the educational system, has largely supported this crude dogma and with it an equally crude practice. It has been said that a change of attitude cannot be expected until science has still more firmly established the fact of individual differences. Sir Charles Grant Robertson, for instance, believes that "If we can once really establish what every one from Aristotle to the present board of education has assumed, that children and adolescents and adults in varying categories and at different age-levels have definite limits of educability, and that it is a waste of time, effort, and money to treat one category as if it were another, the doctrine of equality of opportunity will come to be regarded as a devastating superstition, and the grading of the categories of the educational ladder will be the beginning of an unparalleled social revolution." If every one from Aristotle to the present board of education indeed agrees in the same assumption, it is difficult to see why the social revolution does not come off. We shall probably discover that the formidable barrier to reform is not an insufficiency of scientific evidence but an overplus of humanitarian dogmatism. And until that barrier is scaled we shall doubtless continue to witness, everywhere in American public education, lip-service to the fact of natural inequality and a reluctance to take the practical steps implied by that fact.

What, actually, is the record of American education in dealing with the implications of natural inequality? According to an educationist of high repute, Edward L. Thorndike, "The general spirit of our country for the past

[4] W. M. Lewis, president of Lafayette College, quoted in the *Journal of Higher Education*, January, 1932, p. 41.

hundred years has been to make great efforts to increase the amount of education, but to pay relatively little attention to its distribution. The plea of reformers has been for more education, regardless of who received it. There has been an indiscriminate urge toward more schools, longer school years, and later compulsory ages. . . . The mere volume of education has been taken as a measure of idealism, somewhat as the mere volume of gifts to beggars of all sorts used to be taken as a measure of philanthropy and charity." Unimpressed by pseudo-idealism, Professor Thorndike boldly opposes the growing tendency to keep youth in school and college as long as possible. "Indiscriminate advances in the compulsory school age beyond sixteen seem, in view of the facts, a weak and wasteful procedure. . . . We need laws to prevent greedy or perverse parents from depriving gifted children of schooling, not laws to force them to keep in school children who have neither the ability nor the interest to profit thereby." [5] Clearly, the entire ideology and practice of public education in the United States has tended to be quantitative, not qualitative; indiscriminative, not selective. On the other hand in a country like Scotland, famed for its faith in education, there is a more genuine concern for equality of opportunity, a keen concern for giving all a chance to rise to the top of the educational system. As a former president of the University of Minnesota has recently reminded us, Scotland has a "tradition of giving promising youth, however humbly born, a chance to go from town or village school on through the successive grades to the university. Ministers, teachers, family, and friends are on the lookout for brains and ready to give time and to make sacrifices." "One wonders," he adds, "whether

[5] An address in Chicago, excerpted in the New York *Times*, March 20, 1932.

the search for the exceptional in this country is equally keen, intelligent, and sympathetic." [6]

In the American state university of today, no important steps are being taken to secure the best students and to give them a substantial education, but much is being done to secure the less able and least able and to keep them in college as long as possible by giving them a superficial education.

Rationalizing its expansionist and humanitarian motives, the state university has availed itself of an ambiguity resident in the very conception of individual differences. Differences, it so happens, are of two sorts: differences in ability and differences in interest. It also happens that differences in ability operate in the direction of the selective and limited, while differences in interest operate in the direction of the indiscriminate and unlimited. In this situation, already glanced at in the preceding chapter, what is a university intent upon the widest possible service to do? Obviously, what the state universities have done and still propose to do is to give feeble recognition to differences in ability while making maximum provision for differences in interest. There is occasional talk about raising standards, but incessant action in favor of lower standards by the provision of trivial courses suited to the interests of the average and sub-average. When standards are sufficiently low, it may be said, in the words of an editorial in a university newspaper, that "the dumbest of us soaks up something at college." A very soft form of pseudo-idealism has led the state universities to cater to individual incapacity rather than individual distinction. A truly democratic idealism would seem to involve, not lowering the standard so that everyone could

[6] George E. Vincent, "The Few and the Many in Education," an address at the Johns Hopkins University, February 21, 1936.

find some interesting means of securing a diploma, but rather giving everyone a chance to measure up to an exacting standard. In the schools of Prussia, as Albert Jay Nock remarked a few years ago, "you will indeed see the shoemaker's son sitting beside the banker's son and the statesman's son, over the same lessons; but equality and democracy, as we popularly understand them, have nothing to do with this. The three boys sit there because they are able to do the work." It begins to be plain that the state university cannot afford to develop indefinitely its programme of redefining the work to suit the student. There may be times when this must be done, and the university should stand prepared, after due deliberation, to modify its work in harmony with the changing needs of the society which it serves. This happened, for instance, when various modern languages and sciences were brought into its curriculum. But it does not follow that it should always be casting about, like a commercial home study institute, for some new way of appealing to the endlessly diversified interests of the public, on the assumption that every high school graduate has a right to a university education. As Sir Charles Grant Robertson puts it, "There is and can be no 'right' to a university education, except one based on clear proof of fitness to pursue a real university course, of which the university must remain the judge." Among the obligations of the state university to the social order one of the first is a judgment of what properly constitutes higher education, a judgment which it must form in the light of the more permanent and substantial needs of the state rather than in response to the random pressures of special groups of citizens. At times it may find itself in conflict with certain groups or with a political administration temporarily in power—this will happen in any case—but in the long run it will prosper most securely by serving a high ideal and bending all effort to win the best opinion of the state in support of that ideal.

In the interest of a sound public education culminating in the state university, the primary need of the coming years is a redistribution of education in accordance with individual differences. In the case of most pupils, we are told by the psychologists, differences in capacity should be clear by the age of twelve.[7] If we are prepared to take the psychologists' word for it, most pupils may at that age be divided into three groups. The first is composed of pupils who have reached, or already passed, their natural limits of educability. They are so low in endowment that further instruction would involve definite waste. The second group is composed of pupils who can be trained in preparation for some activities of citizenship and some types of vocation. Receptive of authoritative instruction, they can be indoctrinated in a set of ideas, habits, and attitudes approved by the adult society of which they will presently be a part, and at the same time they can learn how to do some of the things done in the useful vocations; but any education devised for their benefit must take account of the perils of authoritative indoctrination and of the tendency of the acceleration of change to render irrelevant the more specific kinds of vocational training. The third group is composed of pupils who can do more than passively learn items of fact, thought, and habit, who are capable of active assimilation and expression of mind and personality. They have in some degree an intellectual curiosity left unsatisfied by surface

[7] As reported in *News-Week*, December 15, 1934, Dr. Leda S. Hollingworth, of Teachers College, Columbia, is more optimistic: "By means of testing we can tell from the age of three what a man's intellectual position will be for life." "Mental testing is the most important thing in the world today."

But Professor Counts, of the same institution, was reported as saying, "Nobody knows what intelligence is."

explanations, and a desire to use their endowment of personal qualities. They have the gift of human freedom, or the possibility of it. They, and they alone, are capable of liberal education.

A deflated state university serving a high ideal manifestly cannot provide for all pupils of these groups when they have reached the age of eighteen. Whom it can provide for should properly be decided by an entrance examination,[8] though this expedient is regarded as anathema even by educationists enthusiastic over their new science of testing and measurement. At the least, the university could offer a series of advisory tests to all high school students desirous of knowing their promise of success in a selection of liberal subjects. What, then, should be done with those who cannot pass the tests? The answer of the inflated university seeking more inflation would be that they should be invited to the campus conditionally or unconditionally and be given whatever they could be induced to take, at the price of adding to the confusion and agglomeration which an institution of this sort views with complacence. On the other hand, the answer of the deflated university serving a high and clear ideal would be that more appropriate means of providing for them should be found by the state. While such a university may temporarily offer its facilities in an emergency, it must expect the state to begin at once an earnest consideration of what, if anything, the state should attempt to do for young men and women who cannot be absorbed in industry. It is for the state or the nation, not the

[8] A committee report of the American Association of University Professors (*Bulletin*, October, 1926), closely following the recommendations of the College Entrance Examination Board, has called for entrance examinations in Latin, English, mathematics, and a modern foreign language as subjects preparatory for an arts course, or English, mathematics, a modern foreign language, and a science as subjects preparatory for a science course.

state university, to decide whether young people who cannot find remunerative employment should be given certain kinds of employment without wages, or trained to fight their fellows in the next war, or trained to fight nature in conservation work, or placed in schools even if intellectually ineducable or indifferent. If it seems probable that unemployment of youth is to be a long-term problem, and if education is to be called upon to keep youth occupied, the state should recognize a new social need by providing special institutions where those incapable of liberal education will be given the most appropriate training that can be devised. On the basis of records and placement tests, students of a type not suited to the four-year liberal college could be admitted to technical training schools offering two years of specialized education and junior colleges offering two years of training in citizenship. Existing institutions in which these objectives play a large part could be taken over or subsidized by the state, and others could be created. Today nearly every state contains some of the 519 junior colleges in the country; nearly half of them are publicly controlled, and nearly all of them are vague or inconsistent in their aims, awaiting some decisive definition.[9]

Whatever is done for our young people of junior college

[9] California has 55 junior colleges, Texas 43, Iowa 37, Oklahoma 24, North Carolina 23, Missouri 22, Illinois 21. In California they enroll more students than are enrolled as freshmen and sophomores in the University of California, the University of California at Los Angeles, and the University of Southern California combined. According to President Sproul (Charter Day address, 1932), the University of California and the junior colleges of California are harmoniously solving the problem of taking care of high school graduates. The most important function of the junior college, in his opinion, is that it "makes available to boys and girls whose talents do not lie along the lines of a university career but who are interested in further education, training in fields intermediate between the trades and the professions, or in certain activities of home-making and citizenship."

age, be it remembered, will cost immensely. If the solution adopted is that of further education, the result may well prove to be violent resentment against the cost of education in general when viewed in relation to the not very impressive results obtained. As E. R. Embree has pointed out, no nation in the history of the world has ever attempted to provide such educational facilities as we now have in the United States, and yet we are not even successful in teaching children how to read. Within a single decade, 1920 to 1930, school expenditures rose 100 per cent while the national income rose only 48 per cent. This placed a greatly increased burden upon the taxpayer. Today approximately 50 per cent of all state taxes go to education. If the state universities insist upon indefinite expansion, their budgets will also have to enjoy indefinite expansion,[10] and the wisdom of the universities will be increasingly subject to criticism. In 1930 the president of the University of Minnesota acknowledged that "The public has been, and still is, insisting upon a fair return for the money it invests in higher education, and it has been raising questions as to the desirability of attempting to provide college training for all those who are applying." [11] And in the succeeding years, as the president of the University of Wisconsin acknowledged, the entire educational system of the United States was assailed and shaken as it had not been in any previous depression.[12]

In the future the state university may conceivably find it necessary, no longer to advertise its wares in the widest

[10] Income from tuition and other fees that depend on the number of students amounts to only 12 per cent of the budgets of publicly controlled institutions (E. E. Lindsay and E. O. Holland, *College and University Administration*, 1930). The remaining 88 per cent comes chiefly from taxes.

[11] Introduction to *Higher Education in America*.

[12] Glenn Frank. *America's Hour of Decision* (1934).

possible market, but to begin to advise the unfit not to apply for admission. For some years, indeed, this has been done, by bulletin and correspondence, at the University of Michigan. According to a recent official publication, "It is the belief of the University that those students who simply do not possess sufficient ability to meet the ordinary mental demands of college work or sufficient seriousness of purpose and ambition to carry through a college program, should not be encouraged to enter the University. Every effort is being made to avert as much as possible the tragedy of the failing freshmen by admitting only those who have demonstrated their fitness for study at the University." How effective these efforts are may be a matter of opinion. The University of Minnesota, similarly, adopted measures designed to exclude the inapt and the unstrenuous. Minnesota warns the lowest one-fourth of high school classes that they have only a slender chance of succeeding in college work. For other as well as financial reasons, it is frankly said, "nearly half of all students who enter the University drop out before the beginning of the junior year." Inapt pupils graduating from high school are informed that they might well consider enrolling, not in the state university, but in "vocational and trade schools of the better kind" or in "extension courses and correspondence schools." Somewhat inconsistently with this procedure, however, the University has set up a so-called "General College" for the benefit of students not equipped to do the regular work of the four-year liberal college, which, incidentally, is conceded to be not liberal but "specialized study." In this General College such students are invited to follow a less extensive and more popular course, an "overview of modern life and of man's activities," a type of work, one cannot but fear, shallow enough for the unstrenuous to wade through. Among the special courses devised for this purpose are The Practical Applications of Psychology, Human Development and Personal Adjustment, Euthenics, Current English Reading (magazines and newspapers), Current Affairs, Appreciation of Motion Pictures and the Theater, Education in Modern Society, Vocations, University Lectures Course ("a wealth of ideas and new viewpoints" brought to the campus by miscellaneous speakers), and, despite the ban on specialized study, a course entitled Individual Study and Research.

§ 3

If higher education is to deserve the name, it cannot be brought within the reach of the ineducable and the passively educable. To attempt to educate such students at the university, even at the present denatured university, is either to discourage or delude them, as one may see any day by watching the exodus of the unfit from the campus during the first two years and by noting the vagueness of mind and glib utterance of many who stay for four years and attain the illusion of enlightenment. No doubt the "dumbest of us" do soak up something, but it is patent that the good which they receive is more than offset by the harm which they receive and the harm which they do their fellow students by lowering the standard and the tone of the institution. To see the good and not the harm is a mark of sentimentalism, which is quite as rife in the university as in the public. So pervasive is this sentimentalism at times that the very atmosphere of the university seems oppressive with the weight of concern for hopeless inferiority, as if it were an intellectual sick-chamber.

In its healthy estate, higher education is concerned with the fit, the large number of robust young men and women who are able to think, able to feel, able to liberate themselves. In a redistribution of education a maximum share should go to them. They should be given every encouragement to stay in college through the four years, and many of them should then be urged to enter the graduate and professional schools, the presence of which on the campus produces an effect as tonic as the presence of a "General College" (for an equivalent number of the unfit) is debilitating. The intellectually robust are, I think, a much larger body than is usually supposed. The mind that is capable of enough liberal education to justify the effort is not rare; it is common. If it seems rare in the university today, this is because it is stunted or warped by immersion in the low-average of job-hunting students, by financial stringency and the distractions of earning one's way, by a faculty that feels obliged to deal with average students as they actually are, and by curricula that take the vocations seriously and culture frivolously. In case the college of liberal arts, in keeping with its name, were open only to liberal students, its enrollment would be reduced, but it would still be large, and it would grow for a decade at least, so that, along with that of the graduate and professional schools, it would justify the imposing physical plant erected in the era of uncritical expansion. The college of liberal arts would then be enabled to serve the state by an unhampered development of the most valuable resources of the state, its more or less gifted citizens, upon whom the welfare of the state and nation finally depends. These are the persons—a few as leaders, the rest as the middlemen of thought and action—who must be counted upon, in a democratic organism such as ours, to guide public opinion, to assume the responsibility of important positions in their communities, and to set the tone of cultural life.

There are those who assert that the liberal college has already been damaged beyond repair, or that it is in fact extinct, retaining only a name. Giving primary attention to students less and less fit for liberal studies, letting down the bars to more and more young people looking only for quick vocational success, devising courses and fixing standards dictated by the mass of students indifferent to scholarship and culture, adequately providing only for techniques and specialisms, establishing in the faculty a growing cynicism as to the pertinence of high ideals in a state university, the college of liberal arts has come perilously near to abdicating its function. Yet the need of such an institution is permanent. Perhaps it will have to be set up as a new college with a new name. But there may still be time to revive the old college with the old name, by gradually sloughing off the alien elements that have disguised its true nature and by introducing a fresh vision of the spirit and method of a liberal education adapted to the needs of the modern world. It would be folly to continue to concentrate effort upon the unfit and indifferent while wasting the most promising human material entrusted to the care of the university, those who are capable of liberal education.[13]

§ 4

Above all, steps must be taken in favor of the *exceptionally* capable. While step after step has been taken in favor of the

[13] The idea of a liberal education, in relation to the modern world, will be discussed at length in the succeeding chapter. Here, however, it may be remarked that the higher education of citizens of our democracy would seem to involve, in addition to a liberal curriculum, military training and a study of the Constitution or the constitutional history of the United States.—Even a lover of personal liberty like Thomas Jefferson, while opposing a standing army and navy, called for universal military training and insisted that we "make military instruction a part of collegiate education." The right of the University of California and other land grant colleges to require military training was unanimously sustained by the Supreme Court of the United States in a decision handed down in 1934.

relatively incapable, almost nothing has been done in favor of those who, by virtue of natural endowments and fortunate training, give promise of leadership in the professions and in public life. As one writer has said, "It was precisely the ablest student who was, to use Sumner's famous phrase, the 'forgotten man' in American colleges and universities." [14] The ablest are left to shift for themselves—to come to college if they can and to join the campus crowd drifting toward the diploma. The average and the sub-average are taught, coddled, nursed, cajoled, scolded, satirized, given daily lessons, "held up" by quizzes and tests, interviewed by teachers and deans, benefited by special remedial assistance, and are permitted largely to determine teaching methods, standards, and curricula. While every imaginable device is used to drag them through college and send them out at last to serve society, the ablest students are lucky if they find, here and there, an instructor who not only recognizes their ability but has a little leisure to use in their interest, and who believes that a few such students have it in their power to help society more than hordes of the mediocre and deficient. The public welfare demands that this situation be altered. "Does it not seem strange to you," President Sieg of the University of Washington asked in his inaugural address, "that with all our elaborate modern equipment, we are not providing a much greater proportion of intelligent leaders in our country than we did far back in post-revolutionary days, and, indeed, that we are not providing markedly more intelligent followers?"

The acid test of the American state university of the coming decades, the test of the sincerity of the solicitude it sometimes expresses for the ablest students, will be the practical measures which it devises and effectuates with a view to securing such students and developing them into

[14] R. C. Brooks, *Reading for Honors at Swarthmore* (1927), p. 4.

intelligent leaders. From an early age, the state educational system must be concerned with discovering ability for liberal study and opening avenues for its development. It may emerge anywhere, if we are to trust the assertion of psychologists that intelligence is fairly evenly distributed among the population. This has always been suggested by ordinary observation. Jefferson, it will be recalled, found "rubbish" in all classes, and also "genius." In England, Matthew Arnold observed that "In each class there are born a certain number of natures with a curiosity about their best self, with a bent for seeing things as they are," and, long before, Elyot had deplored the "inestimable losse of many good wittes" hastily apprenticed, by foolish parents, to "taylours, to wayuers, to towkers, and sometyme to coblers." A whole social philosophy of education was implied in a remark attributed to Socrates, that "The natures that give evidence of being the noblest are just those that most require education." In present-day America, however, the fair field of which we boast is favoring not the noble but the well-to-do. Our higher education is open to all who can pay for it and denied to those who cannot, and the result is that a very considerable number of our most promising boys and girls are lost to vocations to which they are ill suited and in which they are not needed. Some of the ablest do, indeed, work their way through, sometimes earning every cent of the cost of their college education. While apologists may genially assert that this is the "making" of young people, candid observers recognize that it is more likely to mean their breaking, in health, mind, or character. In any case it means a serious waste of effort upon mechanical and meaningless tasks; at worst, it leads towards disease and death, or psychopathy, or intellectual or moral dishonesty. This is no exaggeration; it could be substantiated by many instances. In recent years, when work has been hard to find even on college campuses, superior students who contrived to get to college have too often found themselves fighting for sheer existence, intent upon economic survival rather than education. Not a few of them have been forced out of college while the inferior have been allowed to slide through. At times the potent sum of five dollars seemed to mean the difference between success and failure in life. University officials did all that they could, but it was not enough. They were not even able to reduce the price of tuition, which, in relation to the general price level, for several years mounted steadily upward. Plainly, "free" higher education was, more than ever, a myth.

The obvious remedy would be to make higher education actually free to at least the ablest students. If the state university is sincere in its expressed desire to discover and train young people of unusual capacity, it will have to set about establishing a system of undergraduate scholarships sufficient to cover the essential expenses of students of proved ability. It already has such a system, far from adequate, for the endowment of special education in the post-graduate years, but it has never seen fit to consider seriously the endowment of liberal education in the undergraduate years, upon which the quality of graduate study depends.

Such assistance would not be one more instance of sentimental humanitarianism, but a form of altruism essential for true democracy. Nor is there anything new in it. Even in the despised Middle Ages, as Rashdall points out, hostels were organized and endowed "to secure board and lodging for poor students who could not pay for it themselves." In contemporary England interest in finding and fostering ability is indicated by a system of scholarships and maintenance grants in the secondary schools, and by the fact that even at Oxford, often regarded by Americans as an institution for a moneyed aristocracy, over half of the students receive scholarships and other aid. In America itself it has long been the practice to encourage the endowment of scholarships for superior young men and women of limited means in the private colleges and universities. The most remarkable instance is the establishment by Harvard College of a system of prize fellowships for undergraduates, ranging in value up to $1200 according to the need of the individual. Invading the region where the state universities are dominant, Harvard made a beginning by selecting ten school boys in the group of states comprising Ohio, Indiana, Illinois, Michigan, Wisconsin, and Minnesota,[15] with the intention of subsequently extending the area and securing as much as ten per cent of its entering class in this way. "In seeking to develop this fellowship plan," said President Conant, "we should note that many potential leaders are today lost because of the fortuitous circumstances that they are not able, for financial reasons, to complete their higher education. . . . We need in our present troubles all the brains that can be brought to bear on our problems and we need to have these brains widely and broadly trained and educated."

Is such a plan for equality of educational opportunity suitable only in a private university, or is it suitable, even more suitable, in a state university also? The answer seems obvious; but it may be clarified and fortified by glancing back to some of the educational aspirations that attended the birth of the American Republic. There is Samuel H. Smith, for instance, who in 1798 formulated twenty-two recommendations, including: "XIII. One boy to be annually chosen on the basis of 'Industry and talents' out of the second division

[15] "The fellowships are attracting boys of high academic rank, even if they fail to obtain one of the awards. . . . The number of students registered in Harvard College from the Middle West has increased 50 per cent since the original announcement of the fellowships was made in 1934" (*Harvard Alumni Bulletin*, May 29, 1936).

of the primary to be sent to college. XIV. That students at college so promoted be supported at the public expense. . . . XVIII. That a National University be established, in which the highest branches of science and literature shall be taught. That it consist of students promoted from the colleges. That one student out of ten be annually chosen for this promotion. . . . XIX. That the student so promoted be supported at the public expense, and be lodged within the walls of the University; remaining so long as he please on a salary, in consideration of his devoting his time to the cultivation of science or literature." Du Pont de Nemours in 1800 presented a plan similar to Smith's. Conceiving that "A single day of an educated man of genius is of more value to the world than the labor of a hundred thousand average men for a year," he devised a plan of education from which natural leaders might be expected to emerge. The selected students were to provide only clothing, on the ground that "There is no family so poor that it cannot clothe its child if the State supplies his education and support." Enough has already been said of Thomas Jefferson's plan for rescuing talents from perishing without use and maintaining a state university in keeping with talents.

State support is equally in harmony with the fundamental motive of the state universities actually established. Though less intent than Jefferson upon discriminating between the fit and the unfit, more prone to the assumption that all men are equally endowed with an intelligence only needing release, the typical state universities of the Middle West were founded for the very purpose of rendering higher education accessible to those whose parents could not afford the cost of such education in the existing institutions. They were founded for the purpose of equalizing opportunity in the interest of those not in the ranks of the moneyed class. The reason that most of the state universities did not, before 1900, build any dormitories appears to be, as Dr. W. H. Cowley has suggested, that "State university students were, in general, poor boys and girls who could ill afford to pay for dormitory residence. . . . They were willing to live in inexpensive rooms and frequently in garrets and cellars. If they could live at home while attending college, so much the better. The great growth of the junior college since 1900 has come about chiefly because of the inability of many parents to educate their children away from home."

The state universities have not carried out their programme of making education higher and making it accessible. Through the extension of the trade school spirit, the type of education has become lower, and at the same time education has been withheld from those unable to meet the expense of it. Prior to the depression, the annual expenses were something like $500, so that the cost of a four-year course for only two children was about $4000. To many families the prospect was nothing short of staggering. Something might be scraped together, something might be earned by the student himself in the summers or by washing dishes at college, but the total sum still looked impossible. Many students came for one semester, or two, or three, gave up the game because the dice seemed loaded, and went home discouraged or bitterly resigned. The state universities often repelled the well-to-do student, who sought a higher standard of living or thinking at some private institution; they attracted the student of limited means, and held him almost regardless of his capacity; and they attracted the poor student and held him until his difficulties became unendurable.

This is not university education as Jefferson conceived it. It does not incorporate the selective principle which he saw was the key to higher education; it is based rather on an humanitarian impulse which has defeated its own ends, and which is not applicable in the field of higher education. The general impulse of the state university today is one making for progress in quantity at the expense of progress in quality. This is in marked contrast with the impulse of the private university, which has used the pressure of quantity to raise the quality. The private university has become more and more selective; the public university, more and more undiscriminating. If this process is suffered to continue, the obvious result will be to widen the gap till the truth dawns on us that the private institutions have nearly all the quality while the public have only the quantity. If that day arrives, the state universities will no longer be able to secure for their faculties men of culture and scholarly distinction; and when faculties deteriorate, swift general deterioration is in sight.[16] Nor will it be easy for the state universities, swallowing their pride, to entrust quality to the safe keeping of the endowed universities. As President Angell of Yale has made clear, the quality of the endowed universities is already gravely imperilled by the prospect of

[16] The situation is not yet irretrievable. In an article entitled "In Order of Their Eminence," in the *Atlantic Monthly*, June, 1935, Edwin R. Embree, appraising the universities of the United States from the point of view of "creative scholarship," includes among the first eleven institutions four state universities: California, Michigan, Wisconsin, and Minnesota.—Speaking through her new president in his inaugural address in 1930, California announced: "We cannot accept the dictum of certain self-styled 'prestige' institutions that state universities must be content to operate on a lower plane for a less gifted group of the population." The same year the president of the University of Minnesota refused to confess "that the states are willing that their universities shall be commonplace, that they shall not exercise the leadership to which they have aspired; for, if they cannot compete successfully with the private universities, they will never be able to attract or retain persons of distinction on their own staffs" (Lotus D. Coffman, presidential address before the National Association of State Universities). No, if the state universities say these things, and act accordingly, the situation is not irretrievable.

taxation measures destructive of the resources which make high quality possible. If the American public is willing to let the public universities deteriorate, it cannot be counted upon to deal more kindly with the private universities.

Indifference, not expense, explains the failure of the state universities to carry out Jefferson's qualitative plan of higher education. They have preferred the maximum numbers, the masses, which satisfy their American zest for magnitude and grandiosity, to the smaller numbers, the more fit, which would appeal to an imagination interested in excellence and magnanimity; and they have buttressed this preference by a pseudo-democratic idealism subversive of higher education and social stability, tenable only in a young, exuberant nation that can afford to be indiscreet because of its security and its easy opportunities. Pseudo-democracy, with its curious mixture of sentimentalism and imperialism, prevents us from adopting the plan of state support of superior students. Clearly, it is not expense that deters us, when we have adopted and rapidly developed the most costly type of university, the university for the masses. Funds have long been available. In the latest edition of *American Colleges and Universities* the annual expenditures of even a comparatively undeveloped institution like the University of Wyoming are given as $1,141,951.61, while those of the University of Michigan are $10,366,-826.44 and of the University of California $16,204,582.36. The state universities are handling large sums of money, but almost none of it in the interest of the most promising and valuable young citizens of the state.

The Jeffersonian plan is not expensive. If one hundred superior students were maintained at one time and each received a stipend of $500, the annual cost would amount to a small proportion of the university's budget. Part of the sum would be returned in the form of tuition and other fees, and the cost would be further reduced if the stipend, instead of being the same for all, were adjusted to the individual's financial need. Clearly, the state could well afford to provide higher education for a limited number of its most promising young citizens, most of whom would in future years discharge the debt, perhaps many fold, by services material or spiritual. Whether all such students should be required to attend the university or whether they should be left free to choose any approved collegiate institution in the state is a question that should be studied in all its bearings. Lest the stipend be regarded as a sinecure, it could be made revocable at the close of any year. Superior students might be selected on the basis of high school records, recommendations, various tests and examinations, and personal interviews. A member of the university staff unembarrassed by other administrative duties might be placed in charge of selection and of the workings of the plan in college.

Along with equally able students coming from well-to-do families, the state-supported students could be placed in advanced "sections" in the first two years, and in the last two years receive the special opportunities implied by an honors programme. Their schedule of studies, throughout, should be so arranged that, instead of trying to juggle with six or seven subjects, they would concentrate, at any one time, upon three or at most four, while remaining free to seek stimulation wherever they could find it by attending lectures in any university course. Intelligent and earnest, these superior students could be given an education truly liberal, escaping, on the one hand, the illusion of enlightenment which besets superficial students when they are educated "widely and broadly" and, on the other hand, the contracted vision of vocational students who receive a prematurely specialized education. In the university of today, as has been pointed out, many of the ablest students desire

a liberal education but actually choose a vocational education, mainly because prudence suggests that the latter
would be more "practical." A sound plan of state support
would overcome this obstacle. It would not only clarify the
nature of a liberal education but make it accessible. The
ablest students could safely embark upon it, without worry-
ing over the imminent problem of self-support. The state,
acting in *loco parentis*, would say to them: "You are here,
first of all, to become men and women—to enter into your
humanity. This you can do, measurably well, within the
customary four years of the college; conceivably in less than
four, if you are already well advanced. Do it measurably
well and I will help you afterward. When you graduate you
may select any career that interests you. If that career demands further training, you shall have your scholarship in
the graduate school or the professional school, as you had it
in college. I shall have faith in you so long as your performance is superior; you shall have help as long as you can
justify it. Do not mistake my motive. This is not simple
kindness, but calculated kindness. I regard your career as a
good investment. I am looking for a return on my investment. I give you not privileges alone, but equivalent responsibilities."

§ 5

State and nation must have leaders, who will possess great
power in despite of all theories of equality. These leaders
should be not the worst or the average, but the best. From
the Revolution to Jackson, the best were theoretically those
qualified by nature, practically those qualified largely by
birth. After Jackson there arose, in time, a crude aristocracy of money, or plutocracy, which perhaps reached its
height of power between 1900 and 1930. Today, notwith-

standing a certain snobbish admiration of distinguished birth and great wealth, American democracy is expressly antagonistic to aristocracy in either of these senses. The alternative is the "natural aristocracy" of intelligence and character. If *aristoi* in this sense are not suffered to emerge, we shall have to put up with *pseudo-aristoi* of a sort not so harmonious with the safety of American democracy. The final test of democracy, according to Tocqueville, will be its capacity to produce and encourage the superior individual. He must be found early, no matter what his "walk" in life, and educated according to his talents: prepared in school for a liberal college, trained in liberal studies till he is ready for special studies, and trained in special studies till he is competent for his special task. Without a sound leadership supplied by superior individuals, democracy will destroy itself in America, as it has destroyed itself in other countries. This we well know, and do nothing.

"The well-being of the many, and not of individuals and classes solely, comes out more and more distinctly to us all as the object which we must pursue. Many are to be partakers of well-being, of civilization and humanization; we must not forget it, and America, happily, is not likely to let us forget it," said an English visitor, Matthew Arnold, in the last century, adding, "but the ideal of well-being, of civilization, of humanization, is not to be, on that account, lowered and coarsened." If the ideal of well-being is sufficiently lowered and coarsened, obviously there will at length be no well-being, worthy the name, of which the many may become partakers. To keep the ideal high, and creatively develop it, is precisely the main function of higher education. Yet to this function our public higher education has grown more and more indifferent, lowering the ideal while striving to care for the inferior. The state universities are accepting every manner of student, includ-

ing many only slightly above the level of the defective, delinquent, and dependent.[17] They are acting upon the devastating assumption, inherited from the romantic conception of original genius, that the special aptitude of each
unique individual, no matter how pitiful it may be, should
be given every opportunity to express itself. Each student
has, it seems, what Walt Whitman called a "precious idioc-
racy"—precious to that student if not precious to the
world—and he should therefore have a chance to be "creative." If this continues to be our ideal of well-being, the
downward course of the state university will be swift. But
if we come to our senses, if we abandon the sentimental
ideology that robs us of vitality, we shall soon regain the
energy and elevation that come of placing first things first.
We shall then remember what a university must always be:
neither, as some think, a school of all things fit to be
studied, nor still less, as many think, a school where all
things may be studied, but rather, as is indicated by the
term *studium generale* (the original *universitas*), a school
for all fit persons. With fit persons the university must still,
as in the Middle Ages, be primarily concerned, only it must
see to it, as the Middle Ages failed to do, that *all* fit persons are enabled to receive training. The modern democratic university should begin by offering its facilities, if
need be *gratis,* to the exceptionally capable, and should not
rest content until it has rendered liberal education accessible to the ordinarily capable as well.

The function of liberal education, President Roosevelt
declared at Jefferson's alma mater in 1934, is that of "training men for citizenship in a great republic." "This," he

[17] Yet J. Howard Beard in "The Teacher's Part in Promoting the
School Child's Health," *School and Society,* December 8, 1934, has stated
that "The enrollment of our institutions for the defective, delinquent,
and dependent is increasing more rapidly than our colleges and universities."

went on to say, "was in the spirit of the old America, and it is, I believe, in the spirit of the America of today. The necessities of our time demand that men avoid being set in grooves, that they avoid the occupational predestination of the older world, and that in the face of change and development in America, they must have a sufficiently broad and comprehensive conception of the world in which they live to meet its changing problems with resourcefulness and practical vision. . . . Every form of coöperative human endeavor cries out for men and women who, in their thinking processes, will know something of the broader aspects of any given problem." While recognizing also the need of those specialists and experts which it is one of the functions of the graduate and professional schools to train, Mr. Roosevelt was concerned essentially with college graduates who, whether or not they become experts, are capable of thinking and acting "not in terms of specialization, not in terms of locality, but rather in the broad sense of national needs." He emphasized the high practicality of liberal education, and he closed with the assertion that "Republican institutions are, in the last analysis, the application to human affairs of those broad humane ideals that a liberal education preserves, enriches, and expands."

Chapter Seven

THE IDEA OF LIBERAL EDUCATION

§ 1

THE EDUCATION OF CITIZENS, UNDER THE American form of government, is simply the education of men and women. Under various non-democratic forms of government which have arisen in the present century, the education of citizens is something very different: it is the shaping of cells in the social organism. The aim of such education is to secure mechanical regimentation rather than personal development, to produce a society composed of fragments rather than a society composed of persons. Fragments, it is conceived, are less than the whole, cells are inferior to the organism, individuals are significant only as parts of society. To this collectivistic view—which rests upon a naturalistic basis—the answer of democracy is that the individual, while realized only in society, is both the source and the end of society. Whatever the dependence of man upon the social organization, man is superior to the social organization—an affirmation which must rest finally upon a humanistic or religious basis. Democracy seeks men and women, not automata, persons not tools, freemen not slaves, and its collegiate education is properly liberal not special, postponing the formation of experts to the formation of citizens, or men and women. Under the American

200

polity, it should make no difference whether we speak of the education of citizens or the education of men and women—the education will be the same, it will be liberal.

President Roosevelt was quite right: liberal education is hostile to regimentation, to vocational grooves, to narrow specialisms and expertnesses: it should make men and women resourceful, prepared to face with elasticity of mind whatever situations life may bring, ready for the unpredictable requirements of a world in which the tempo of change has become bewildering. The resourcefulness which was a prime virtue in the pioneer days is still, because of the rate of change, a prime virtue in our mature civilization. Within the space of a single lifetime we are now witnessing such an alteration of circumstances, of opportunities, and of responsibilities, that neither the young nor their teachers can foresee the problems that must be dealt with a quarter of a century hence. Those who are to be leaders must be trained for life in a world which does not exist. What today seems an education for efficiency may turn out to be merely fixation in maladjustment. Many of the special powers and services that have been useful in the past may be fundamentally altered or may disappear. In the Victorian era, when the acceleration of change was only beginning, even a writer like T. H. Huxley, product in so many ways of the humanitarian movement, demanded a liberal education, of which one of the results should be an intellect "ready, like a steam engine, to be turned to any kind of work," not a special kind of work. Today, far more than in the Victorian era, a narrow *ad hoc* education, enabling the individual to do one thing acceptably and disabling him from doing other things because the variety of his capacities has been stunted by neglect, is a grave disservice to our young men and women and a menace to the society in which they are to live.

§ 2

The background of our American education for power and service, as we saw in an earlier chapter, is the humanitarian tradition that grew up in Europe in the seventeenth and eighteenth centuries. The American state university has now carried the educational implications of that tradition to something like completion. The background of the old American liberal education, and of any new liberal education we may hereafter seek to set up, is the humanistic and religious tradition which governed the culture of Europe prior to the seventeenth century and then gradually declined in prestige, though to this day it retains a vitality that is commonly underestimated. Still supported by this tradition, liberal education plays a great rôle in Europe, a dominating rôle in France and England. Human culture, not mechanical efficiency, is still the central object; the formation of men and women is still insisted upon as prerequisite to the formation of experts. Europe is not lightly abandoning, even under the impact of three centuries of increasing humanitarianism, the old liberal education stretching back something like twenty-five centuries.

In view of repeated distortions of the concept of liberal education by modern sophists, it will be worth while to review here its historical meaning. The concept of liberal education, as John Henry Newman pointed out, "is illustrated by a continuous historical tradition, and never was out of the world, from the time it came into it. There have indeed been differences of opinion from time to time, as to what pursuits and what arts came under that idea, but such differences are but an additional evidence of its reality." And what is this concept? According to Newman, its best expositor since Elyot, it is simply the cultivation of the mind, the development of intellectual excellence. It is not the acquirement of useful knowledge or useful habits in doing specific things, but the development "of judgment, of clear-sightedness, of sagacity, of wisdom, of philosophical reach of mind, and of intellectual self-possession and repose,—qualities which do not come of mere acquirement." Its object is "to open the mind, to correct it, to refine it, to enable it to know, and to digest, master, rule, and use its knowledge, to give it power over its own faculties, application, flexibility, method, critical exactness, sagacity, resource, address, eloquent expression." And thus "the intellect, instead of being formed or sacrificed to some particular or accidental purpose, some specific trade or profession, or study or science, is disciplined for its own sake." This is its sufficient justification, this culture of the mind, comparable with the culture of the body for its health and vigor. But further: it so happens that, as a healthy body can do what an unhealthy one cannot, "so in like manner general culture of mind is the best aid to professional and scientific study, and educated men can do what illiterate cannot; and the man who has learned to think and to reason and to compare and to discriminate and to analyze, who has refined his taste, and formed his judgment, and sharpened his mental vision, will not indeed at once be a lawyer, or a pleader, or an orator, or a statesman, or a physician, or a good landlord, or a man of business, or a soldier, or an engineer, or a chemist, or a geologist, or an antiquarian, but he will be placed in that state of intellect in which he can take up any one of the sciences or callings I have referred to, or any other for which he has a taste or special talent, with an ease, a grace, a versatility, and a success, to which another is a stranger." Finally, as intellectual culture leads to professional skill and success, so it exerts influences upon the moral nature, tending to produce such qualities as "veracity, probity, equity, fairness, gentleness, benevolence, and amiableness," although the full development of the moral nature is possible only through the offices of religion.[1]

This is not merely Newman's theory of education; it is the dominant British theory, which may be traced back to its formulation in *The Boke of the Gouernour* during the English Renaissance. In the French Renaissance, we encounter much the same conception in one of the most vigorous essays of Montaigne. According to Montaigne, mere acquirement, the blind learning by rote, is servile education. Liberal education, on the other hand, consists in the training of judgment. The student is to "examine and thoroughly sift everything he reads, and lodge nothing in his fancy upon simple authority and upon trust." When he encounters differing opinions he will choose, if he can; if not, he will remain doubtful. What he acquires, he must digest and assimilate, as the bee culls sweets from thyme and marjoram and makes a honey which is no longer thyme and marjoram but purely his own—for assimilation, unlike acquirement, is a form of creative originality. Education is liberal when the judgment is free. The effect of such education will be, above all, wisdom or self-knowledge, that is, the science of how to live and how to die, the most useful knowledge man can secure. Through philosophical study the young student may approach virtue, which is not, as the schoolmen say, situated upon the summit of a steep and inaccessible cliff but seated on a fair and fruitful plain. Yet wisdom and virtue are not the whole of life, and Montaigne therefore calls also for excellence of the body and manners through the discipline of running, wrestling, dancing, fencing, and the like. " 'Tis not a soul, 'tis not a body that we are training up, but a man, and we ought not to divide him."

[1] *The Idea of a University,* especially Discourses V-VIII (4th ed. 1875).

This education of body and mind, together with Montaigne's emphasis on wisdom and virtue, had already been set forth in theory and carried out in practice by the humanist educators of Italy. The theory of liberal education has perhaps never been put more broadly and clearly than in the familiar words of Vergerius. "We call those studies *liberal*," he says, "which are worthy of a free man; those studies by which we attain and practice virtue and wisdom; that education which calls forth, trains, and develops those highest gifts of body and mind which ennoble men, and which are rightly judged to rank next in dignity to virtue only." The humanists of Italy were intent upon a practical education, an education that should best prepare men for the actual conduct of life. This explains why they did scant justice to the natural sciences, for, while it is true that the science of that day was inadequate for educational purposes, the fundamental reason for their neglect of it lay in their conviction, as humanists, that men should be directly concerned with human affairs. Even the Spanish Vives, exceptional in his interest in science, maintained that it was not proper "to push research into causes and principles, which are beyond our reach, but to order all our inquiry with reference to the practical needs of life." For the same reason the humanists limited philosophy to ethics, eschewing metaphysical subtleties such as fascinated the schoolmen. Among the studies befitting a free man, the place of honor was given to letters, the literatures of Rome and Greece, which the humanists prized, as Sir Richard Jebb puts it, as "not only models of style, but treasure-houses of wisdom, guides of life, witnesses to a civilization higher than any which could then be found upon the earth."

While dominated by practical purposes, humanist education was not practical in the ordinary modern sense: it proposed no easy short-cuts to vocational efficiency. In the Mantuan school, conducted by the most amiable of the humanists, Vittorino da Feltre, no technical or professional training was offered. His aim, as Woodward says, was "to lay foundations in liberal culture to serve as the necessary preliminaries to specific training for careers." Students stayed with him till they had passed their twenty-first year. Whether a student was destined for law, medicine, or theology, whether he was to enter business or banking, humanist education conceived that he must first be humanized. His first practical duty was to become, in the full sense, a man; his second, to become competent in a vocation. In his training due provision was made, especially by Vergerius, for leisure, that part of life in which a free man is most conscious of his freedom. In Vittorino, who realized the humanist education of the Renaissance at its best, the whole theory and practice were religious in spirit, since, unlike many a "mere" humanist, Vittorino was profoundly Christian. His aim was nothing less than to fuse, in vital harmony, the two great European traditions, classical and Christian. "He himself," says Woodward, "took a leading part in the religious teaching of the school; and by addresses, by private conversations, and above all by his own example, he brought the full force of his personal character to bear upon his pupils in the critical years of their life." From the Mantuan school of Italy to the Protestant and Catholic colleges of modern America, liberal education has frequently provided a place, sometimes predominant, sometimes incidental, for Christian instruction.

Since the best liberal education of the Renaissance was deeply indebted to the Christian faith of the Middle Ages, we must go back to classical antiquity for a clear conception of a liberal education independent of religion. Tracing the liberal tradition to its primary source of inspiration, we come at last to the theory and practice of education in ancient Athens. The general object of Athenian education was to produce citizens, but the citizens must be free men, not slaves of the state as in other ancient civilizations and some civilizations of today—free men, able to govern, to engage in war, and to set the tone of cultural life. They must be, above all, men of character, and, since weakness in one part of man's nature may undo the strength of the rest, this meant that they must be symmetrically developed in body, mind, and taste. They would then attain wisdom, or self-knowledge, which would guide their conduct better than the arbitrary authority of the old religious and social traditions. Developed on all sides, seeking due proportion in all things, resourceful and flexible in all the situations of life, they would realize fully the idea of humanity. They would be, first of all, persons, not individuals; for personality could be attained only through effort, while individuality would take care of itself.

Education, so conceived, is liberal not vocational—the antithesis of the terms was sharply brought out by Aristotle. Vocational training, as he views it, is illiberal because it looks toward money-making rather than freedom. It narrows instead of broadening the mind. Training for a specific occupation is inferior in excellence to liberal education because it is concerned with only a part of life and not the most important part. Over-cultivation of any one of the liberal arts is similarly to be deplored, for the young specialist's devotion to a liberal study with a view to attaining professional skill in it is degrading to the intellect. Indeed it makes a great difference, says Aristotle, for what purpose we do or learn a thing.

What lies behind these Aristotelian distinctions is a conception of "leisure," σχολή, which is typically Greek and sundered far from the usual trivial associations of the word today. On the one hand leisure is distinguished from labor, and on the other from recreation. In labor we pursue what is necessary, in recreation what fits us for further labor, these two, labor and recreation, alternating, as it were, on a low plane. On quite another plane is leisure, for it is in leisure alone that we pursue what is good and productive of happiness. To put the matter in another way: our recreation is less serious than our labor, and our labor, in turn, less serious than our leisure, for we recreate in order that we may labor, and labor in order that we may have leisure. As Bosanquet has well stated the matter: "Leisure—the word from which our word 'school' is derived—was for the Greek the expression of the highest moments of the mind. It was not labor; far less was it recreation. It was that employment of the mind in which by great thoughts, by art and poetry which lift us above ourselves, by the highest exertion of the intelligence, as we should add, by religion, we obtain occasionally a sense of something that cannot be taken from us, a real oneness and center in the universe; and which makes us feel that whatever happens to the present form of our little ephemeral personality, life is yet worth living because it has a real and sensible contact with something of eternal value." This leisure, this free activity of the higher self, this enlargement and elevation of our humanity, is the end of liberal education, and no education which does not attain this end is in the true sense liberal. And it is for those only who are gifted with the possibility of freedom.

§ 3

Historically, liberal education has always been founded on humanism, often on religion as well. To this day it sometimes has both foundations, most plainly in the Catholic

institutions of learning. Any future extension of this twofold basis must depend upon the possibility of a Christian
revival—at present a remote possibility, at least in America.
Meanwhile we may still avail ourselves of humanism, since
humanism, ever since it became self-conscious in the Renaissance, has been one expression of what we call the "modern spirit." Now, the modern spirit is at bottom the ancient spirit, the spirit of Horace and Cicero, of Aristotle
and Plato, of Athens in the age of Pericles. When this ancient quest of knowledge and the good life regained its
prestige in the Renaissance, it entered upon a complicated
development. Following one line, it cultivated the humanities and maintained a humanistic view of life, usually
within the framework of a Christian view of life, as in the
grand siècle of France. Following another line, it cultivated
the sciences and formed a naturalistic view of life in conflict with both humanism and Christianity. The issue of
this conflict did not long remain doubtful. As naturalism
advanced, Protestant Christianity retreated, step by step
compromising, at length surrendering almost wholly to the
rising secular and scientistic spirit. Similarly, humanism,
relaxing its distinction between man and nature, more and
more took on the color of the new age, and came to believe
that its salvation lay in a factual, scientific scholarship and
in a naturalistic type of art and philosophy. In vain did a
few humanists and Protestants, in vain even did a Catholic
church, firm in doctrine and powerful in organization, attempt to stem the tide. Today naturalism is triumphant.
But so, very nearly, is chaos. In all fields naturalism is showing its inability to give human life order, meaning, or happiness. It may be that the fulfillment of the movement
which began so gradually in the seventeenth century will
be followed by swift disintegration. Near or far, the time is
apparently approaching when the modern spirit, if it can-

not bring itself to an acceptance of Christianity, will have to express itself once more in the line of humanistic development which it entered upon in the Renaissance.

§ 4

When the Renaissance opened the modern age, humanism found itself in a situation different from that of the ancient humanism from which it drew its inspiration. The Middle Ages lay between; and the task of humanism was now conceived to be that of affirming its vision of life in opposition to an excessive devotion to otherworldliness. Men like Vittorino, Erasmus, and Milton, it is true, were too profoundly Christian to desire a sharp break with the great ages of faith; by precept and example they showed that humanism and religion have much in common and can live well together. The fact remained, however, that a new enthusiasm had arrived—a confidence in man, in human powers, in the possibility of a good life in the world—and that this new enthusiasm seemed to need justification as against an otherworldly religion and an authoritative Church.

Today, the humanistic tradition faces a different antagonist: not religion, but naturalism. It is, indeed, the ally of religion, i.e., dualistic religion, opposing as a common enemy the monistic naturalism of the day. Itself without a systematic philosophy, the humanistic tradition is opposed to metaphysical absolutes—above all, in the present situation, to the absolutes set up by naturalism.

Since the naturalistic tradition today claims the immense prestige of science, humanism, in opposing naturalism, is often mistakenly regarded as opposed to science. The presumption seems to be that when the one is attacked, the other is attacked also. But science is not the private property of naturalism: it is the product of the human spirit, and is prized as such by humanism. Clearly, humanism could not be hostile to science without being hostile to the Hellenism from which it ultimately derives. The attitude of humanism toward science has a sufficient spokesman in a Hellenist like John Burnet, who has said: "Man is ignorant, but he knows that he is so, and he cannot rest in his ignorance"; "Whatever else science may be, it is one of the spiritual conquests of mankind"; "Science depends upon Humanism . . . since it is only the Humanist point of view that can furnish an adequate motive for its pursuit or even a justification of its existence." [2] Consequently, if the day ever arrives when science is imperilled by obscurantism, humanists will be found fighting side by side with scientists against the forces of darkness. For humanism believes in light, in knowledge as a good in itself and in knowledge applied for the use and benefit of mankind. Without science we should assuredly be more ignorant than we are and less able to shape nature to our human ends.

Yet it must be recognized, as humanism reminds us today, that it is idle to look to science for any knowledge that can be called absolute. Science operates within artificial limits of its own choosing, and attains only relative knowledge. It adopts a certain point of view and can see only what is visible from that point of view. Its observation is rigidly selective; what it cannot use, it simply disregards. The value of its discoveries is limited by the conditions under which it set out to make discoveries. It provides us with abstractions, which are valid only on the basis of the assumptions underlying them. Not that the scientist is necessarily aware of these conditions and assumptions. He may never have given them—such is our higher education—a moment's thought, supposing that his programme is nothing more or less than to find out some things not known before. Many

[2] *Essays and Addresses* (1929), pp. 113, 119, 124.

a scientist today would be surprised to learn what he has really been doing, much as M. Jourdain in Molière's comedy was surprised to learn that he had been speaking prose all his life. However he may choose to look upon his work, every scientist operates within the limits of a very definite enterprise, and the enterprise itself does not afford him any means of criticizing the final validity of the abstractions which he attains: that is the function, not of science, but of philosophy.

The moment the scientist claims final validity for his abstractions, the moment he asserts that whatever must be termed true for science is true for man, the moment he declares that science gives us everything that deserves to be termed knowledge and that everything conflicting with the findings of science is of necessity false, the moment he informs us that science is gradually taking the place of philosophy and making it superfluous, the moment he does any of these things, he ceases to be a scientist, he abandons his high calling, and adopts instead a calling he is wont to spurn—the calling of the philosopher.

As scientist he weighed all the evidence relative to his task; as philosopher he now pretends to weigh all the evidence there is. In the laboratory he worked within the limits of science; in the lecture, the interview, or the magazine article, he ventures opinions outside the limits of science. What he learned in the laboratory has the authority of science; what he thinks afterward has the authority of philosophy. As a man he has, of course, the right to be both scientist and philosopher, and the duty to take both of his occupations seriously, lest he appear in the light of a philosopher ill at ease in science or a scientist ill at ease in philosophy. Ideally, he should undergo equal discipline in the two fields. Unfortunately, in the present age, nothing is commoner than to see scientists who, while exacting of themselves a stern discipline in science, recklessly embark upon the perilous seas of philosophy with the scantiest equipment. In any case, whether well prepared or ill, the scientist, because of his zealous appreciation of science, is likely to adopt some form of the philosophy of naturalism which he finds everywhere about him. He lives comfortably in the intellectual climate of the day. He is quite at home in a naturalistic philosophy that appears to be erected on the solid foundations of science. Perhaps shy of the term philosophy, he likes to think that he is merely following science "in her most exalted mood." And thus he arrives at the world-view which elevates science to a supreme court, a monistic world-view which holds that the only reality there is is the reality of nature as interpreted by science. All other reality is illusory, all other reality can be explained away by the corrosive force of a science that has no room for wishful thinking. Deep in his heart he may doubt whether, after all, reality is so simple, and he may show another side of his nature to his family, or in his church; but officially he is committed to a naturalistic monism, officially he believes he must obey the *Einheitstrieb* by means of which this philosophy unites man in his entirety with nature.

For it is the philosophy of naturalism which effects this perfect union, not science. As a physical organism, to be sure, man is part of the life of nature, as nineteenth-century biology made far clearer than it had been; this was the work of science, rather than philosophy. But latterly all the rest of man has been melted into nature; and this is the work of philosophy, rather than science. For while the authority of science is plain in the realm of the physical, its authority in other realms depends entirely on the philosophy one adopts. A psychology, for example, may be elaborated which studies man as an assortment of natural wishes and drives like those which apparently dominate the lives of other animals. When this point of view has been taken and the evidence sedulously gathered, the abstractions may well turn out to be scientifically true; that is, true within the arbitrary limits of the enterprise. But it by no means follows that henceforth man must be viewed as an assortment of natural wishes and drives, since it is just as possible as it was before to view him in other ways, the validity of which will depend upon these other ways of viewing him and the evidence in favor of those ways.[3] The declaration that man is an assortment of natural wishes and drives and nothing else, can never issue from scientific observation but must always rest upon dogmatic naturalism.

At no time between Socrates and the present day has humanism been willing to endure this claim of the scientistic rather than scientific mind. Rightly considered, the spirit of science is modest; science has no desire to assert an hegemony to which it is not entitled. Properly, the spirit of science is unprejudiced, unwilling to deal roughly with what does not fit its preconceptions, laying aside rather than destroying what seems irrelevant to its immediate work. Properly, science is as gentle as firm. Scientists also, if they are genuinely religious or humanistic, may be as gentle as firm. As a rule the best scientists of today, even when tinged with naturalistic philosophy, are chary of dogmatism. But there is scarcely any limit to the assurance of some of the best, and of the generality of workers below the

[3] "Dewey said then [in his *Psychology*, 1886], as philosophers say now, that an exposition of psychology depends upon the philosophical assumptions implicit in it, and that it is better to have these assumptions explicit and out in the open than to use them, pretending that they are not there. This argument, however, has never made headway with the psychologists, who are inclined to point to the unphilosophical nature of the other sciences in explanation of their own philosophical naïveté" (Boring, *op. cit.*, p. 533).

best, if one may judge from their published utterance, that their mode of study is the one avenue to truth, that nothing human is alien to exact analysis, and that the ways of nature embrace the whole of reality. They are quite oblivious of the fact that dogmas of this sort are derived not from science but from naturalism, that such dogmas are speculative in the philosophical sense, and that they will be rejected as soon as some philosophy other than naturalism gains the supremacy. Like other philosophical systems, naturalism will presently appear to be forced and exclusive, and some other philosophy will then proclaim the importance of elements that were depreciated or omitted, perhaps with a new prejudice as marked as the old, while the common sense of mankind yawns. "Materialism and mentalism—the philosophies of 'nothing but.' How wearily familiar we have become with that 'nothing but space, time, matter and motion,' 'nothing but sex,' that 'nothing but economics'! And the no less intolerant 'nothing but spirit,' 'nothing but consciousness,' 'nothing but psychology'—how boring and tiresome they also are! 'Nothing but' is mean as well as stupid. It lacks generosity. Enough of 'nothing but.' It is time to say again, with primitive common sense (but for better reasons), 'not only, but also.' "

As Aldous Huxley here suggests, there is such a thing as an enduring common sense, which sooner or later becomes aware of an exaggeration, then wearies of it, and finally revolts against it. Edmund Burke termed it the "permanent sense of mankind." It is the basis of any sound humanism. An affirmative outlook on life which persistently seeks the mean between conflicting extremes, humanism prefers the flexibility and inclusiveness of the permanent sense of mankind to the rigidity and exclusiveness of rational systems. Content to define and formulate only within the bounds set by common sense, it refrains from the construction of a systematic philosophy. It is merely a working philosophy, and is sound in proportion as it represents what men normally live by. With the critical and positive spirit of science but without the exclusiveness of naturalism, it rests upon experience, the whole of human experience, primarily experience open to us in the present, secondarily, for verification, experience open to us in the records of the past.

Unhampered by the logical necessities of naturalism, humanism has nothing to explain away, or even to explain. It does not seek to show how life came from non-life or consciousness from unconsciousness, or perhaps why consciousness is not a fact at all; it is not troubled to prove that man is a creature of the planet, a curious bit of the ceaseless flow of nature, subject wholly to her law; it need not perplex the common sense of humanity by explaining into absurdity or nothingness the realities of ethics, religion, and art, or how it comes about that so deluded an animal is capable of the constructions of science and naturalistic philosophy. Ungoaded by the *Einheitstrieb* of any such monism, humanism is content to accept, without explanation, the "doubleness" of human experience, experience shared with nature and experience not shared with nature. It is willing to acknowledge two realities, the reality of nature and the reality of the human spirit, without subsuming either under the other. It affirms, as in the succinct lines of Emerson, that

> There are two laws discrete,
> Not reconciled,—
> Law for man, and law for thing.

There are two different orders of reality, two series of events in personal or racial life, each secure in its own right. The reality of nature and of man in his purely corporeal existence is suited to scientific investigation; the reality of the human spirit, as we know it in normal experience, is in a realm to which science, because of its initial assumptions, has no access. Today, as in the past, humanism can only accept the paradoxical terms on which we live. When Carlyle heard that Margaret Fuller had decided to accept the universe, he said, "Gad, she'd better!" The incident has pleased naturalists, who forget that the very act of accepting implies something in us which has a choice between accepting or not accepting, something which differentiates the accepter from the thing accepted. No doubt it is important for us to accept the physical universe outside us; but it is even more important to accept the humanity within us, upon which our knowledge of the physical universe depends. The most relevant knowledge we have is self-knowledge.

Once we affirm that two discrete kinds of reality are indicated by the permanent sense of mankind, it should be clear that a single method of seeking knowledge will not suffice. The reality must determine the method; not the method, the reality. The method of science has proved so fruitful in modern times largely because that method was more and more clearly adjusted to the subject-matter—this, indeed, is the prime lesson which the humanities should have learned from science, instead of being satisfied with applying its method to their very different subject-matter. The restricted method which science employs in the investigation of nature may be applicable to certain peripheral aspects of the humanities, but is not suited to the center of the subject, which is the human reality of conscious purpose. To study man as a purposive being by the methods of physics or chemistry is about as inept as to study atoms or elements by the methods of ethics or aesthetics.

There is a fundamental distinction between scientific

knowledge and self-knowledge, which has been very clearly stated by Robert Shafer. "Scientific knowledge," he says, "is external, concerning sensible appearances; it is fully communicable and verifiable, and thus becomes public property—a possession of society—as rapidly as it is achieved; and it is impersonal. Self-knowledge, on the other hand, is personal, private, and inward. A man may know himself as no one else may know him, and as he may know no one else. Though others may help him, and indeed must if he is to go far in this direction, he alone can discover himself and learn what is to be learned; and he can never directly or fully communicate his self-knowledge, which begins and ends with him, and is, like himself, unique or individual. . . . A developed, conscious self cannot be passed on to a succeeding generation as science is; though self-knowledge and scientific are both knowledge in the same sense of the word, and the latter is not more genuine or final or trustworthy than the former—perhaps, indeed, is never as real as the former may be."[4] For each man the task is new, as if the human race were just beginning; yet this is not to say that the history of the race is irrelevant, since it constitutes, in a sense, a vast laboratory in which he may test what he knows of human life, a laboratory of institutions and literary and artistic records, of experiments in living and confessions of experience, in endless variety. Here is inexhaustible wealth to supplement the poverty of his personal experience, and yet he can draw upon it only in proportion as his personal experience gives it vital meaning. A masterpiece of the human spirit will not speak to him till he is ready to be spoken to—till he has in some measure lived the truth which it expresses. The method of human knowledge, unlike the method of scientific knowledge, is inescapably personal. If we wish to study poetry,

[4] *Paul Elmer More and American Criticism* (1935), pp. 144-45.

for example, we may go to science for an objective description of its physical nature when read aloud, because poetry then enters the realm of physical sound and may be analyzed with the exact instruments which we owe to modern technology; yet poetry is vastly more than the voice of a reader, and its intangible essence will never be amenable to the impersonal method of science. It is something to which personal experience alone can give access. This is why, as the quantity and quality of our experience changes, our judgment of the meaning and value of certain poems changes also. To most of us a few masterpieces remain forever relatively meaningless, never reborn in terms of life as we know it, so that our knowledge of them is superficial and indirect, not profound and intimate. Intellectually, we may concede their greatness, for when many competent persons in many periods of time have given a strong inner response to them, the probability is that our own excellence, rather than that of the works, is in question, but for us personally they are not important, indeed scarcely exist.

Human knowledge is thus, basically, self-knowledge, direct, intuitive, subjective. And yet from the personal experience of many individuals something more emerges than a mere chaos of conflicting observations. While we are single persons, we are also human beings, endowed with similar traits and confronted by similar conditions of living. Through the ages of recorded history the unity of human nature is so marked that we commonly say there is nothing new under the sun. Those who assert that human nature is going to be different tomorrow are nearly always deficient in knowledge of the past. The unending repetition of much the same problems and much the same ways of dealing with them makes it possible for us to transcend the subjectivity in which human knowledge begins and to attain an objectivity analogous to that of science. Beginning with the self, widening our study to include more and more selves of the present and the past, we may attempt the formulation of general truths concerning life and then use them for the purpose of self-fulfillment. These general truths, be it noted, are not the statistical averages that science offers. They do not concern merely what has been and is, but rather the *best* of what has been and is, the best which is possible under the law for man. They are *ideal* truths, the truths of a conscious and purposeful creature.

Following the subjective-objective method of human knowledge, we come at once upon the central affirmation of humanism: the duality of human nature, the distinction between the two selves. The evidence for it is not inferred but direct, that is, is found not through scientific abstraction but through concrete experience. It is an immediate perception, a datum of consciousness. Its validity is almost universally recognized in the practice of living, though denied by many in their theory of life. Its corroboration lies in the "wisdom of the ages," Occidental and Oriental. So much is quite clear. The precise definition of the two selves, however, is more difficult. Graeco-Roman humanism defined the two selves as impulse and reason. In the words of Cicero, "The natural constitution of the human mind is twofold. One part consists in appetite, by the Greeks termed ὁρμή (impulse), which hurries a man hither and thither; the other is reason, which instructs and makes clear what is to be done or avoided." It was the way of classical antiquity to enthrone reason, and Occidental humanism has ever since given it a high place. Yet even as early as Plato there are many adumbrations of an ultimate truth not accessible to reason, and in Aristotle, notwithstanding his desire to give a rational basis to life, there is more than a suggestion of a reality that refuses to be reduced to rational terms.

The doubleness of human nature likewise underlies the wisdom of the Orient, in the form in which it spread over the Occident: Christianity teaches the primacy of the will and finds the true dualism in a conflict of desire and will. Profoundly affected by the teachings of Christianity, the humanistic tradition of Europe, notwithstanding its derivation from ancient Greece, has generally suspected that the characteristic confidence of the Greeks in the competence of reason to plumb the depths of reality and bring about the good life was itself a form of excess requiring a corrective. To the pride of reason and all other forms of overconfidence it has opposed humility, regarded even by a humanist like Burke, in the midst of eighteenth-century rationalism, as "the low, but deep and firm foundation of all real virtue." This is something other than that modesty which worldly humanists have often praised, for humility, unlike modesty, looks toward something elevated above ordinary human excellence, something which the religionist is wont to call the supernatural but which the humanist (unless also a religionist) prefers to regard simply as experience of the higher self.

Humanism affirms, then, two selves, desire and will, or, to avoid misunderstanding, two wills, the will which endlessly desires and the will which restrains desire within due limits, the temperamental will and the ethical will.[5] This does not imply any disparagement of nature; our expansive instincts and energies are essential for any human achievement, and are evil only when uncontrolled. In art, in science, in social

[5] Any terminology dividing human nature is, of course, more or less forced, and open to criticism. The criticism that has been levelled against the rigid "faculties"—intellect, will, reason, and the like—is justified. But it is noteworthy that modern psychologies that have cast out the faculties have not succeeded in establishing anything in their place. Somewhat like "periods" in history, they are a practical necessity for fruitful thinking. I have not hesitated to employ them in the following pages.

and political life, in all forms of outer action, they are so much material and power at our disposal, and yet they cannot be suffered to express themselves without control or guidance. Nor can they—notwithstanding current naturalistic views of human nature—be trusted to check each other, since all the evidence indicates that one or another of them will run wild; this is why sympathy, if viewed as itself an expansive instinct, is so easily overruled by some other instinct. Man alone, among all animals, displays a power of control of instinct, a power of staying the flux at the command of conscience, the inner veto. He alone has a means of saying "no" to his instincts and energies and shaping them for the attainment of some end set above nature. In childhood this power is revealed to him by external discipline, and as he matures he can exert it more and more by self-discipline. Accidents of heredity and environment will prevent his bringing this power to perfection and using it with uniform wisdom, for freedom of will is not unlimited. Yet the will possesses freedom, the seal of humanity.[6]

While assigning the primacy to will, humanism does not, however, depreciate reason. It does not make the error of romanticism in looking upon reason as "the false secondary power that multiplies distinctions." Though secondary, reason is not always false, for there are real distinctions as well as fanciful ones. There is, for example, the real distinction between science and scientism, or between leisure and recreation, or between the true mysticism of the "Divine Comedy" and the pseudo-mysticism of "Tintern Abbey" or "Prometheus Unbound." Men are often the dupes of words and phrases, as "progressive," "self-expression," "realism,"

---

[6] On the insoluble question of free will, the most realistic attitude is that of Dr. Johnson, who said: "All argument is against it; all experience is for it." As a practical view of life, humanism uses the verdict of experience.

"idealism," "social justice," "the war to end war," "Nordic," "Americanism," and "loyalty," to name a few current in this century, so that one of the main functions of reason, though a badly neglected function ever since the Middle Ages, consists in a careful discrimination in the use of general terms. Without scrutiny of meanings, we are certain to be misled by some charlatan or demagogue or sophist who uses fine words as a cloak for the false or ignoble. In the daily conduct of life, no less, we need rational guidance to make clear to us what the right action or attitude is—when or how far to say "yes" or "no." The humanist, as well as others, needs such guidance, for his doctrine of the mean, the application of which varies with the person and the circumstances, requires the keenest discrimination. "It does not follow," says Aristotle, "if ten pounds of meat are much and two are little for a man to eat, that the trainer will prescribe six pounds; that would be little for Milo, but much for a beginner in gymnastics." What is true in the physical realm is true also in the ethical: "For instance, it is possible to fear or feel bold, to desire, to get angry, to feel pity, and in general, to feel pleasure or pain, in a greater or less degree, and in both cases wrongly; but to have these feelings at the right times and on the right occasions and towards the right persons and with the right motive and in the right way is the mean." Evidently, the mean is not to be found without a sensitive intelligence.

The sense of proportion is closely connected with the sense of the comic. Having faith in common sense and using reason to lay hold of the sensible amid the clutter of nonsensicalities that hide it from view, humanism does much of its work through "the first-born of commonsense, the vigilant Comic." Whenever men, as Meredith says of the comic spirit, "wax out of proportion, overblown, affected, pretentious, bombastical, hypocritical, pedantic, fantastically delicate; whenever it sees them self-deceived or hoodwinked, given to run riot in idolatries, drifting into vanities, congregating in absurdities, planning short-sightedly, plotting dementedly; whenever they are at variance with their professions, and violate the unwritten but perceptible laws binding them in consideration one to another; whenever they offend sound reason, fair justice; are false in humility or mined with conceit, individually or in the bulk—the Spirit overhead will look humanely malign and cast an oblique light on them, followed by volleys of silvery laughter." This is the spirit that resides in the gentle irony of Plato, the keen perception of folly which is so much of the wisdom of Erasmus and Shakespeare, the clear reason of Molière warring against every manner of unreason, and in the pillory of snobs by Thackeray, of sentimentalists by Lowell, of overweening modernists by Chesterton—all of them seekers after the permanent sense of mankind. But the critical spirit of comedy is by no means to be associated only with literature; it operates in life, and indeed is a main instrument in the art of humane living. It is a happy means of destroying excess, whether in others or oneself. Directed by the intellect, it laughs at any inclination of temperament to depart absurdly from the mean.

Now temperament, forever tugging to free itself from reason and shrinking from the ridicule of the comic spirit, has a powerful ally in what we call the imagination. Imagination, as Napoleon rightly said, rules the world, and it does so because it lends enthusiasm to either side of human nature, the temperamental or the ethical, either the side that tells us what we desire to be or the side that tells us what we ought to be. Through its images it can make any excess, however perverted, attractive and often irresistible; restraint is shaken off, reason is put aside or reduced to mere rationalization, and the thing desired is blindly pursued. Where images of glory are concerned, or power, or wealth, or sex, the mental picture may become an obsession determining the quality of life in an individual, a country, or a whole epoch of civilization. It is the nature of the temperamental self, goaded by the imagination, never to be satisfied for long but always to be seeking satisfactions that lie beyond. Its genius is endlessness. All the finance ministers and upholsterers and confectioners of Europe, as Thomas Carlyle said, could not make one shoeblack happy "above an hour or two," because he would need, "for his permanent satisfaction and saturation, simply this allotment, no more, and no less: *God's infinite Universe altogether to himself*, therein to enjoy infinitely, and fill every wish as fast as it rose." In varying degrees all men, save perhaps a few saints, are lovers of folly, cherishing dreams of somehow contenting the endless desires of temperament. But there is another part of our nature, a centripetal power resisting the centrifugal impulses of temperament, drawing us back towards the very center of our being; and this other part, the ethical will, uses the imagination no less. It is the imagination which enabled Greek humanism to envisage for the guidance of daily living, and to represent in artistic forms which fired the imagination afresh, an image of man as he "ought to be," a βέλτιον, or higher reality: an image so grand that it could be rendered, in epic, in drama, in sculpture, either through human beings conceived as elevated above their ordinary selves or through gods conceived as human beings idealized. It is the imagination which led Christianity to find inspiration in the image of the cross, the Virgin Mary, the example of Jesus, to picture Heaven and Hell, to build edifices suited to the high purposes of religion. It is the imagination which gave passion to the Revival of Learning, the Renaissance expansion of personality, the faith in the good life here and now, the growing curiosity to understand the physical world and master it for human ends. It is the imagination which, in any age, induces men to work for the realization of what is permanent in themselves, to withdraw from the flux of things, the natural realm of *endlessness,* in which the only law is perpetual change, and to seek the human realm of the *infinite,* an abiding reality which makes for peace and elevation and to which men have access in ethical or religious experience.

Humanism as here conceived—as a way of living in which the ethical self controls the temperamental and employs reason and imagination as its allies—holds forth the possibility of individual progress and social harmony. It is not impressed with the evidence in support of any natural law or tendency to general progress such as the past two centuries have cherished; but it recognizes, as the wisdom of the ages has always recognized, that progress is open to individuals. That many individuals *do* progress is a matter of mere observation. That individuals *may* progress is owing to the freedom of the human will, which enables them, within limits, to realize in themselves, more and more, the idea of humanity—to become persons rather than mere individuals. Inasmuch as idiosyncrasy is less desirable than humanity, inasmuch as individual differences are less important than the likenesses of individuals, humanism is concerned in the first instance that men and women should progress by becoming human, and only in the second instance that they should progress by becoming the particular persons they tend to be. It is not in sympathy with the current emphasis on one-sidedness—the sacrifice of the ideal of humanity on the altar of specialization, a lingering form of the sentimental cult of original genius fostered in the eighteenth century—because nature itself seems amply to assure the expression of whatever is unique in individuals, as may be seen in many periods of culture when men gave no thought to being peculiar. If anything, the originality of St. Francis and St. Augustine, of Phidias and Michelangelo, of Shakespeare and Goethe appears to have been the greater because it was unsought. On the other hand, the progress of our humanity, which does not come naturally but is imposed upon nature, demands that individuals work upon themselves, seeing to it that their energies may really flourish because controlled and directed instead of being frustrated by each other, or dissipated and lost, or expressed in absurdities.

The progress of the individual towards a fulfilled personality, it should go without saying yet needs to be said, is the very opposite of selfish progress, since every increase of self-control limits further that temperamental imperialism which we call selfishness. The individual, while learning to live wisely, becomes progressively more fit to be lived with. Two fools will live badly together; one fool and one wise man will do better; and two wise men will do best. The reason was indicated in a saying of Aeschylus which impressed Goethe: "The wise have much in common with one another." All men who have attained a high degree of inner order and justice and peace will tend to produce, in their social relations, outer order and justice and peace. Self-cultivation is the root, social harmony the fruit. Self-control precedes any desirable form of social control. The sound individualist, beginning with himself, progressing towards self-fulfillment, will become the social man.

What we see everywhere today, however, is the social animal; we see societies rather than communities, we see gregarious unities far inferior to those of certain insects rather than human groups dominated by a quality of will not to be found in the animal creation. Our societies are little more than arbitrary alliances of self-seeking individuals, who disguise their self-seeking with the pseudo-idealism of the humanitarian tradition. As late as the close of the eighteenth century, many men still possessed "a just estimate of that love of power and proneness to abuse it which predominates in the human heart," such as Washington commended to his fellow countrymen in his Farewell Address. Many were realistic enough to see, as Aristotle had seen long before, that the majority of men prefer a disorderly to a sober life and that the fundamental cause of social conflict is nothing other than "the wickedness of human nature." Not that men are hopelessly wicked, for, in the humanistic tradition as in the central tradition of Christianity, humanity is characterized, not by natural and total depravity, but by a propensity toward evil accompanied by a capacity for goodness. The crux of the problem of social welfare accordingly lies in man's divided will, the dual constitution of man. But as we saw in an earlier chapter, the humanitarianism of the age of Rousseau made the blunder of substituting, for an unwarranted notion of total depravity, an equally unwarranted notion of natural goodness. There was now one self, and it was good, and it seemed to follow that the source of evil must lie outside of man in institutions, economic, political, and ecclesiastic. Accordingly the old dualism of human nature gave place to the new dualism of the individual versus society. In the eighteenth century, sentimentalism and romanticism took sides with the individual against society; in the nineteenth century, when the economic man increasingly dominated, "rugged" individualism similarly arrayed the individual against society. In the twentieth century, this anarchic individualism was shaken to its foundations by the martial and economic conflict of nations seeking a secure place "in the sun," and men felt themselves forced, by the pressure of fear, to turn their hopes toward national collectivism, taking sides, now, with society against the individual. Collectivism has produced some strange ideologies and strange practices; it adds to the conflict of nations the conflict of social groups, postponing the classless utopia to a future that steadily recedes. Fascism, socialism, and communism alike begin with the externals of life, with mechanisms for the organization and distribution of the instruments of living and killing. All three attempt, by regimentation, to attain the maximum of power, power for security and prosperity in peace or in war, while they incidentally profess service of cultural values and international coöperation.

From the point of view of humanism, as of religion, this absorption of the individual into the mass and this development of the mass into a means of attaining the maximum of economic and martial power, is a return to primitivism, not an advance toward the great society. To substitute the social animal for the social man is to renounce the dignity of man, which rests upon the freedom of individuals. No society can be better than the individuals who compose it, and none of the individuals who compose it can become better without self-discipline. Reform, like charity, begins at home. Not merely discovery and invention but all the goods that society prizes owe their origin to individuals. As Mill said, "The initiative of all wise or noble things comes, and must come, from individuals; generally at first from some one individual." What one individual attains becomes public property, or rather, the property of all those who, by imitation, follow the leadership of that individual. Followers, in turn, become leaders and acquire followers; and thus wisdom, like folly, has a tendency to spread.[7] There is no way to assure

---

[7] "What used to be talked about in the drawing-room is repeated in the streets," was the observation of a traveler returning to France at the beginning of the reign of Louis XVI. Revolutions are not started by masses of men, though of course conditions must appear to justify change. The direction of change is determined by individuals.

the dominance of wisdom over folly, for the means of social control, such as legal and educational institutions, may come into the hands of either the wise or the foolish. All we can say is that a society will be wise if enough of the individuals who compose it are wise, and that it will move toward wisdom in proportion as its naturally superior persons, or leaders, are moving in that direction.

For in the end everything depends upon leaders and followers, example and imitation. "Example," as Burke said, "is the school of mankind; it will learn at no other." Of imitation, Jefferson said, "Man is an imitative animal. This quality is the germ of all education in him." [8] Christianity itself may be briefly described as the imitation of Christ; humanism has imitated an ideal envisaged by the imagination and this ideal has always owed its efficacy to particular human examples, from, let us say, Socrates to Goethe; and naturalism, no less, has imitated its sentimentalists, its supermen, its captains of industry, and other types through the compelling attraction of examples. This is why society grows, or decays, first at the top. What is believed or done there is presently found to be believed or done at the bottom. Jefferson was therefore quite right: the source of progress lies in the uncommon men who, whatever the social class they are born into, compose a natural aristocracy, exemplary persons who are "representative" in a wider sense than the political because they express what is best in common men and set the standard by which common men may seek to develop themselves. According to Professor Chinard, Jefferson soberly concluded "that each people have the government they deserve, and that durable improvements can come only as a result of

[8] Repeating the thought of Aristotle, who wrote that "Man . . . is the most imitative creature in the world, and learns at first by imitation."

the improvement of the moral qualities of every citizen—
from within and not from without." [9]

Whatever progress may be possible for a society—between
periods of regress—depends, then, on the leadership of a
persuasive minority composed of men of intelligence and
character. To such leaders we must look for constructive
wisdom and administrative integrity. Hope does not lie
in dictators thirsting for power, nor in social groups identifying their alleged rights with the general welfare, nor
in average men and women doing the best they can under
leaders no better than themselves. Nor does it lie in any
new form of control designed to operate well no matter
who plans the machinery and runs it. Once we have sound
leaders, we may safely entrust to them the administration
of our economic, social, and political arrangements. If
our present arrangements are defective, they should be
altered by the wise and not the foolish. Whether the wise
exist and whether they will be elected as the people's representatives, will depend almost wholly on the kind of education conducted by the nation and the distribution of education according to ability.

As for the relation of national states to each other, again
everything depends in the end on intelligent and moderate
leaders. Such men will tend to produce a political state
which is intelligent and moderate, which refrains from
both commercial and "idealistic" imperialism, and which
is therefore an example that other states may properly
imitate. Any state that has become ethical through an
ethical leadership will find it feasible to coöperate with

9 Chinard, *op. cit.*, p. 501. The author adds: "Such a moderate conclusion may surprise those who are accustomed to damn or praise Jefferson
on a few sentences or axioms detached from their context; but, after
careful scrutiny of the evidence, it seems difficult to accept any other interpretation."

any similar state, for between ethical states, as between ethical individuals, is a deep-seated community. There can be no other avenue toward peaceful internationalism. It is idle to hope that an ethical state can long succeed in coöperating with an unethical state; there can be no permanent peace with the wicked except at the price of suffering injustices even more subversive of the values of civilization than resort to arms. And as for the hope of a world-wide union of unethical states, this is a dream that may end in a terrible awakening. There is no short way to the universal peace for which we yearn, and every anodyne of false hope in which we indulge but makes the way longer.

§ 5

Such, as I conceive, is the present outlook of humanism—very different, certainly, from the outlook offered by humanitarianism, with its emphasis on the natural goodness of man, on environment and mechanical organization, on a scientistic and naturalistic ideology. By means of humanism, an attempt could hereafter be made, not only to revive the idea of liberal education, but also to give to modern life the order, meaning, and happiness which naturalism cannot give. Humanism in the twentieth century suggests a way by which we may carry out the full implications of the "modern spirit," by being positive and critical in both the natural and the human realms, instead of continuing our one-sided absorption in scientific method and naturalistic speculation. To be fully modern, we need the two approaches to reality, the subjective and the objective, the inner life of the human spirit and the external observation of nature and of man as part of nature.

To which naturalism will offer the short rejoinder: "This is a scientific age." Science, it seems, has arrived, and all the future belongs to science. We are done with your "inner life," your weak-kneed religion, your mystical humanism, your "wisdom of the ages" (the blind leading the blind), your traditions, folkways, and prejudices, your "common sense" and guess-work. You can't believe in those things and be modern. The modern spirit is just the scientific spirit, the rational procedure of science, the way the mind works when it is honest. It gives us more and more knowledge, steadily reduces the darkness in which men have so long groped. We must go forward to ever greater light—not go back, defeated, to the darkness of the past. We must believe in strict observation, experiment, and measurement, in hypotheses and the testing of hypotheses; we must have faith in science, the lamp of human reason.

Increasingly, however, the same persons who are proclaiming the arrival of a scientific age are lamenting, with Mr. Laski, "All over the world the lamps of reason are going out." [10] Now, how can an age of science be an age in which reason is being abandoned, if we are to assume, as is commonly done, that modern science and reason are identical or at least inseparable? An answer has already been suggested: the leading character of our age has not been science, but an emotional scientism and naturalism. Yet our scientists have not stopped to examine closely the faith that sustains their activity; absorbed in their empirical research, they have made only the most superficial use of rational analysis. They have increasingly set the tone of an age that, compared with antiquity and the Middle Ages, is hostile to reason. To the assertion that ours is not an age of science we must add the assertion that ours is not an age of reason.

The unintellectual nature of modern science has been well brought out in an article by President Hutchins, of

[10]"Universities in These Times," *New Republic,* January 23, 1935.

the University of Chicago, whose thesis is "that in modern times we have seldom tried reason at all, but something we mistook for it, that our bewilderment results in large part from this mistake, and that our salvation lies not in the rejection of the intellect but in a return to it." [11] Our conception of empirical science, placing primary emphasis on the accumulation of observed facts, is essentially anti-intellectual. Our modern programme has divorced science and reason. Dr. Hutchins reminds us "that the fundamental constituent of a science is the analysis of its basic concepts, and that without this a science cannot exist. The proper immediate subject matter of a science is its abstractions, as can be seen as soon as the question is asked, What is the basis of the division, classification, and selection of the concrete material? The answer, contrary to Francis Bacon, is that the basis must be found in the rational analysis, which is logically prior to the empirical operations involved." We have been so busy collecting the facts that we have failed to grapple with the fundamentals. Indeed, "as the Renaissance could accuse the Middle Ages of being rich in principles and poor in facts, we are now entitled to inquire whether we are not rich in facts and poor in principles."

This mention of the Middle Ages will horrify many a scientist, who will suspect Dr. Hutchins of advocating a new scholasticism concerned with the question how many angels can rest on the point of a needle.[12] But even this

[11] "The Issue in the Higher Learning," *International Journal of Ethics*, January, 1934.

[12] In an editorial entitled "Dr. Hutchins Turns Scholastic?", in a Jesuit publication, the *Modern Schoolman*, March, 1934, the scientific upholder of the lamps of reason will read with some perplexity: "The Scholastic has always looked upon himself as the defender of human reason. . . . In a world that is vociferous in proclaiming its rationalism he claims to stand alone as the only true rationalist."

derided question, which, one infers from many modern books, was the only question that concerned the Middle Ages, has the prime merit of involving the nature of the human mind and is actually closer to human interests than are many of the facts of science. Thus we are presented today with the astronomical fact, slightly colored with communistic humanitarianism, that if all the stars of heaven were equally divided among the earth's inhabitants, "there would be about one hundred for each person." Unfortunately, it would be as hard for us to claim our stellar property as to lay hold of the angels shining out of "the intellectual darkness of the Middle Ages." Facts as well as dreams may be fantastic, when they are viewed in relation to the essential problems of mankind. To these essential problems the Middle Ages dedicated a supreme effort of the human intellect. Even if one finds many of its conclusions unacceptable, one must grant, I think, that the intellect itself then attained an astonishing keenness and penetration which it has since progressively lost. How far we should go now in a return to reason depends, it would seem, on one's faith in the ultimate power of the human intellect to encompass reality. Whatever the scholastic or the naturalist may profess, the humanist, as I have indicated, finds himself compelled to refrain from the construction of a rational system of philosophy or theology, offering instead merely a working philosophy based upon concrete human experience. To him the prime use of reason is not constructive but regulative.

At all events, those who lament that the lamps of reason are going out cannot hope to rekindle them by means of empirical science. As Boutroux has said, "Science cannot order us to do anything, not even to cultivate science." Our orders come from other sources, philosophic or religious. Once we have our orders, science can greatly help us to carry them out. If we have determined what we want, science can provide many ways of securing it. If we have decided what we are living for, it can supply instruments of living to that end. Science has been compared to a time-table which tells us how we may proceed in any direction but which is silent as to our destination. A wise and prudent world will first decide upon its destination. But the unwise and imprudent and quite irrational modern world is busy elaborating the time-table in the hope that it may prove useful some day. Hence it is that the leading characteristic of the modern world, according to Dr. Hutchins, is bewilderment. "We do not know where we are going, or why; and we have almost given up the attempt to find out." Another voice crying in the wilderness, Ortega y Gasset, has well described the intellectual and spiritual impotence of modern man. "We live at a time," he says, "when man believes himself fabulously capable of creation, but he does not know what to create. Lord of all things, he is not lord of himself. He feels lost amid his own abundance. With more means at his disposal, more knowledge, more technique than ever, it turns out that the world today goes the same way as the worst of worlds that have been: it simply drifts. Hence the strange combination of a sense of power and a sense of insecurity which has taken up its abode in the soul of modern man. To him is happening what was said of the Regent during the minority of Louis XV: he had all the talents except the talent to make use of them."

But the habit of an age is not easily changed; and so the belief is expressed in many quarters that salvation may yet come through science. It is argued that in developing science for the control of nature we have attended to only one side of the problem, and that we must now seriously undertake the development of science for the control of man. Our proper programme now is to push the social sciences forward. Too lightly did we assume that social well-being would be carried along with natural knowledge—like the Scot who bought only one spur, on the theory that if he made one side of the horse go, the other side would have to go, too. It is now argued that we need the other spur. We can hardly hope to solve the social problems that plague us till we have collected and organized a great body of social knowledge, economic, political, sociological, and the like. Upon this all-important branch of knowledge we should hereafter focus our research and our education.

Unhappily, there is no prospect that this programme could ever give us a science of man. The subject is not only far more complex than the science of nature—if that were all, it might eventually be conquered—but it is also, from the laboratory point of view, hopelessly intangible. Adequately controlled experiments are impossible, and without them solid results are impossible. This alone, candor compels us to admit, vitiates the whole enterprise from the start. Furthermore, the social investigator, unlike the natural investigator in his laboratory, is not clearly differentiated from his subject-matter. He cannot enjoy the sardonic satisfaction of the chemist or physicist in running into cold, hard facts and finding his errors shattered. Preconceptions and prejudices arising from his social training and his membership in social groups will strongly tend to shape his conclusions, while he is unaware of what is going on in him or, if aware, unable to cope with it. Because of these barriers to truth, it has been suggested that the social sciences must have a different technique from that of the natural sciences; but no one has been able to devise, or is likely to devise, a special technique as workable and trustworthy as that of the natural sciences.

There is another way of stating the difficulty. An accumulation of social facts, without interpretation, is insignificant, and yet interpretation of social facts inevitably carries the investigator far afield from science into the realm of values. Suppose that the investigator is a Roman Catholic and his subject sociology. "The Catholic student of sociology presupposes the following: . . . 1. The existence of God. 2. God created all things, man included. 3. Man has a soul which is supramaterial. 4. Man is endowed with freedom of will. 5. Man's soul is immortal. 6. Man is by nature subject not only to physical (necessary) laws, but also to a moral law. 7. Man has certain rights and duties which are common to all mankind." [13] Not one of these postulates, not even the last of them when understood in the Catholic sense, is acceptable to the naturalistic sociologist, who would say that a sociology thus established may be good Catholicism but is not good science. But the Catholic (and with him the humanist, though he could not accept unreservedly more than one or two of the postulates above) would promptly reply that the postulates which the naturalistic sociologist would substitute, make his subject good naturalism but not good science. From naturalism, not from science, does the typical modern sociologist derive his postulate, for example, that man must be viewed as merely one species of animal among others, as merely the most remarkable social animal in natural history. He professes, to be sure, to base his science on other sciences, particularly biology and psychology. But the psychology he refers to is, of course, naturalistic psychology—philosophically naturalistic in its assumptions

[13] "These are the seven postulates of reason," according to E. J. Ross in *A Survey of Sociology* (1932), pp. 15-16.

and conclusions while superficially scientific in its method. The support of sociology by psychology therefore involves question-begging. As for biology, "It is manifest," says a sufficiently typical writer, "that sociology must depend upon biology, since biology is the general science of life, and human society is but part of the world of life in general." [14] But this involves distortion of a noble science, which deals with living matter, including the physical organism of man, and which has nothing to do with the ethical and spiritual life of man in society. Human society, for all biology knows, may in certain aspects be specifically human or even divine, marked off in either case from the life of the world in general. The insistence of the sociologist that man is "but" part of nature derives not from natural science but from naturalism. From this unstable vantage-point he then proceeds to survey human life in terms of such biological concepts as the efficiency of organisms and the survival of species, which, because of the bewildering complexity of human nature, human behavior, and human aspiration, soon lead him to the formulation of every manner of undemonstrable assertion interpenetrated and guided by his own aspirations, which are commonly humanitarian.

To the humanitarian reformer disguised as social scientist, the control of man means primarily the control of other men by the reformer, so far as he can bring that about. To the humanist, it means primarily the discipline of free men by themselves, "from within and not from without," a responsibility which each individual must undertake for himself, though it may be lightened by sound education and the imitation of examples. The

[14] The quotation is from "an elementary text in sociology for use in high schools, colleges, and reading circles," C. A. Ellwood, *Sociology and Modern Social Problems* (1910, 1913, 1919, 1924).

knowledge which most illuminates this discipline is self-knowledge—human knowledge, not scientific knowledge. The control of man is concerned with values rather than actualities, with what ought to be rather than what is— with what humanly ought to be rather than what naturally is. If the task assumed by nineteenth-century naturalism was to place man wholly in nature, the task to be assumed by humanism in the twentieth century is to take him out of nature again insofar as he does not belong there. Naturalism, with one spur or two, places nature in the rider's seat:

> Things are in the saddle,
> And ride mankind.

Humanism places man in the saddle, directing nature in the service of his human ends.

The clarification of these ends is the prime function of the intellect in the coming years. What is needed first of all is a critical reëxamination of the human "wisdom of the ages" to enable us to distinguish between that permanent wisdom and the arbitrary conventions in which it was often enswathed. This is incomparably more urgent than a further accumulation of facts through empirical science, for, while the accumulation of facts should continue if nature is to be made to serve man, no quantity of facts could, of itself, achieve individual human happiness and social community. Indeed, the situation in which the world now finds itself should abundantly show that our unrestrained thirst for knowledge and power, far from assuring mundane blessedness, is threatening unimaginable destruction and suffering. This would seem to be the logical upshot of a furious development of science combined with a naturalistic conception of man. If man and nature are one and inseparable, man must be viewed as basically aggressive and cruel—"red in tooth and claw" —accomplished in disguising his rapacity or rationalizing it into "service," accomplished also in devising engines of destruction for the times when the rapacities of social groups clash. If it is necessary to believe that men are sunk in the immediacy of nature, it is necessary to believe that they partake of the irresponsibility of nature.

Fortunately the actions of modern men have often belied this naturalistic pessimism. Despite Baconian science and Rousseauistic sentimentalism, we have not yet witnessed a genuine "return to nature." Only in part have men lived in terms of the naturalism which they have professed. In another part they have continued to live in terms of that very wisdom of the ages which they affected to despise. In the actual conduct of life they have pressed into service many elements of the rejected Christian and humanistic traditions. The sense of responsibility, the assumption of free choice, the perception of an inner conflict of a higher and a lower principle, the belief in common sense, the quest of the middle course, the comic spirit roused by gross disproportion, the desire to reason things out, the occasional visitation of reverence and humility, these and many other elements of human experience still feel the momentum of the old established views of life. When it is said that the modern world demolished the values of the past and now rests upon science, both parts of the assertion are untrue. In its practice, the modern world still uses to a large extent, however unconsciously, the capital it inherited from the past, and in its creed it rests not upon science but upon scientism and naturalism. We may say even more: in its very scientism and naturalism it has drawn heavily upon the old capital. Thus, the scientific movement beginning in the Renaissance restored the Greek love of knowledge, with a difference: it became the love of facts and the love of material utility of facts. Similarly, the sentimental movement, upon the close of the Renaissance, took over and parodied the Christian virtue of charity and the Christian belief in the equality of human souls, giving them secular meanings curiously tinctured with old spiritual meanings.

Yet the values of the past are fast fading, as everyone knows. The ethical and spiritual values of humanism and religion have lost momentum as the material values of naturalism have gained it. The inherited capital has depreciated, till it is now so attenuated that it can hardly go on offering serious resistance to the process of disintegration. Force, the arch virtue of naturalism, threatens to be our only means of attaining order, and in the long run can lead only to the gravest disorder. Unchecked, naturalism must progress downward from civilization to barbarism to primitivism—a primitivism in which science and the humanities would founder together. The critical stage in this progression has apparently not been reached, but may be nearer than we like to think. If what has been said in this chapter has any validity, this critical stage cannot be averted or postponed by placing fond hopes in the social "sciences," or by emotional propaganda in favor of socialism, fascism, communism, or any other social and economic utopisms, all of which becloud the central issue. That issue is one which transcends external facts and external mechanisms. The central issue is whether we shall continue to regard man as merely part of the flux of nature, or as, at the same time, *sui generis*.

Once this issue has become inescapable, expediency, if nothing more, may cause us to reassert the inner life. When that time comes, we shall once more look upon the humanities seriously not frivolously, turning to them for help in the construction of values. We shall turn to the studies most useful in the furtherance of human as opposed to scientific knowledge. I repeat: a programme of human knowledge must have no hostility toward science, since the creation of science is one of the signs of man's humanity; but the preoccupation of human knowledge must be with the direct, not indirect, study of human nature. The proper study of mankind is still man, not man as known through a naturalistic psychology (which, so far as it is positive, is really physiology), or through a naturalistic sociology (which views human society as merely a form of animal society), but man as known directly, in his inner life and its manifestations in social and political history, in literature and the arts, in philosophy, in religion.

In the pursuit of this human knowledge lies our surest way of transcending the bewilderment of a world that has acquired all the talents except the talent to make use of them.

Chapter Eight

EDUCATION OF MEN AND WOMEN

§ 1

IF THE FOREGOING ANALYSIS IS SOUND, IT should now be apparent that liberal education will not be revived till a humanistic outlook on life is reëstablished. Liberal education cannot be achieved by naturalism. Naturalism, with its exclusive devotion to the sciences, to scientific as opposed to human knowledge, to fact as opposed to value, to means as opposed to ends, is not concerned with the making of free men and women but with the shaping of human tools for vocational efficiency and the advancement of specialized scientific knowledge, a programme eminently appropriate to the natural and economic man. Naturalism cannot educate the human man, because it denies his existence. Taking seriously the sciences alone, it neglects the humanities or cultivates them merely as ornaments—pleasant adjuncts to the real business of life, desirable only because there is an urge in the human animal that functions in terms of the beautiful dreams of religion, art, and literature. Exercise in the functioning of this urge is recommended to the young because a part of their mature life will be given to leisure, by which is meant recreation. But this exercise is to be incidental, for of course the dreams of life, which are the

244

province of the humanities, are of little moment in comparison with the realities of life, which are the province of the natural and social sciences.

While naturalistic learning is in practice almost wholly a matter of mere acquirement, of amassing items of accurate information (certainly this is suggested by the examination questions set before the student), one often hears it said by defenders of naturalistic education that the central object is, or should be, "teaching how to think." This sounds a good deal like the object of liberal education as defined by Cardinal Newman: the cultivation of the mind, the development of intellectual excellence. But in truth it means something very different. "Teaching how to think," as this slogan is commonly used today, means far less than Newman had in view, for it means, simply, teaching how to think scientifically. Its object is "the scientific mind," the mind that has become habituated to the application of scientific method to everything. It is in harmony with the dictum of Huxley, not Newman, that there is only one kind of knowledge and one method of pursuing knowledge: scientific knowledge and scientific method. Thinking may deal, to be sure, as Huxley states in his essay on liberal education, with "men and their ways" as well as with "things and their forces," but law for man and law for things are only two aspects of Mother Nature and are to be studied in the same fashion. And thus it turns out that teaching how to think scientifically means, in the end, teaching how to think naturalistically.

Higher education has always professed to teach thinking. That was its aim in the intellectual Middle Ages: that was its aim even in the anti-intellectual nineteenth century. It has been the aim of the naturalistic university, and it has been the aim of the humanistic university. Only, there are many ways of thinking, one of which will always tend to dominate. In the naturalistic university of today, one way of thinking so overwhelmingly dominates that other possibilities are quite lost to view. To assert that the university of today teaches the young "to think for themselves" is sheer cant. Within the pattern of scientific and naturalistic thinking, no doubt, the student may be given considerable range, but if his mind wanders outside that pattern he is generally disregarded as hopeless or reproached for his prejudice. Such is the attitude toward the Catholic student, for example, on the part of many professors singularly ignorant of the doctrines of the Church. Any student who sets out to think for himself, outside the pattern, will find many obstacles and little if any assistance. Doubtless the same is true, *mutatis mutandis,* in the Catholic and in the humanistic university, as one must in all candor admit, though in both of these a dualistic conception of life provides a certain generosity unknown in the naturalistic university. Thus, in the humanistic university, there is room for thinking on either the natural or the human plane; room for both scientific knowledge and human knowledge. Thought of the one sort does not encroach upon thought of the other sort, or disparage it, or deny it. And more: access is left free to the third plane of experience, the religious. Since human knowledge finally confronts a higher reality, or the illusion of a higher reality, for which the religious name is the supernatural, the passage is easy, for many minds, from a dualistic humanism to a dualistic religion. While humanism makes no claim to knowledge of the divine, the possibility of this supreme knowledge is left open—a stand which, if it does not help the student, at least does not hinder him.

From the humanistic point of view, what is meant by thinking? It is the domination of facts by principles, it is the process of reflecting, relating, weighing, and judging, it is a means of developing a critical mind, and wisdom, and taste: "that humane endeavor," in the words of Irving Babbitt, "which it is the special purpose of the college to foster—that effort of reflection, virile before all others, to coördinate the scattered elements of knowledge, and relate them not only to the intellect but to the will and character; that subtle alchemy by which mere learning is transmuted into culture." "The task of assimilating," as Babbitt goes on to say, "what is best in the past and present, and adapting it to one's own use and the use of others, so far from lacking in originality, calls for something akin to creation." [1] Thoughtful assimilation, the function of collegiate education, is thus different from reception, or mere acquirement, which necessarily predominates in the lower schools, and different again from original inquiry at the frontiers of knowledge, which is the distinction of graduate study. The specialist mind, in its passion for original inquiry and its indifference to culture, has a way of casting aspersions upon assimilation, as if it meant a passive process, an aimless reception of items of information, whereas in fact it means an active process of conversion and appropriation.

For what is taken in must be transformed into "a system consisting of parts, related one to the other, and interpretative of one another in the unity of the whole." Progressively the general scheme of knowledge is discovered by the student, all that he learns taking a place, an ever clearer and firmer place, in the expanding scheme. Mathematics, for instance, comes to be seen as closely related with science—the prime language of science, no less—and with logic as a branch of philosophy. The sciences become more than a mass of facts about nature; they suggest, more

[1] *Literature and the American College* (1908), p. 101.

and more impressively, the vast power which natural knowledge gives man for human ends, and they invite ways of looking upon the theatre of human existence that challenge comparison with the ways of religion and poetry. A foreign language, once the student is really immersed in it, reveals to him for the first time the character of his native language, together with the ties that bind language to life and language to the act of thinking. Literature opens the way to the fine arts, and the arts illuminate each other and literature as well. History, rightly studied, shows that the present cannot be understood without the past, and that the meaning of the past is always reinterpreted as the present advances. Philosophy brings all fields together, speculating as to their special claims, their types of evidence, their relevance to each other and to the conduct of life.

But this is not all: for knowledge is not something apart from the learner, a formula to be blindly mastered, but something that deeply concerns the learner himself, and therefore to be brought into intimate relation with his own personality and experience. The student is not possessed of a special faculty, an intellectual machine for registering knowledge; he is a human being, who, as he grows in knowledge, alters in character and taste. Without effort on his part, what he learns will affect what he does and what he likes. Encouraged and aided in making a deliberate effort, he can bring his intellect into the most fruitful relationships with the rest of his nature. While a liberal education makes clear to him that his first task is the cultivation of intellectual excellence, it makes clear, at the same time, his responsibility for relating his mind to his sense of conduct and his sense of beauty and for developing them as a whole. His education is, in a word, progressive self-mastery. In the lower schools a pupil, in college he becomes a scholar—not a thinker, but *Man Thinking*.

If the young scholar is thus to shape himself into a thoughtful human being, it follows that he must work upon a carefully selected group of subjects—such as those already named—representative of the scheme of knowledge. Only a university drifting without standards will declare that all subjects should be free and equal, that one subject is as good as another, and that selection should therefore be relative to the students' "individual differences." Even in such a university it would be difficult, as a matter of fact, to find educators who really believe in the equivalence of subjects. It would be difficult to find professors of the liberal arts proclaiming that study of the liberal arts should be wholly optional, or professors of the sciences proclaiming that study of the sciences should be wholly optional. In their franker moments perhaps all professors would be willing to name *some* subject which they regard as naturally inferior to their own. Indeed, an enthusiastic advocacy of their own subjects is the foremost reason for the inability of faculties to agree upon uniformly required subjects; they take their stand in favor of parity because they severally fear they may otherwise get less than parity. While they frown upon fixed requirements in general education, they do not hesitate to formulate fixed requirements in the various special curricula; there the belief in equivalence mysteriously evaporates. Even the department of education, most literal in the interpretation of individual differences and the equivalence of subjects, generally imposes fixed requirements, such as "Introduction to Education," "Technic of Teaching," and "Educational Psychology," upon all who desire certification for a teaching career. In sum, a university faculty that renounces its obligation to select subjects suited to the education of men and women gladly accepts its obligation to select subjects suited to the education of specialists. In the field of liberal education, where it is indifferent, it refuses to be "arbitrary"—something to be avoided at all costs. In the field of special education, where it is interested, it is bold enough to fix require-ments, though occasional changes in these requirements suggest that some of them may be arbitrary.

Arbitrary or not, a selection of studies pursued in common must always form the heart of a liberal curriculum. If the university is to be an intellectual community, its members must have much in common. The university must combat, therefore, not only those "centrifugal forces which tend to separate our faculties into an ever-increasing number of subdivisions" (in the words of President Conant), but also those centrifugal forces which tend to separate our students and which, if not resisted, will produce at last the chaos of "a curriculum for each student." Owing to these centrifugal forces the intellectual atmosphere of the university is becoming thinner and thinner, an atmosphere in which the vital communication of mind with mind will presently be impossible. If students talk of little else save sports, grades, and "dates," the main reason is that they have little else to talk about. According to Samuel Johnson, the ends of education are three: "to develop the moral nature, to train the judgment, and to furnish material for conversation." We are not achieving the third end any better than the others; indeed, it might plausibly be asserted that we are furnishing material for silence. For, the more specialism succeeds, the more it isolates the learner and narrows the possibility of communication with other learners, so that the ideal society of the specialist educator would logically be one in which nobody knew anything which anybody else knew.

A true university is not a mere assemblage of learners. It is a community, a communion of minds, a society in which the essential principles of thinking and living are shared, a society animated by a common set of cultural memories and the same ideal purposes. "Surely as Nature createth brotherhood in families," said Bacon, "so in like manner there cannot but be fraternity in learning and illuminations." He did not foresee that this fraternity could easily pass into alienation, unless education provided men with a common fund of intellectual experience. Putting the idea of community in its strictest form, Dr. Meiklejohn once defined a college as "a group of people, all of whom are reading the same books." Pursuing the same thought less rigidly, Irving Babbitt remarked that "two men who have taken the same course in Horace have at least a fund of common memories and allusions; whereas if one of them elect a course in Ibsen instead of Horace, they will not only have different memories, but, so far as they are touched by the spirit of their authors, different ideals." In the eighteenth century, it was possible to quote the works of Horace in the House of Commons with confidence in a certain warmth of recognition—a situation symbolical of the cultural unity, at that time, not only of England but of Europe as a whole. Europe then had an essentially common education, based upon a common classical heritage, which promoted a cosmopolitan spirit such as it has never had since the French Revolution. Later the aim of educational community came to be not cosmopolitan but nationalistic. Thus in Germany, long before the totalitarian state of Hitler, we have the amazing spectacle of the Pangermanists, who "object to the teaching of foreign languages as tending to undermine patriotism, and especially to the teaching of Classics, which has for its object what is common to western Europe, the Graeco-Latin *Kultur*. . . . Nor do they care about the classical literature of Germany itself. The writings of Goethe and Schiller are suspect of cosmopolitanism. . . . As for Science, that is frankly international. . . . Even the Christian religion is dangerous, . . . and the Hotspurs of the party, the out and out *Deutschtümler,* are all for reviving the cults of Odin and Thor. Of course the German Emperor does not go to these extremes, but he is undoubtedly accessible to ideas of this kind, and he too advocates a 'national German education.' " [2]

Since the war, in country after country, violent efforts have been made to achieve solidarity through education—solidarity with reference to the nation, separatism with reference to humanity—and these efforts are succeeding only too well. The spread of a militant nationalistic education to the United States is by no means unthinkable, for inner community is a deep and permanent human need, which will assert itself in inadequate or dangerous forms if no sound and worthy form is made attractive. At present the higher education of the United States is attempting to discourage every form of inner community. A university moving toward a curriculum for each student is headed toward chaotic individualism, the final decadent extreme of the *laissez faire* principle. It will reach its goal when, like the "child-centered school," it totally abdicates its responsibility and becomes "pupil purposed, pupil planned, pupil executed, and pupil judged."

The type of community appropriate to a democratic polity is neither individualistic, in the current American sense, nor nationalistic, in the current European sense, but humanistic. For the United States, as for England, as for any nation determined that democracy shall not perish from the earth, "the grand aim of the higher education," as Chancellor Robertson maintains, "is the fullest and

[2] Burnet, *op. cit.,* pp. 178-80.

freest development of human personality—which is the imperishable message of a true humanism." [3]

The fullest and freest development of human personality, it is necessary to insist, is to be carefully distinguished from the unilateral "self-expression" introduced by the sentimental movement of the eighteenth century and promoted by the naturalistic psychologies of the present day. Ever since Rousseau reduced the sublime Christian esteem for each person to the bathetic declaration that he was different from every other individual, educators and educationists have confused personality, which brings men together, with individuality, which separates them. Many of our educational leaders have inconsistently supported the gospel of "individual differences" while urging a social programme that would regiment individuals in terms of some scheme of social planning. They have had a mystical faith that individuals dispersing as fast and far as possible would somehow also march in line. While their social purpose has remained mere planning, their educational purpose has been put into action: more and more they have acted upon the assumption that every student is educable because he possesses some aptitude, if not for this then for that or the other, some aptitude, precious to him even if slight or trivial to others, which is to be found, nursed, and pushed to its natural extreme while he is relieved of the necessity of pursuing studies for which he has no aptitude and from which he cannot therefore profit. From the point of view of a true humanism, however, this unilateral self-expression is not enough. The soundest and highest development of a natural aptitude demands that other elements of the student's nature be developed also, for, if this is not done, the aptitude will reach its natural extreme in an attenuated form—thin, starved, and shrill. And furthermore, human-

[3] *British Universities* (1930), p. 69.

ism insists that men do not exist to be the slaves of their
natural aptitudes, but, first of all, to enter freely into their
humanity. Humanism is not content to let Nature take her
course. Education does not consist in throwing down the
reins. As Aristotle suggested, we become human largely by
resisting our own natural tendencies, pulling ourselves
back toward the mean just as people straighten pieces of
wood that are warped. The child, the youth, must be preserved from his imperious natural temperament and from
the tyranny of his special aptitude by the imposition of human culture.[4]

Primarily, education is cultural transmission, as generation is physical transmission. In the words of M. Maritain,
"It is clear that the teacher must adapt himself to the child,
but education properly so called does not begin until the
child adapts himself to the teacher and to the culture, the
truths, and the systems of value which it is the mission of
the teacher to transmit to the child." [5] If the culture, the
truths, and the systems of value are those of Catholicism, as
M. Maritain assumes, the rôle of education is transmission;
if they are those of humanism, the rôle of education is
again transmission; and if they are those of naturalism, the
rôle of education is, once more, transmission. This is apparently conceded even in the cautious report of the American Association of University Professors, which informs us,
it will be remembered, that to teach effectively is to lead,
to inspire, and to guide the learner, though the professors
resolutely refuse to tell us in what direction they are taking, or should take, the learner. The direction proposed by

[4] "A nation," similarly, "is really civilized by acquiring the qualities it
by nature is wanting in" (Matthew Arnold, *Letters*, 1895, I, 280). A
nation moving in the opposite direction tends to become monstrous and
dangerously unsocial.

[5] Preface to De Hovre, *Philosophy and Education* (American Edition,
1931).

humanism has now been amply indicated: it is the development of free human beings, with all that that implies, through thoughtful assimilation of "what is best in the past and present," both in the sciences and in the humanities.

§ 2

From the point of view developed in this chapter, the "best" is composed of what G. R. Elliott has termed "human masterpieces"—the great human persons, and the great human works of literature, art, science, history, philosophy, and religion that are competent to transmit to the future the knowledge and wisdom and beauty of the past and present. Freedom of election in the college of today, says Professor Elliott, actually means "freedom from the human study of human masterpieces. Not many of these are included in the courses taken by the typical undergraduate and he studies very few of them indeed with anything like human freedom. He is free to become a Bachelor of Arts by missing the chief works of human art, of human making, from the *Odyssey*, let's say, down to *Faust;* and by acquiring only a faint acquaintance with a baker's dozen (if his luck runs thus high) of the noblest persons in human history, from Confucius to Lincoln. Amazing lists could be made of the little things with which the young Bachelor's head is stored and the important things from which it is free." [6] The core of the curriculum proposed by Robert Shafer similarly consists of human masterpieces in the forms of great books, such as Plato's *Republic*, Aristotle's *Politics*, Dante's *Divine Comedy*, Bacon's *Novum Or-*

[6] See the penetrating article by G. R. Elliott on "The American College" in the *American Review*, November and December, 1933; also the address of Henry Lester Smith as president of the National Education Association, published in *School and Society*, July 6, 1935.

ganum, Book I, six plays of Shakespeare, Hobbes's *Leviathan,* Parts I and II, Gibbon's *Decline and Fall of the Roman Empire,* Boswell's *Life of Johnson,* and Mill *On Liberty.*[7] Pursuing the same general educational aim, Columbia University issued more than a decade ago an *Outline of Readings in Important Books* which covered some half a hundred works—not precisely "the world's best books" but rather a selection especially designed for college students. It may be worth while to set down here the headings of the outlines:

Homer	Galileo
Herodotus	Grotius
Thucydides	Montaigne
Aeschylus	Shakespeare
Sophocles	Cervantes
Euripides	Francis Bacon
Aristophanes	Descartes
Greek Art	Hobbes
Plato	Milton
Aristotle	Molière
Lucretius	Locke
Vergil	Montesquieu
Horace	Voltaire
Plutarch	Rousseau
Marcus Aurelius	Gibbon
St. Augustine	Adam Smith
The Song of Roland	Kant
The Nibelungenlied	Goethe
St. Thomas Aquinas	American State Papers
Dante	Hugo

[7] Robert Shafer's analysis and suggested reconstruction of "University and College" in three numbers of *The Bookman,* May, June, July, 1931, is one of the weightiest contributions to educational discussion in recent years.

Hegel	Pasteur
Lyell	Marx
Balzac	Tolstoy
Malthus	Dostoevsky
Bentham	Nietzsche
Mill	William James
Darwin	

The past hundred years, in this list, are represented somewhat injudiciously. The present is not represented at all, and indeed could not be through great books alone; there would have to be, for one thing, lectures and demonstrations illustrating the principles and modern history of science. Nor is it to be taken for granted that the best way for the student to cover such a list is to read the books in the order given, or outside the usual academic courses. Somewhere—perhaps it matters little where—reading of this quality should be given a central place among the responsibilities of every student in the liberal college. It is a curious symptom of the times that the Columbia outlines were prepared for a "General Honors" course, not for all undergraduates. Unhappily the proportion of such reading accomplished by American students during the past half century has steadily declined, while the proportion of reading in contemporary textbooks has correspondingly increased —a situation nothing short of alarming in view of the fact that more and more of the textbooks used in our colleges are the work of undisciplined minds, loose, nerveless, sometimes all but illiterate, especially in such fields as economics, sociology, psychology, and education.[8] How students are to learn to think by contact with fifth-rate or tenth-rate

[8] The softening of our textbooks by such minds is partly deliberate. Typical is this advertisement: "A new approach to English literature, simpler, lighter—in step with changed teaching attitudes and the widely varying social background of today's students."

minds is a mystery "not yet" explained by the science of education. Small wonder that one sometimes hears of a student, even an aspirant to the Φ. B. K. key, who boasts that he has never read a book.

We have indeed travelled a long way since the time when Thomas Jefferson received his thorough classical training. "Whatever may be said against a classical education," Charles A. Beard remarks, "it has at least one virtue: it brings young students into contact with some of the first minds of the ages, with those dead but sceptred sovereigns who rule us from their tombs. It can give them the historic sense—a feeling of the sweep of centuries, in which our little plans of the moment are as dust in the balance. Unlike education in textbooks written by pedagogues, now all too common, the classics introduce young spirits to great and masterful spirits and to grand actors in the making of civilization." [9] The old American education which put leading minds of antiquity in the foreground apparently did not render the recipients of that education inept in practical and contemporary affairs. As the president of the Carnegie Foundation for the Advancement of Teaching reminds us, "The signers of the Declaration of Independence and the designers of the Constitution were for the most part college graduates who during their immature years in college were fed a steady and exclusive diet of languages which for practical purposes were almost as dead then as now. Yet these graduates, according to a carefully documented study by Father Walsh, led a political revolution that rocked the world. They studied Latin, Greek, Hebrew, literature, history and philosophy, rather than material recommended by a Social Science Commission. They defended their right to graduate by disputation in Latin rather than by participating in open forums on social prob-

[9] "Jefferson in America Now," *Yale Review*, Winter, 1936.

lems, as advocated so convincingly by our contemporaries. They revolted and risked their necks thereby. They set up a constitutional government that has outlasted any of its time."[10]

A proposal to restore the old classical curriculum in the state universities of today would, of course, not even gain a hearing. But the time has plainly come for the establishment of a new liberal curriculum as firm in conception and solid in substance as the old. The initial step in this direction might well be the requirement of direct contact with some of the first minds of the ages, as the primary means of learning how to think. If this were sufficiently insisted upon, it would soon begin to force a pruning of the curriculum, for there are many fields of study in the present state universities in which great minds have never interested themselves. The subjects which have absorbed the great minds, the subjects which represent the best that man has thought and done, would presently define themselves with ample clearness.

After all, there is little mystery as to the best subjects— except among naturalistic educators. Are there any subjects, President E. H. Wilkins inquires, "of such outstanding significance that they should certainly appear in the typical individual curriculum? My answer is, distinctly, 'Yes.' And the subjects I should designate, with full recognition of the fact that there is room for difference of opinion in this matter, are hygiene, psychology, logic, and English." [11] But naturalistic educators are rarely so forthright. As a rule they refuse to designate subjects (except English

[10] Walter A. Jessup, address at the meeting of the Association of American Colleges, January 16, 1936. The quotation above, taken by itself, may seem to imply too much. The point is not, of course, that the United States of America owes its establishment to the Classics, but that our early leaders received a rather substantial education.

[11] *Higher Education in America*, p. 447.

studied as a "tool") on the ground that they will not dog-
matize; besides, "individual differences" and "the equivalence of subjects" really preclude any choice. How dare one
say that unique individuals must have a common education, or that a subject professed by one specialist is superior
to that professed by another? In any case, how could you
ever get a faculty of specialists to agree? The answer, in
truth, is that you never could, so long as they dealt with
their general educational responsibilities from the point of
view of specialism. Even if they tried to transcend that
view, they would still be deeply confused, since their naturalistic philosophy offers no scale of human values to guide
them in forming a curriculum. The harder they tried to
think, the more perplexed they would become, till in the
end they might offer some proposal as bizarre as that of
President Wilkins. With less thought, indeed, they might
do better, for then many of them would avail themselves of
their share of the permanent sense of mankind. On *this*
basis there would, I think, be a fairly clear consensus in
favor of (1) mathematics and natural science, (2) history,
(3) literature, and (4) philosophy and religion.

Until so much is agreed upon, little would be gained by
an attempt to define the curriculum more closely, suggesting just what ground is most valuable in each of these
broad subjects, what fields of history, for instance, are
worthy of cultivation by all students. Obviously any more
definite selection of studies would be, or would appear to
be, arbitrary. If various institutions determined upon a
more or less arbitrary selection, the normal workings of
trial and error could be counted on gradually to bring
about an harmonious conviction not only within but
among these institutions.[12] Before the matter is thus re-

[12] The common curriculum of the University of Chicago—much discussed at the state universities and adapted by at least one of them, the

ferred to the test of experience, however, something must be said concerning one or two of the most difficult problems that will have to be faced.

Aside from English, the great literature of the Occident is locked within six principal languages, Greek, Latin, Italian, French, Spanish, and German. While it is possible to offer a survey of the principles and history of science, it is evidently impossible to offer a survey of foreign literature read in six different languages. Again, while it may suffice to read works of science or philosophy in translations, it does not suffice so to read works of imaginative literature. The solution of the problem cannot be a survey course in comparative literature or "world literature" read in translations, even if translations were better than they are. As in science the student should see with his own eyes, so in literature he should have direct not secondhand contact with creations of the imagination. Since he cannot read in all the languages, a selection is necessary, and, if this selection is to harmonize with the principle of community or shared experience, it must be the same for all students. Assuming that we cannot expect the mastery of more than two languages in the secondary school and the college, what two

University of Florida—I have tried to evaluate in an article entitled "Chicago and General Education," in the *American Review*, September, 1935. Whether general education can successfully be limited to two college years depends, as Chauncey S. Boucher recognizes (*The Chicago Plan*, 1935), on the ability and willingness of the high school to accept a sufficient share of the task of general education. But the high school of today is not primarily interested in preparing students for college, and its graduates, consequently, cannot be counted on to bring to college such modest attainments as some skill in mathematics, a reading knowledge of one foreign language, or even an ability to read and write in their native language. Finding high school graduates unready for serious work, the state university ordinarily permits them to begin the study of any high school subject (except English) at any time prior to the conferring of the baccalaureate. The whole situation threatens to become worse before it becomes better.

languages should they be? For the present, I think, the answer is: any two of the six. Eventually the logic of the situation might well send us back to the despised classical languages, for Greek especially, even if a "dead" language, is far more alive, more vital to us, than many "living" languages, such as Portuguese—not to mention the African dialects—which do not unlock comparable treasures. But a firm selection of two modern languages, say French and German, if the mastery of these languages were insisted upon, would mark a vast improvement over the situation at present, when students have usually pursued the study of several languages without learning how to read in any of them. If French and German were studied for three or four years before the beginning of college work, the undergraduate would be prepared to study to advantage the great books in those languages, as well as source materials and modern works of scholarship to which instructors in non-literary subjects would like to refer him. Then his work in foreign literature would be higher education in literature, whereas today, for nearly all students, it consists solely of high school education—preparatory courses which prepare for nothing, since nothing follows.

In English literature, a common curriculum should obviously provide for an intimate acquaintance with such human masterpieces as the *Canterbury Tales,* the best plays of Shakespeare, and *Paradise Lost,* along with some representation of later English and American writings down to the present day. To this might well be added, for the proper understanding of English literature (and, indeed, modern foreign literature as well), reading in the two great sources of inspiration of that literature, albeit this would have to be done in translation: the Bible and the masterpieces of ancient Greece. As for "composition," it is plainly the responsibility of the department of English to afford training in well-organized communication of facts and ideas, by means of constant criticism of constant writing done in the required course, although, if this training is to produce a regular habit rather than a casual capacity, all the other departments must unite in insisting that the writing done in reports, examinations, and the like possess a decent correctness and clearness—and perhaps, as President Conant would add, some degree of "grace."

The problem of language and literature is difficult enough; more so is that of religion, especially in a state university. Notwithstanding the separation of church and state, "I believe," says President Sproul of the University of California, "that the university which makes no effort to stimulate in its sons and daughters a sensitiveness to the issues of religion is likely to be a danger rather than a benefit to the state." [13] If that is true, one is bound to suspect that most of our state universities are a danger to the state which they profess to serve. Certainly the efforts they have made so far are anything but effective. Not without justice are they regarded as irreligious, when they receive freshmen who are eager for ideal values in which intelligent men and women can believe and four years later send them out naturalized, skeptical, or cynical. Much as the intellectuals of the eighteenth century frequently conceived of religion as the artifice of the cunning, so the intellectuals of the twentieth century frequently conceive of it as the wishfulness of the stupid. The destruction wrought by professorial intellectuals of this sort (freedom of speech having, of course, its price) far more than offsets the construction accomplished by the university in its decent espousal of university sermons, denominational organizations, discussion groups, and the Y. M. C. A. But certainly a university that can adopt these feeble devices might adopt others more effective, without

[13] *The Obligation of Universities to the Social Order*, p. 383.

encroaching upon the domain of the churches. If it refuses to do so, if it is content with the policy of "keeping off," it fosters the assumption that, however meritorious religion may be, it is not for intellectual people—an assumption which may sometimes seem justified by particular ministers but which no church worthy the name could accept for a moment.

What more can the state university legitimately do? "Is religion itself a legitimate field of learning in the university?" inquires President Sproul, though he gives no certain answer. In a naturalistic university, it would seem proper to include "the science of religion," as we have seen this interpreted by Professor Haydon. In a humanistic university, it would seem proper to include a sympathetic study of the place which religion has occupied in our Occidental culture—the history and literature of Judaism and Christianity. As Professor Hocking of Harvard suggests, "It would be particularly appropriate for the university to present to its students as historic facts those great value schemes which we call religions—each one presented by some one who believes in it!"[14] More than a century ago, something of the sort was desired by Thomas Jefferson for the benefit of the University of Virginia. An advocate of religious freedom and toleration, he deemed it expedient to encourage "the different religious sects to establish, each for itself, a professorship of their own tenets, on the confines of the university, so near as that their students may attend the lectures there, and have the free use of our library." By this means Jefferson hoped to round out the curriculum, and at the same time disprove the idea that the university was "an institution, not merely of no religion, but against all religion." Freedom of religion was not to mean absence of religion.

[14] *Ibid.*, p. 340.

The first state university to act upon, and improve upon, this suggestion was the University of Iowa. Its school of religion, founded in 1925, not "on the confines" but within the structure of the college of liberal arts and graduate school, provided a means of viewing religion intellectually as a subject of higher learning, under the instruction of professors representing, respectively, the three religious groups of the state, the Jews, the Catholics, and the Protestants. The University of Iowa has thus set about the task of showing that, whatever else religion may be, it is a subject of importance to educated persons and an integral part of liberal culture. The task is not easy. Schools and departments of religion will be inclined to imitate other departments of the university by offering superficial and "practical" courses and by devising a "laboratory" for "efficiency in religious activities." That way lies cheapness—the "degradation of the noblest of human interests. Only by observing academic and religious dignity will such schools be able to maintain religion in the curriculum. Only by keeping the subject on a high plane will they retain the support of the faculty of the university and of those churchmen whose opinions carry most weight. The university will then be looked upon, not as a foe or rival of organized religion, but as an invaluable ally, for it will tend to lead the sons and daughters of the state not away from but toward the church.

§ 3

Abeunt studia in mores. Since studies pass into habits, the curriculum is of high importance. This has been well understood throughout the history of education from ancient Greece to present-day Europe—not so well, latterly, in the United States. A body of educable students follow-

ing a given course of studies, without any guidance by
teachers, would tend to be shaped in mind and character
by that course of studies, even though their progress were
slow and blundering. Education is primarily learning, not
teaching. And yet it is impossible to separate the processes
of learning from those of teaching. The arrangement of a
curriculum is itself a form of teaching. The reading of
books in a library is a form of teaching, the writers becoming the readers' teachers. If in addition a body of masters
in knowledge and wisdom is given the task of guiding
young and impressionable apprentices, the possible value
of teaching is incalculable. Once the right students and the
right teachers are brought together, most of the perplexi-
ties of education are quickly simplified.

But who are the right teachers? Clearly, right teachers
must be right from a certain point of view, good teachers
must be good for something, effective teachers must have
effects of such or such a kind. Clearly, we cannot say which
teachers are right, or good, or effective, or successful, or
best, till we have determined the object for which they are
educating. The American Association of University Professors, it will be remembered, asked the very pertinent question, "Can anything be accomplished in the way of improving the quality of college and university teaching unless it
is preceded by an agreement concerning the purpose for
which the teaching is done?" As in the case of stock-breeding
or human eugenics, we are not ready to undertake improvement in quality till we have decided what qualities we wish
to improve. Unless the purpose of the teaching is agreed
upon, we have no means of knowing whether experimental
changes in method are making things better or worse; nor
can we say which members of a faculty need to improve the
quality of their teaching, or which should be rewarded by
promotion because of the high quality of their teaching. If

the purpose is ruled out of consideration, it is perfectly futile to rank teachers according to opinions of them secured
from colleagues, students, alumni, leaders in the subject,
and other institutions (as expressed by "calls"). No collection of measurements, or legerdemain in interpreting
them, can then be anything but irrelevant and confusing.
Even when the purpose is clearly understood, opinions will
be insignificant unless secured, not from any and every
judge, but from those who render their judgment in accordance with this purpose. In this case it is evidently necessary for the administrator to judge the judges before he
judges the teachers. He cannot shirk his responsibility of
proceeding intelligently from an initial conception of the
purpose of the teaching to a final judgment, direct and indirect, of particular teachers.

If the liberal college is devoted to liberal education, the
purpose of the teaching is at once defined: it is the cultivation of a critical intelligence. Today, however, the liberal
college of the state university is devoted to special education, and the purpose of its teaching is the making of specialists, the bulk of whom will perform the routine work
of the world with some skill, while a few will reach the
frontiers of knowledge and press beyond. It is not concerned, unless by lip-service or sundry pitiful measures,
with the making of men and women, permitting the young,
on the contrary, to become malformed and mutilated, progressively remote from that balance or consent of human
faculties which is the basis for common sense and uncommon
judgment. Now if the prime purpose of the college is specialism, what is a good teacher? He is a specialist, a master
of his subject, competent, by virtue of personal qualities
and intellectual force, "to lead, to inspire, and to guide" in
the direction taken by himself. The real basis of his success
in doing this is not his teaching method but his stimulating

example. As Charles W. Eliot observed, "The influence which develops the necessary motive in the thinking child or youth is, in most cases, a personal influence, which is partly stimulus, but more example. . . . The student will probably get the chance of coming under the influence of an enthusiastic specialist in the subject which the student affects; and this specialist" (Eliot adds somewhat falteringly) "may be a thinking man who leads his pupils to think." [15] Beneath the inspiring specialists are many, far too many, whose teaching is merely methodical, or even mechanical, commonplace men who in an age of scientific activity attain a prestige exceeding their intellectual capacity. As Ortega y Gasset remarks, experimental science has progressed "thanks in great part to the work of men astoundingly mediocre, and even less than mediocre. That is to say, modern science, the root and symbol of our actual civilization, finds a place for the intellectually commonplace man and allows him to work therein with success." Very ordinary persons, by dint of a reputation for being constantly active in the production of very ordinary contributions to the sum of knowledge, rise rather quickly to the status of full professors. On the whole, however, it must be granted that the teaching in our universities answers well the end of specialism. That end agreed upon, a considerable part of it must be called definitely good teaching, and if the students and the public do not think so, the reason is presumably that students and public maintain a current of doubt as to the sufficiency of specialism.

Dimly both students and public realize the truth of Newman's dictum that "You must be above your knowledge, not under it, or it will oppress you," the truth of Mr. Laski's remark that the specialist tends "to make his subject the measure of life, instead of making life the measure of

[15] *Education for Efficiency*, pp. 17-18.

his subject." Students and public, that is, even in an age
dedicated to science and specialism, continue to feel the
need of that liberal education which the universities still
profess to give but do not give. They sense the absurdity of
the attempt to provide liberal education by means of teachers who themselves were not liberally educated. For the
purposes of special education, the universities have an adequate faculty of specialists, soundly trained in their special
subjects. For the purposes of liberal education, the universities have—an adequate faculty of specialists.

There are exceptions. Intermingled in the mass of specialists are a few teachers who perceive that youth craves
something more than specialized knowledge. Seeking to be
liberal, these teachers are usually only popular. Seeking to
rise above specialism, they usually fall beneath it into su-
perficiality. They wish to make the ways of learning easy
and pleasant; they wish to invite the free play of the mind
unhampered by too many facts and too much method; they
wish to be stimulating, provocative, and entertaining. They
try to make their courses broad in scope, their assigned and
suggested readings interesting or even journalistic, their
lectures inspirational or picturesque or intimately personal,
their standards of attainment reasonably genial. They are,
in a word, pseudo-liberals or dilettanti. They subdivide
into such types as the sentimentalist, the sophist, the demagogue, and the clown. It should be added that they are not
always sharply differentiated from the specialists: they may
be specialists en déshabillé. It should also be added that the
most effective dilettanti are often inconsistently regarded,
by specialist colleagues and by administrators, as the university's best teachers.

If the purpose of the liberal college, however, is neither
special training nor popular culture but liberal education,
we must look for the best teachers in another minority

group, the small band of genuine liberals. They are sometimes confused, by the uncritical, with the dilettanti because, having a curiosity about the general scheme of
knowledge, they appear not to belong with the narrow specialists. But assuredly interest in a special field does not
force a scholar to be narrow, since he can contrive to place
himself above his subject rather than under it. The truly
liberal teacher, like the specialist, has a special field, which
in its larger sense is simply the subject he professes and in
its smaller sense is some part of that subject, but at the same
time, having managed to educate himself liberally, he
maintains in his thought, study, and teaching a vital relationship between his special subject and other subjects and
indeed the whole encyclopedia of knowledge. For every department of knowledge, as Burnet says, possesses "its universal side, the side on which it comes into touch with every
other, . . . the most important side of it for the educator.
To insist upon this is the true function of Humanism in
Education." The professor of a subject must obviously himself be oriented if he is to orient his students, so that in a
liberal faculty there will be no need of a catch-all "orienta-
tion course." The professor of a subject must bring his subject into vital relation with other subjects; if he does this
there will be no need of ambassadors between the provinces
of learning, such as the "roving professors" of Harvard.
The professor of a subject, teaching within the framework
of a curriculum much of which is shared by all students,
will be in a position to relate his subject to the common
subjects, to illuminate them as they illuminate his own; if
he does this there will be no occasion for trying to settle
the pseudo-problem of "transfer." While the specialist dis-
dains to speak of other subjects, which "belong" to other
specialists, or else interprets other subjects in terms of his
own specialty, consciously or unconsciously forcing them

into the groove of his special set of abstractions, the liberal pursues his task of developing the critical mind by keeping all the avenues open, by protecting all points of view, by suggesting the samenesses underlying differences and the differences insusceptible of reconciliation, by revealing the various types of evidence and their claims upon us, by persistently seeking to instill in the student the spirit of intellectual justice. Like the specialist, he expects the student to acquire a substantial body of facts, only the facts must be reflected upon and used, not merely learned. Like the specialist, he offers the thrill of discovery: not the discovery, however, of something never before known by anyone, but simply the discovery of something never before known by the student, some principle, some point of view, some relationship that opens up a new domain of experience or throws a flood of light upon a multitude of facts previously obscure or inert; not the discovery of new items of fact, but the rediscovery of keys to the understanding of life. The liberal teacher is never content with fact as such, which is, humanly speaking sterile, nor with technical tricks and skills useful in a calling, but insists upon bringing to whatever subject he teaches a critical attitude, a philosophical breadth, an awareness of its place in the general scheme of knowledge and its relevance to the contemporary world.[16]

Because his teaching is humane rather than factual and vocational, the liberal teacher meets young men and women at the college stage on their own terms. He does not bore students by assuming that they are still in the high school stage of receptivity, or that they have reached the graduate school stage of professional specialization; he recognizes

---

[16] For this reason an inferior subject like carpentry may be liberal in the hands of the right teacher, while a superior subject like Latin may prove to be vocational even when taught by "eminent specialists." See L. B. Richardson, *A Study of the Liberal College* (1924), pp. 19-20.

that educable youth is first of all assimilative and reflective, desirous of wide experience and understanding, eager for self-knowledge and knowledge of the world. Interested in young men and women rather than in children or in mature specialists, he enters readily into the minds of his students. He is the "right" teacher for the purpose of awakening and guiding the college undergraduate. This was the view of Henry Suzzalo while president of the Carnegie Foundation for the Advancement of Teaching. "When we have more college teachers," he said, "with an interest in human beings as vital as their interest in academic subjects, and with the sympathetic ability to see the problems of life as the youth perceives them, then students will be interested intellectually." Close to the minds of his students and in constant association with them, the liberal teacher naturally becomes, furthermore, the friendly adviser of his students concerning their work, their life in the university community, and the life to which they look forward. If the college faculty is indeed liberal, there is scant need for the provision of courses in adjustment to university life or to vocational problems, or for the mechanism of a non-teaching bureau of advice ("the sleek data-dominated efficiency of our personnel services"), or for a system of faculty advisers composed of specialists living in a groove —all of them simply ameliorative devices resulting from unsound education.

As instructor and adviser of youth, the liberal teacher is usually successful in exact proportion as he is himself exemplary. What he is—in mind, personality, character— his students will tend to become. It is important, consequently, that he should be himself, and that his self should be worthy of conscious or unconscious imitation. He cannot succeed by putting on a good show, sentimental or melodramatic; nor can he succeed by subordinating himself to any "teaching methods" formulated by the science of education, flimsy crutches for the uncreative mind. He will constantly experiment with methods of presentation suggested by the problem in hand, in the manner of the artist seeking the fullest communication, and his best methods will be *his,* best for himself, conceivably worst for others. During the sixteen or eighteen years of his own schooling, he learned much, by observation, of the art of teaching; once become a teacher himself, he will continue to learn by "doing"—i.e., by practical experience in his art. So important is the teacher himself—his quality of mind, personality, character—that the college administrator may safely act upon the suggestion that "For picking a man to teach any subject the motto is that shrewd Middle English proverb, *Send the wise and say no thing."* [17] If he is wise, his wisdom will discover methods for communicating itself to his students, though the best of it will pass from him to them in ways too subtle for description, so subtle, indeed, that often he himself will not know when or how this is happening. His most casual remarks, long forgotten, will be brought back to him years later by old students whose lives have been deeply affected by them, though they may seem, when repeated, the merest commonplaces. The fact is that the values conveyed by the liberal teacher are not so much taught as caught, not so much perceived intellectually as experienced sympathetically, so that a subject like ethics pursued under a scientistic logician may easily prove less valuable, in its ethical effects, than a subject like history or natural science pursued under a humanist. High-minded himself, the liberal teacher tends to elevate the interests of his students; if he cares for what is higher and finer and his students are

[17] Professor J. S. P. Tatlock, "Early English in the Universities," *English Journal,* September, 1935. p. 556.

capable of caring for it, there is every likelihood that they will learn to do so. Hence the prime test of a teacher, we may say, is "his power so to stimulate his students as to raise their interests to a higher level. From the point of view of the college the vital question is not whether a teacher inspires interest, but what kind of interest he inspires and in what quality of undergraduate." [18]

Throughout our institutions of higher learning, and especially in the state universities, the number of teachers who have themselves been liberally educated and who are capable of serving the purposes of liberal education is steadily declining. Apparently the situation was already serious as long ago as 1914, when President Butler of Columbia declared, in his annual report, that it was "increasingly difficult to secure good courses of instruction for those who have the very proper desire to gain some real knowledge of a given topic without intending to become specialists in it." Ten years later, in the proceedings of the National Association of State Universities, President Kinley of the University of Illinois deplored "the absence from our faculties of men who have either the knowledge or the ability to correlate their particular subjects of instruction with collateral or allied subjects." In 1931, in the proceedings of the Institute for Administrative Officers of Higher Institutions, Dr. Suzzalo condemned the conduct of college education by men who have "specialized on near ignorance instead of on broad knowledge," and set down as the first requirement of a teaching scholar that he be "a civilized or cultured man in his intellectual understandings and appreciations." Even the 1933 report of the American Association of University Professors, which showed a real concern for good teaching along

[18] Babbitt, *op. cit.*, p. 198.

with central confusion as to the nature and conditions of good teaching, acknowledges that the profession is failing to attract to itself "a sufficient number of broadly cultured young men and women," and suspects that the professors now teaching in the colleges are not "portraying by their own careers and example to the younger generation of scholars the kind of profession which strikes the youthful imagination in a favorable light when compared with other callings." The best college youth, it would seem, are now turning to medicine, law, engineering, and business, not so much because they are attracted by the higher financial rewards in those callings, as because they are repelled by the type of teacher who prevails in higher education.

For the future, the fundamental questions of higher education are those stated by President Conant in his report for 1934–1935: "What type of individual will teach in our colleges and universities in the coming years, and what will be the quality and character of the student body? Knowing the answers, one could predict all the rest. . . . If we are to plan for the future, therefore, we must plan in terms of men." In the liberal college, as I have affirmed, the right students are those capable of profiting from liberal education, and the right teachers those capable of imparting it. Now that the number of such teachers is dwindling, our most urgent task is to develop a large number of right students into liberally educated persons interested in the teaching profession. And here we encounter a vicious circle.

A faculty of specialists naturally tends to reproduce its kind indefinitely. Far from being experimental in a large sense, it assumes the permanent validity of its tradition of education for efficiency, and works persistently for the maintenance of that tradition. A faculty dominated by

the habits of scientistic and naturalistic speculation inculcates these habits, consciously or unconsciously, in the
students who will succeed them in the profession of college teaching. Can this perpetually circular repetition be
interrupted? The answer indicated by the history of institutions is not only that it can but that it will. In all
human affairs, for better and worse, there is not only a
principle of permanence but a principle of change. History itself denies the assumption of the naturalist. So does
logic, at least his own logic, since his whole philosophy is
couched in terms of endless change. If all things change,
the specialist education he has set up will change.

It will begin to do this when a sufficient number of
influential specialists become aware, as a few are already
aware, of the folly of specialization on near ignorance,
perceiving that specialization itself, the thing they value
most, suffers when not based on broad knowledge. Once
enough of them come to agree with President Coffman
that "the more an individual is sharpened to a point, the
broader the base should be," they will take steps toward
the revival of general education. Then, in due course, it
will become apparent that general education cannot thrive
unless it is liberal, and that liberal education cannot thrive
unless it is humanistic. Events shaped by the will of man
in the outer world may either hasten or prolong this series
of changes, or cause a quite different series to work itself
out; such matters are in the laps of the gods. If the forces
making for a worthy form of liberal education are suffered
to proceed, the quality of teachers in our colleges will
improve until the youthful imagination is once more attracted to the profession, and from that point on further
improvement will be swift. At the same time this process
of change will work downward into the secondary schools,
since the teachers in these schools receive their training

in college, and upward into the graduate schools, where we may eventually witness, as in the English and French universities, the subordination of "research" to creative culture. The key to educational reform is thus the college of liberal arts.

INDEX

PREPARED BY E. A. C.

279

posals, 255-257; Jefferson's plan, University of Virginia, 20. *See also* Elective system *and* Vocational training

Cushing, Dr. Harvey, on status of science, 138

Darwin, Charles, idea of progress, 50; theory mentioned, 55

Degrees, requirements, 96-101, 109-114; decline of significance, 111-113

De Hovre, Frans, book quoted, 254

Departments, university, importance in organization, 91-93; increasing subdivisions of faculty, 250; required subjects and departmentalism, 249, 250

Depression, effect on universities, 135, 145-147; students' attitudes, 145

Descartes, René, Condorcet's estimate, 46

Dewey, John, cited on psychology, 214n.3; quoted on scientific attitude, 118; nature of influence, 7

Diderot, Denis, quoted on value of feeling, 38

Dualism. *See* Humanism *and* Religion

Duffus, Robert L., cited on science, 141n.6

Dupont de Nemours, Pierre S., plan for higher education, 191

Durie, John, humanitarianism, 30

Education, departments of, fixed requirements, 249. *See also* Teacher training

Elective sytem, 87-88; new definite curricula, 101-104; majors, 92, 93, 100-104

Eliot, Charles W., educational ideal, 94; nature of influence, 7; elective system, 88; influence on graduate schools, 106, 107; quoted on Christian humanitarianism, 41, 42; on Spencer, 116; on nature of teaching, 268

Elliott, G. R., on elective system, 255

Ellwood, C. A., on relation of sociology to biology, 239

Elyot, Sir Thomas, on education and government, 5; on individual difference, 174, 188; conception of progress mentioned, 44; mentioned, 202

Embree, E. R., quoted on school system, 182; on high school enrollment, 153n.11; rating of universities, 193n.16

England, aims of British universities, 252, 253; liberal education tradition, 202; secondary education, 153n.11; theory of education, Newman as expositor, 202-204

Enrollment, effect of depression, 150, 151; growth, 153; several periods, 81, 82

Entrance, to universities, restrictions, 183; inequality of opportunity to talent, 170; students unqualified, 151-157

Erasmus, Desiderius, comic spirit, 224; religious attitude, 210

Faculties, Conant on increasing subdivisions, 250; on importance of teaching, 275; liberal teachers, 269-274; indoctrination of naturalism, 115-121; selection of, 166-170; specialism, 267

Flexner, Dr. Abraham, on graduate schools, 106

Florida, University of, curriculum, 261n.12

Fontenelle, Bernard de, ideas on progress, 44
Foster, Sir Michael, quoted on scientific progress, 48, 49
Fox, Charles James, humanitarianism, 31
France, liberal education, tradition, 202; secondary education, 153n.11
Francis, St., originality, 227
Frank, Glenn, cited on depression, 182
Freedom, academic, 161-170; loyalty oaths, 160, 161
Frontier, influence on universities, 21-26
Fuller, Margaret, incident mentioned, 217

Gardiner, Gov. W. T., campaign incident, 172
Germany, state of academic freedom, 162, 163; literacy, 172; doctrines of Pangermanists, 251, 252; schools of Prussia, 178; secondary education, 153n.11; uniformity, 168
Gilmore, Eugene A., quoted on needed changes, 158, 159
Godwin, William, quoted on progress, 46
Graduate schools, commercialism, 70; growth, 106-108; handicaps, 108-115

Hamilton, Alexander, dangers of disunion, 13; distrust of men, 15
Harvard University, graduate school, 107; prize fellowships, College, 190; roving professors mentioned, 270
Haydon, Albert E., scientific religion, 122, 123
Helvetius, C. A., equalitarianism, 170

Herklots, H. G. G., on vocationalism, 69n.1
High schools, mixed aims, 261n.12; growth, 152, 153
Hobbes, Thomas, naturalism, 33; Rousseau's answer to, 34
Hocking, W. E., on education in religion, 264
Holland, E. O., cited on finances, 182n.10
Holmes, Justice O. W., on free thought, 163
Hoover, Herbert, individualism, 55, 56; on insatiability of wants, 53; on numbers in universities, 81
Hubbard, Elbert, 76
Hugo, Victor, on compulsory education, 170
Humanism, dualist basis, 32n.4, 220-222; educational ideals, historical view, 202-221; individual progress, 226; relation to religion and science, 246; to science, 216-218; as road to internationalism, 231, 232; as answer to present needs, 242, 243, 252-254. *See also* Liberal education
Humanitarianism, as basis of American education, 202; influence of Bacon and Rousseau, 28; history of, 29-55; inadequacy as modern philosophy, 232-243; individual *vs.* society, 228; utilitarianism, 43-56; position of psychologist, 131, 132
Hume, David, humanitarianism, 33; quoted on Rousseau, 38
Hungary, state of academic freedom, 162
Hutchins, Pres. R. M., on reason and science, 233, 234
Huxley, Aldous, on common sense, 215; novel cited, 42
Huxley, Thomas Henry, on liberal